HISTORY AND THEOLOGY
IN SECOND ISAIAH

HISTORY AND THEOLOGY
IN
SECOND ISAIAH

A Commentary on Isaiah 35, 40-66

BY

JAMES D. SMART

THE WESTMINSTER PRESS

PHILADELPHIA

LIBRARY OF CONGRESS CATALOG CARD No. 65-17000

Published by The Westminster Press®
Philadelphia, Pennsylvania

PRINTED IN THE UNITED STATES OF AMERICA

CONTENTS

PREFACE

THE SPECIFIC CHARACTER of this commentary requires some explanation. It combines in one volume an attempt to establish a new approach to the writings of Second Isaiah and an exposition of those writings that is addressed not just to the scholar but also to the ordinary Bible student. The former purpose necessitates a running debate with other commentators that the ordinary reader may be inclined to dismiss as beyond his range of interest, whereas the scholar may be impatient with an exposition that seems to him too "homiletic," since it goes beyond historical exegesis in an attempt to grasp both past and present significance of the theological content.

But need one be so reluctant to involve the ordinary Bible student in an extended debate on questions of interpretation? There is a tendency in many books on the Bible that are aimed directly at such readers to assume that they have time and interest only for a very simple exposition of the message of the text and that on critical questions they need only be told what is "the generally agreed standpoint among scholars." But this conveys a totally false impression of the state of Biblical scholarship and encourages a far too complacent trust in the "authorities." Both on critical questions and in their understanding of the content of the text, the "authorities" have frequently been wrong in the past and there is no reason why the ordinary Bible reader should not be encouraged to use his own eyes on the text that he has before him and to ask himself which interpretation is most convincing to him. Surely we need to encourage ministers and laymen in the church to interrogate the Biblical text for themselves, not content merely to take either their critical views or their understanding of the message ready-made from anyone.

On the other hand, need any apology be offered to the scholar for asking him to interest himself in an experiment in hermeneutics that proceeds on the principle that we have no access to the theological content of a Biblical text except through the present meaning of that text for living persons? The idea has long been firmly established that the scholar's task is only to determine what the text meant in its original historical situation. Present meanings have been regarded as the domain of the preacher who has merely to take over the conclusions of the Biblical scholar and make them meaningful for present-day life. But in recent years this simple order has begun to be recognized as grossly inadequate. A clergy trained in a historical exegesis that passes lightly over the question of theological content has frequently found itself helpless and confused in the face of the problem of letting Scripture speak its own message in the modern world. There is a problem here that demands the attention of scholars. It is already receiving wide consideration in the debate on hermeneutics in Germany and is likely to come more and more to our notice in America. The solution attempted in this commentary may not be the most adequate one, but it is not just a "homiletical" expansion of the exegesis. Its intention is to do justice to both the historical and the theological character of the text.

A second point at which the commentary goes contrary to general practice is in the precedence that it gives to the theology of the prophet. It is usual to consider historical questions first and by themselves, and then, having established the prophet and his writings firmly in their historical situation, to give attention to his theology. This procedure, applied to Second Isaiah, has in the past had disastrous results, for the simple reason that the historical evidence has about it a very considerable haziness and uncertainty. But the prophet leaves us in no uncertainty about his basic theological convictions. Few prophets ever revealed their minds with the clarity and decisiveness of Second Isaiah. Therefore, on the principle that we should start, not from uncertainties, but from certainties, we give precedence to the theology of the prophet and proceed with the expectation that a right understanding of his mind may have real value in arriving at a right understanding of his historical situation.

A third peculiarity is the placing of certain basic discussions that are of decisive importance for one's total approach to the book, not in the introduction where they are usually found, but in the body of the exposition. An instance of this is the treatment of the references to Cyrus and to Babylon-Chaldea. The usual procedure has been to deduce from the references to Cyrus a historical context for the book as a whole and then to interpret the chapters from ch. 40 on in this context—or with Torrey, to expunge the references to Cyrus and construct a quite different historical context. Interpretation has been so vitiated and confused by such assumptions that it may be worth trying a different procedure: to begin the exposition with the fewest possible assumptions, to read ch. 40 as though we knew nothing of the prophet except what he himself tells us in the text of the chapter, then to read ch. 41 in the light of what we have learned in ch. 40, ch. 42 in the light of chs. 40 and 41, and so on throughout the twenty-eight chapters. Particular problems will thus receive consideration in the context that the prophet himself provides, and it may be possible to liberate him from some of the theoretical constructions that have been built around his book with little or no justification.

It will be noted that the comments on the earlier chapters are much fuller than on some of the later ones. Chapter 40 occupies a space out of all proportion to the others. But this arises from the necessity of dealing with distinctive themes of the prophet at some length when they first occur, which then makes a much briefer treatment possible when they appear again.

The commentary will be found incomplete in many respects, not only because of limitations of space but also because of limitations in the competence of the author. No attempt is made to analyze the poetic structure as Muilenburg has done so extensively in *The Interpreter's Bible*. Parallels in Near Eastern literature will have to be sought elsewhere. The history of the various theories concerning the Servant will be found adequately presented in H. H. Rowley's *The Servant of the Lord and Other Essays on the Old Testament* and C. R. North's *The Suffering Servant in Deutero-Isaiah*. There is a vast literature on Second Isaiah, with most of which I am familiar, but in the main, I have confined references to four commentaries, two in German by Bernhard Duhm and Paul Volz and two by Americans, C. C. Torrey and James Muilenburg. Duhm is still important after seventy years because of the fact that his theories have dominated the interpretation of Second Isaiah for three quarters of a century, most existing commentaries in English and German being largely variations upon Duhm. Volz and Muilenburg remain in the stream that stems from Duhm, but both have a theological penetration that Duhm lacked. Muilenburg's appreciation of the theological depth and poetic power of the prophet is most notable. C. C. Torrey represents a massive repudiation of Duhm's theories and a fresh approach to the problems of the book. My agreement with Torrey in his dissent from Duhm and in his dismissal of Cyrus may create the impression that my approach is largely dependent upon his, but, as a matter of fact, my investigations and the development of a distinctive interpretation began in 1930 when suddenly the character of the prophet's eschatology dawned upon me and the whole of his writings opened up with new meaning. At that time I had not seen Torrey's commentary, published two years earlier. I am grateful for what I have learned from him—but it has not been in the realms of eschatology or theological interpretation. Even where my critical conclusions are similar to his, I have reached them usually by a different route and have found a somewhat different basis for them.

In order to avoid footnotes as much as possible, references to the views of other commentators are identified merely by the name in parentheses. The relevant passage will be found in their commentaries under the chapter and verse that are being discussed.

I have to thank Union Theological Seminary for a sabbatical leave and the American Association of Theological Seminaries for the financial support that provided the opportunity of finally working out a full-length commentary. I am grateful also to Prof. George Landes of Union Seminary for a careful reading of the manuscript and a number of helpful criticisms and suggestions.

J. D. S.

Union Theological Seminary

ABBREVIATIONS

BWANT—Beiträge zur Wissenschaft vom Alten und Neuen Testament
JBL—Journal of Biblical Literature
KAT—Kommentar zum Alten Testament
RSV—Revised Standard Version
ThZ—Theologische Zeitschrift
ZAW—Zeitschrift für die alttestamentliche Wissenschaft

COMMENTARIES CITED IN THE TEXT

Calvin—John Calvin, *Commentary on the Book of the Prophet Isaiah.* Wm. B. Eerdmans Publishing Company, 1948.

Duhm—Bernhard Duhm, *Das Buch Jesaja,* 4th ed. Göttingen: Vandenhoeck & Ruprecht, 1922.

Frey—Hellmuth Frey, *Das Buch der Weltpolitik Gottes.* Stuttgart: Calwer Verlag, 1958.

Klostermann—A. Klostermann, *Deuterojesaja.* München: Oskar Beck, 1893.

Marti—Karl Marti, *Das Buch Jesaja erklärt.* Tübingen: J. C. B. Mohr, 1900.

Muilenburg—James Muilenburg, "Isaiah 40-66," *The Interpreter's Bible,* Vol. V. Abingdon Press, 1956.

Skinner—John Skinner, *The Book of the Prophet Isaiah*. Cambridge: Cambridge University Press, 1915.

Smith—George Adam Smith, *The Book of Isaiah,* Vol. II. London: Hodder & Stoughton, Ltd., 1890.

Torrey—C. C. Torrey, *The Second Isaiah*. Charles Scribner's Sons, 1928.

Volz—Paul Volz, *Jesaja II. KAT*. Leipzig: Deichert, 1932.

I

Introduction

1. THE SHAPING OF THE PROBLEM

THE PROPHET whose writings are preserved in Isa., chs. 35, 40 to 66, but whose name is lost beyond recovery, has with good reason been called "the evangelist of the Old Testament." The very word "evangel," which Jesus used to describe his own message, was borrowed by him from this prophet, and more than once he drew from the same source words to describe his mission—to preach good news to the poor, to proclaim release to the captives, and to restore sight to the blind (Luke 4:18; Matt. 11:5; cf. Isa. 61:1 f.). There was undoubtedly a pastoral element in the ministries of many of the earlier prophets, but it is concealed by the concentration of their public oracles of judgment upon the nation as a whole. Their dealings with individuals have left only a slight residue in the records. We can discern it, however, at a number of points: the circle of disciples around Isaiah (Isa. 8:16), the letter of Jeremiah to the exiles in Babylon (Jer., ch. 29), and Ezekiel's indictment of prophets for failing to be true shepherds or pastors who would seek the lost sheep and bind up the wounded (Ezek. 34:4 ff.). But in Second Isaiah the intimate concern of the prophet as pastor of his people comes clearly into the foreground and attains decisive expression. The broken and discouraged Israelites knew in him a man of God who moved through their midst with a word that was bread to the hungry—bread, milk, wine, water (ch. 55:1,10,11)—all that was needful to sustain life. He strengthened the weak hands, made firm the feeble knees, and said to those who were of a fearful heart: "Be strong, fear not! Behold your God . . . will come and save you" (ch. 35:4). Passionately he proclaimed to his people the power of God to transform the desert places of their life into fruitful gardens and to open before them an unbelievable new future. Like a true evangelist, however, he had no word of comfort and hope that was not at the same time a word of judgment and a call to repentance. To hope in God is to renounce all false bases of hope and confidence, and perhaps most difficult of all, it is to renounce the lassitude of despair. To drink from the fountain of living waters one has to give up drinking from a number of other fountains. The comfort the prophet offered his people was no minor encouragement but was the mighty word "God with us," and therefore it was a comfort that was to be possessed only by a people that was prepared to respond with its whole being to God in faith and obedience. Those who turned a deaf ear to God, who insisted that the obstacles in their way were too formidable even for God to do anything about them, who clung to their idols, who put their trust in fasting and sacrifices, who showed their heedlessness of God by their heedlessness toward their naked and hungry brothers, heard from the prophet biting words of judgment. There was no contradiction in this, but only a clarification of the costly and demanding character of the comfort offered by the prophet and evidence of his integrity as an evangelist.

Such is the impression that Second Isaiah makes upon our minds: evangelist, pastor, poet, profound theologian, interpreter of history. Almost every reference to him in present-day Old Testament literature acclaims him as representing the highest point in the prophetic tradition. Yet when the work of interpretation begins, at once serious disagreements and uncertainties appear. Which chapters belong to Second Isaiah, the whole of chs. 40 to 66 with one or both of chs. 34 and 35, or only chs. 40 to 55? Where did he live and work: Babylon, Palestine, Syria? What did he expect of Cyrus, a limited political act that would permit Jewish exiles to return to Palestine, or that Cyrus would be God's agent in the world's transformation? Or does Cyrus not belong in the book at all? Could a prophet of comfort who proclaimed the forgiveness of Israel's sins revert to thunderings of judgment on the stubbornness of the nation in sin? Did he at one time denounce the Temple and its sacrifices, but at other times regard it with a friendly interest? Is the Servant who plays such an important part as the agent of God's purposes to be identified with the nation or with some historical individual or with the Messiah? All of these positions have been put forward and defended at some time or other.

We shall understand the wide diversity of interpretations to which Second Isaiah has been subjected only when we take account of what seems to be the contradictory character of the evidence. In chs. 40 to 55 he frequently addresses Jerusalem and in chs. 56 to 66 the people with whom he deals are clearly in Palestine, yet in chs. 40 to 55 his mind seems at times to be reaching out to exiles who are located far from Palestine. In the two specific references to Cyrus the anticipation is that Cyrus will "fulfill all God's purpose" and establish a great new era on earth, yet the agent of God's redemptive purpose elsewhere in the book is the Servant. In some passages Israel is told that God has already forgiven her sins and her salvation is about to dawn, but in others the hypocrisy and brutal paganism of the community is denounced and there is no prospect except a fiery judgment. In ch. 44:28 the future rebuilding of the Temple is the crowning point of the promised restoration, but in ch. 66:1-2 an attempt to rebuild the Temple is condemned, whereas in ch. 56:4-7 the existence of the Temple and its worship seems to be assumed. In ch. 49:3 and elsewhere the Servant is definitely identified as Israel, yet in chs. 50 and 53 the figure of the Servant is so intensely individual that the collective interpretation seems insufficient.

Such contradictory phenomena received little attention so long as the entire book of Isaiah was attributed to the eighth-century prophet. As early as Calvin the exilic situation presupposed by chs. 40 to 66 was recognized, but it was explained by the hypothesis that Isaiah projected his mind forward two centuries and delivered messages that were intended for that future era. Then, when at last the evidence of a sixth-century provenance had become conclusive and chs. 40 to 66 were acknowledged to be the work of a later prophet, attention was focused so strongly upon what distinguished them from the writings of eighth-century Isaiah that discordancies within the chapters were not allowed at first to set their essential unity in question. But it was only a matter of time until such problems would demand their due.

When chs. 40 to 66 were finally recognized as an independent work, their author was called "the prophet of the exile." It was the evidence of his ministry falling in the time of the exile that had been chiefly instrumental in securing recognition of his independent existence. But "time of the exile" in the latter half of the nineteenth century was taken at once to mean "Babylonian exile." The historical schema of the Chronicler was unquestioned: that the main line of Israel's life was transferred to Babylonia in 597 and 587 B.C. and continued there until in 538 B.C. Cyrus permitted a return of the Babylonian exiles to Judah. Palestine was thought to have been denuded of its Israelite inhabitants during the exile years, at least of all who were of any significance, so that the possibility of a sixth-century prophet such as Second Isaiah ministering in Judah seemed to be out of the question. Thus to define him as "the prophet of the exile" seemed automatically to place him outside Palestine and most likely in Babylon. His anticipation of a restoration of exiles to Palestine and a rebuilding of Jerusalem, his prophecy of the radical humbling of the Babylonian tyrant, and his two specific references to Cyrus (to which some other somewhat veiled references were usually added) were taken to make the matter conclusive.

Therefore, in 1875 and 1892, when Bernhard Duhm published his epoch-making work[1] on Second Isaiah, it was taken for granted by most scholars that "prophet of the exile" meant "prophet among the exiles." George Adam Smith in his commentary in 1890 never hesitated a moment in placing the prophet in Babylon, and in the intervening years most commentators have done the same, all of them so confident of the location that they do not even bother to assemble the evidence for it. Duhm, however, seems to have been aware of the slenderness of the evidence for Babylon and left the location vague, suggesting that the prophet may have been among exiles in Phoenicia or Lebanon, but it never occurred to him to consider Judah.

The negative judgment was universal that the "prophet of the exile" could not have lived in Judah, and this judgment had important consequences for the critical analysis of the writings. The

[1] In his *Israels Propheten* (Tübingen: J. C. B. Mohr, 1875; 2d ed., 1922) and in his commentary on Isaiah in 1892.

background of chs. 56 to 66 was clearly Palestinian, reflecting a community firmly established in Judah. Therefore, since chs. 40 to 55 were assumed to be by a Babylonian prophet, chs. 56 to 66 had either to be assigned to a different prophet or explained as the product of the period after the return of the prophet and his exiles to Palestine. The severe condemnations of the community in some of the later chapters seemed hardly to represent how Second Isaiah, the prophet of comfort, would address the "cream of the exiles" whom he had led back from Babylon and who would be engaged in the work of restoration. It was simply inconceivable that the denunciation of the building of a Temple in ch. 66:1-2 could have been directed against the project encouraged by King Cyrus. Such considerations as these, plus the evident changes in tone from ch. 56 on, brought general approval for Duhm's proposal that chs. 56 to 66 be assigned to a disciple of Second Isaiah who was then called Trito-Isaiah. He explained the remarkable similarity in style and content between the writings of the two as the disciple's imitation of his master, and assigned him, as an imitator, a very low status among the prophets. A really great prophet would have shown more initiative and independence.

Duhm proceeded to a second act of surgery, this time on chs. 40 to 55. Here the central problem for him was the contradiction between passages in which the prophet expected the liberation of his people, the restoration of the national life in Palestine, and eventually the transformation of the world to be achieved either by the Persian monarch Cyrus or by Israel itself, and other passages in which the agent of God's redemption was conceived in purely spiritual terms, a Servant of truth who would win his way to victory, not by force, but through suffering and death. Again Duhm showed his acuteness, more penetrating than many later commentators, by recognizing how impossible it was for the same prophet to cherish these contradictory expectations. He thought he could see in brief passages in chs. 42 and 49, and in larger ones in chs. 50 and 53, a distinctive style and a superior content that would justify him in separating them from their context, assigning them to a different prophet, and labeling them "Servant Songs." Naturally, as a result of this surgery Second Isaiah, like Trito-Isaiah, lost much of his glory and became a much less admirable prophet.

For more than a generation the discussion of Second Isaiah proceeded within this general pattern established by Duhm.[2] Various questions were debated. Were there not some parts of chs. 56 to 66 that might be assigned to Second Isaiah? Were the "Servant Songs" composed by a prophet who preceded Second Isaiah and then had his poems incorporated in the larger work, or did he come after him and himself insert them, or were they perhaps composed by Second Isaiah himself and later merged with his other writings? Who did the composer of the "Songs" have in mind as the Servant? How much did the prophet know of Cyrus' career? The dreariness of most of this literature derives from the fact that neither a prophet who goes into ecstasies describing how the world is to be redeemed by a Persian king nor one who is content to imitate his master in a stumbling fashion is likely to command much respect. All the glory was reserved for the author of the "Servant Songs."

An attempt was made by C. C. Torrey in 1928 to cut through this confusion and to liberate the prophet and his writings from the tangle of interpretations in which they had become involved. To him Second Isaiah was a philosopher and poet with a universal outlook whose writings in chs. 34, 35, 40 to 66, were a perfect unity, set in this order by the author himself "like pearls in a necklace." He quite arbitrarily placed the work late in the fifth century after eliminating all references to Cyrus and Babylon. Unfortunately, certain features of Torrey's commentary earned it an unwarranted neglect: an arrogance in the assertion of his own views, a tendency to assume that earlier works of his own had totally discredited the Chronicler as a historian, and an insistence upon categorizing Second Isaiah as a philosopher rather than as a prophet. He was also devoid of any appreciation of the prophet's eschatology. Yet, however one may disagree with his interpretation, the boldness with which he cut

[2] A somewhat different line of interpretation was attempted by German scholars such as Ludwig Köhler, *Deuterojesaja (Jes. 40-55) stilkritisch untersucht,* (Giessen: A. Töpelmann, 1923); J. Begrich, *Studien zu Deuterojesaja, BWANT,* IV, 25 (Stuttgart: W. Kohlhammer, 1938)—treating the text of Second Isaiah as a compendium of seventy independent oracles and applying to them the methods of form criticism in order to discover the original character and context of each. This could be done only by ignoring the continuity of meaning in larger units. But so far as the book as a whole is concerned, these interpreters remained generally in the bann of Duhm and produced merely variations upon the themes introduced by him.

through a mass of baseless assumptions and opened the way for a fresh approach to the text itself is a contribution of the first order. European scholars have ignored his work to the detriment of their own researches.

The commentary of Volz in 1933, like that of Muilenburg in *The Interpreter's Bible* in 1956, gives much more attention to the theology of the prophet than earlier commentaries, and especially to the eschatology, but neither of them breaks free from the network of assumptions that have conditioned the mainstream of interpretation since Duhm. Both give Cyrus a place of central importance in the prophet's thought, Volz especially so, and both locate the prophet in the context of the Babylonian exiles. Consequently, in spite of their insistence upon the prophet's greatness, his writings remain broken apart and he himself remains burdened with the prophetic absurdity of having expected a Persian conqueror to inaugurate a new era in which all nations would find their salvation in the acknowledgment of the sole sovereignty of Israel's God.

2. A PROPOSAL
FOR A NEW APPROACH

IT HAS BECOME evident in our brief preliminary survey of the interpretation of Second Isaiah's writings that a number of assumptions concerning the prophet and his historical situation that attained the prestige of obvious facts when actually they were based on very slender evidence had a profound influence upon the analysis of the problems. It seemed incontrovertible that the prophet was concerned with the Babylonian exiles on the eve of their return to Palestine, and that the appearance of Cyrus was the event that roused his hopes to such an ecstatic pitch. These and other assumptions are open to challenge. We must examine them one by one.

When we search for evidence of the prophet's residence in Babylon, we are perhaps surprised how hard it is to find any that is convincing. The fact that he addresses himself to exiles does not signify that he was among the Babylonian exiles. His exiles are scattered to the four corners of the earth, north, south, east, and west (chs. 41:9; 42:10-11; 43:5-6; 49:12; 60:9). We have the impression almost everywhere in chs. 40 to 55 that the prophet is writing to a widely dispersed people rather than speaking directly to a local community. Exiles in Babylon would be just one element in the nation to which he appeals. But what has changed the situation at this point most radically since 1890 is the revision that has taken place in the historian's picture of sixth-century Israel. According to the Chronicler, nothing worth mentioning happened in Judah between 587 B.C. and

538 B.C. The country was denuded of its inhabitants, and the continuity of Israel's life and faith was maintained in Babylon alone. However, when even the most liberal estimate is made of the number who were exiled to Babylonia and fled to Egypt and other neighboring countries, it has to be recognized that the majority of Judeans remained in Judah. Only the more prominent citizens were removed. Farmers and ordinary workmen with their families would remain. They might retreat into the ample caves of the Judean hills in a time of invasion, but they would come out in time to plant and harvest the next season's crop. Life would go on. Jeremiah 41:5 indictates that sacrifices continued to be made at an altar among the Temple ruins. There would be drastic poverty, but soon some would be doing very well for themselves while others starved. Martin Noth[1] in his *History of Israel* disputes the Chronicler's schema of sixth-century history and maintains that the main line of Israel's religious development was in Palestine, for the Deuteronomic authors had their residence there. John Bright,[2] in his version of the history, gives greater credit to the Chronicler, accepting his report that the cream of the nation was exiled in Babylon and sustained the purest tradition there, yet he admits frankly that the larger part of the nation spent the whole of the sixth century in Palestine.

How the idea has arisen that the Babylonian exiles preserved such a pure tradition is puzzling. Jeremiah may have regarded them more hopefully than he did the degenerate community in Judah, but he had no illusions about the purity of their faith. The same may be said of Ezekiel. That the exiles were drawn mainly from the upper classes is hardly a basis for declaring them the "cream" of Israel, especially in the light of what Jeremiah tells us about the Judean aristocracy of his time. Was the purest tradition of Israel's faith kept alive more truly among the nobles and priests and wealthy citizens rather than among the poor workmen and farmers? What was to prevent a prophet growing up in a peasant home in Judah during the years of its devastation and poverty? This does not necessarily convince us that Second Isaiah had his ministry in Palestine, but only that Palestine in the sixth century cannot be excluded from consideration as a possible location.

[1] Martin Noth, *The History of Israel* (2d ed., Harper & Row, Publishers, Inc., 1960).
[2] John Bright, *A History of Israel* (The Westminster Press, 1959).

The threefold mention of Babylon and Chaldea (chs. 43:14; 48:14, 20) gives no convincing indication of the prophet's residence. The text in all three instances is problematical (as will be considered in detail in the exposition), but even were the existing text accepted as original, it does not require its author to be present in Babylonia. So also in regard to the exultant anticipation of the destruction of Babylon in chs. 46 and 47. An Israelite in Palestine or Syria who at a distance had felt the heavy hand of the Babylonian tyrant could rejoice at the prospect of his fall as well as one in the immediate neighborhood. Again, the "highway" in ch. 40:3 has frequently been taken to be the road from Babylon to Jerusalem that is to be traveled by the returning exiles. But in ch. 40 there is no mention of exiles returning. The highway is one element in a theophany, the way by which God himself is to return to his people. In ch. 35:8-10 it is a road in which on the day of redemption *all* God's people return to Zion. In ch. 49:11-12 there are highways over the mountains from all directions on which the scattered exiles find their way home.

The polemic against idol worship has sometimes been cited as evidence of a Babylonian situation, but it would need to be shown that the form of idol worship attacked was peculiarly Babylonian, since Israelites in Egypt or Syria or Palestine were equally tempted to worship the gods of their neighbors when they lost faith in the God of Israel. Surely it is curious also that a prophetic oracle such as ch. 40, which is addressed specifically to Jerusalem and the cities of Judah, should so generally have been assumed to have been intended for exiles in Babylon. "Jerusalem" and "the cities of Judah" may, like the terms "Jacob" and "Israel," represent the nation as a whole, both in Palestine and in the regions of exile, but it could hardly be used *exclusively* for exiles in Babylon at a time when they were only a minority of the nation and the whole nation was being addressed.

The simple fact, which should be frankly acknowledged, is that the author of chs. 40 to 55 nowhere makes clear to us his geographical location. The reason for this we shall have to consider later. He differs from other prophets such as Amos, Hosea, Isaiah, or Jeremiah in this respect, and it is one of his most striking peculiarities. Why then should we presume to know what we do not know as we approach his writings? The situation seems to call for a suspension of judgment at this point until the prophet has been allowed to tell us more about himself. Torrey's assumption that he was in Palestine, Duhm's that he was in Phoenicia or Lebanon, and the more widely held one that he was in Babylon are all open to question, so that the investigation of the book and the reconstruction of the historical situation that forms its context should not be based on any such flimsy foundation.

A second assumption has been that Cyrus was of preeminent importance in the life and thought of Second Isaiah. His name occurs only in two successive verses (chs. 44:28; 45:1), both of which are seriously open to question (as will be demonstrated in the exposition). Additional veiled references to him are usually found in chs. 41:2, 25; 45:13; and 46:11, but these passages are capable of a quite different significance in their context. Undoubtedly what has made scholars reluctant to question the validity of the references to Cyrus is the seeming parallel between the role assigned to him here and that which the Chronicler gives to him in his story of the return from exile and the rebuilding of the Temple (Ezra, chs. 1 to 6). The Chronicler may exaggerate the deference that Cyrus paid to the God of Israel, but Cyrus' action in releasing exiles and restoring a local sanctuary is quite in keeping with his character as known from other records. But actually the function of Cyrus in chs. 44 and 45 goes far beyond anything suggested in Ezra, chs. 1 to 6. In ch. 44:28 he is to be God's shepherd (which definitely suggests a Messianic office) and he is to bring "all" God's purpose to fulfillment, a purpose that in Second Isaiah's thought comprehends not just the reconstruction of Jerusalem and its Temple but the establishment of God's rule over the whole earth. Then in ch. 45 he is specifically named "Messiah" and is promised God's help in subduing the nations and seizing their treasures, not for his own sake, strangely enough, but for the sake of Israel (ch. 45:4), and with the direct consequence that God's sole sovereignty will be revealed to all men! In short, Cyrus is to achieve the world's salvation on God's behalf! Attempts have been made to whittle down the function of Cyrus to more reasonable and historical dimensions and to allow him only a political task,[3] but it cannot

[3] Ernst Jenni, "Die Rolle des Kyros bei Deuterojesaja," *ThZ*, July-August, 1954, p. 255. But G. von Rad, *Theologie des Alten Testaments* II (München: Chr. Kaiser Verlag, 1960), p. 257, asserts that the naming of a foreign king as God's Messiah is not only without parallel in the Old Testament but is inconceivable in the context of Israel's Messianic expectations.

be done without ignoring the plain meaning of the text or tearing the text apart. The argument that to see Cyrus as the divine agent in Israel's deliverance is little different from Isaiah's identification of the Assyrian king as the rod of God's anger is faulty. The rod of God's anger had a very limited task and then was himself brought to judgment, but Cyrus as Messiah, if the present text of Isa., chs. 44 and 45, is valid, has an unlimited task, ushering in nothing less than the great day of divine salvation for the whole earth (ch. 45:8).

Here nothing less than the integrity of Second Isaiah as a prophet of God is at stake. How are we to understand his passionate assertion that the *only* hope both of Israel and of the whole world is in the redemptive action of God in his word and through the Servant of his word? No one would dare suggest that Cyrus should be identified with the Servant of the Word. Must we then follow those[4] who say that the prophet began by fixing his hopes on Cyrus and then, when Cyrus failed him, developed his doctrine of the Servant? Or shall we suppose him to have been confused and careless in his thinking and terminology, so that in his enthusiasm for Cyrus he attributed to him functions that actually he expected only of the Servant? On either count the stature of the prophet is seriously diminished. Frankly, who can take seriously a prophet who in God's name proclaims the impending *salvation* of humanity through the agency of a pagan conqueror?

The question must be faced whether this contradiction was present in the prophet's thought or has been introduced into his writings by the clumsy though well-meaning activity of a later editor. In the Judean community in the fifth century the name of Cyrus would be held in high honor as the liberator of exiles and the instigator of the restoration of Jerusalem. In such a community the references in the writings of Second Isaiah to a conqueror who would subdue the hos-

---

[4] Begrich, *op. cit.*, is not alone in portioning out the various chapters to the various periods of Cyrus' conquests, debating which chapters were written before Cyrus captured Babylon and which were written afterward. M. Haller, "Die Kyros Lieder Deuterojesajas," *Eucharisterion. Studien zur Religion and Literatur des Alten und Neuen Testaments*, ed. by H. Schmidt (Göttingen: Vandenhoeck & Ruprecht, 1923), pp. 261 ff., has Second Isaiah traveling in Cyrus' entourage, composing oracles to glorify his exploits and hoping thereby to win him and his influence for the Israelite faith!

tile nations, send the exiles home, and begin a new day for Jerusalem would seem to point directly at Cyrus—and in such a poor faltering community as it was, it would seem impossible that Israel itself should be the conqueror. A very slight retouching would be sufficient to bring the whole book into line with the accepted tradition concerning the restoration. Perhaps at first only the name of Cyrus was entered in the margin to make clear who was meant. This must at least be admitted as a possibility, and once admitted as possible, it necessitates a withholding of judgment concerning the place of Cyrus in the thought of the prophet and certainly cautions us against making the movements of Cyrus the context in which the whole book is interpreted.

A third assumption, which stems from Duhm but has gained wide acceptance and has had profound consequences for the understanding of the prophet's thought, is that there are a number of "Servant Songs" embedded in the text of the book. For Duhm there were four, chs. 42:1-4; 49:1-6; 50:4-9; and 52:13 to 53:12. Some of these were extended by other scholars, and other passages were added. Some held them to be compositions of an earlier prophet that Second Isaiah incorporated into his writings, some attributed them to a later prophet who was under the influence of Second Isaiah and inserted them into his master's compositions, or, the better to account for the remarkable similarity of style and vocabulary between the "Songs" and the writings of Second Isaiah, some have supposed that they were composed by the prophet himself at a different period from the remainder of his writings. Always there have been scholars who have been unable to see any dividing line between the "Songs" and their immediate context.[5] The impression of diverse authorship seems to have arisen not from any demonstrable diversity of style or language, but rather, from the conviction that the Servant in these passages has a different *character* from what he has in the remainder of the book and that, whereas in them the salvation of the nations is to be achieved by the faithful witness and patient suffering of the

[5] Karl Budde, *Die sogenannten Ebed-Yahwe-Lieder* (Giessen: J. Ricker, 1900). More recently Muilenburg, *loc. cit.,* and M. D. Hooker, *Jesus and the Servant* (The Seabury Press [S.P.C.K.], 1959), have shown how each "Song" belongs perfectly in its context, yet both continue to use the misleading term "Servant Songs." Torrey abandons any distinction between these passages and all others.

Servant, elsewhere in the writings either Cyrus or Israel as God's agent is to bring the new day by compulsion. A sharp contrast has been drawn between the Servant who is endowed with such wisdom that he can teach the nations righteousness and guide them into the true way of life and the Servant Israel who is blind and deaf. The former is gentle and wins men by self-sacrifice, whereas the latter tramples upon its foes. The former is blameless before God; the latter is sinful through all its history. What seemed to clinch the distinction was the fact that in ch. 49:5-6 the Servant of the "Songs" has a mission to Israel to recall the nation to its destiny and restore it to its homeland.

These antitheses, however, arise from a basic misunderstanding of the prophet and his eschatology. He had to make seemingly contradictory statements concerning Israel in order to comprehend the full reality of the nation's life. From its beginning Israel had been blind and sinful, rebellious against God's purpose (chs. 43:27; 48:8), but with equal truth he could say that from its beginning it had been called by God to be the bearer of his word and the agent of his redemptive purpose (chs. 44:2; 49:1-3; 59:21). There is also in the mind of the prophet a distinction between the Israel of the present hour of darkness and humiliation and the transformed Israel of the future hour of glorious vindication. Today Israel is blind and deaf (ch. 42:19), but suddenly tomorrow this same Israel has eyes and ears (ch. 43:8 ff.) and becomes God's witnessing Servant before the world. The humiliated and rejected Servant of the opening verses of ch. 53 becomes in v. 12 the triumphant Servant who divides the spoil with the strong. The true and faithful Israel is hidden even now within the unfaithful Israel. Therefore, the prophet can speak of a mission of Israel to Israel, just as there has always to be a mission of the faithful church not only to the world but also to the unfaithful church. These considerations should be sufficient to restrain us from any overhasty agreement to separate a series of "Servant Songs" from the body of the writings.

A less important yet widespread and influential assumption has been based upon the opening words of ch. 40, "Comfort, comfort ye my people." The label "prophet of comfort" has sometimes been fastened on Second Isaiah as though he would be incapable of speaking biting words of judgment such as we hear from the earlier prophets. Therefore, passages in which the sins of the community are denounced with severity have been regarded as incongruous in the mouth of Second Isaiah and have been denied to him.[6] But behind Second Isaiah's message of comfort and encouragement was the recognition that reconciliation with a righteous God meant the abandonment of all unrighteous ways. The good news of Second Isaiah was that God had forgiven his people and by his forgiveness was opening before them a new day, but such forgiveness had to be received and the receiving of it entailed a radical break with the established practices of the past. In short, the comfort he offered was the comfort of a costly grace that brought new responsibilities and tasks. Just as with Amos there was mercy hidden in the judgment he proclaimed, so with Second Isaiah the judgment of God was hidden in the mercy. The one is inseparable from the other. No one can know God's mercy or comfort without coming under his judgment.

We have already mentioned the influence of the Chronicler's schema of Israel's history upon the interpretation of Second Isaiah. Writing in 1890, George Adam Smith trusted the Chronicler's account so implicitly that he drew a completely idealized picture of the returning exiles: "When Israel returned from Babylon the people were wholly monotheist; when Jerusalem was rebuilt no idol came back to her."[7] Religion pure and undefiled was preserved only among the Babylonian exiles and on their return to Palestine they had to be prevented from mingling with the "people of the land," who were little better than heathen.

The validity of the Chronicler's picture of the sixth century was first seriously questioned by W. H. Kosters[8] in 1895 and by C. C. Torrey[9] in a series of studies that began in 1896. A careful analysis of the oracles of Haggai and Zechariah as primary records concern-

[6] Both Duhm and Volz do this.

[7] George Adam Smith, op. cit.

[8] W. H. Kosters, Die Wiederherstellung Israels in der persischen Periode (Heidelberg: J. Hörning, 1895).

[9] C. C. Torrey, The Composition and Historical Value of Ezra-Nehemiah (Giessen: J. Ricker, 1896); Ezra Studies (The University of Chicago Press, 1910); The Chronicler's History of Israel (Yale University Press, 1954).

ing the period of restoration in Jerusalem disclosed no evidence of any massive reconstruction or radical fresh beginning in the years immediately before 520 B.C. They make no mention of any attempt to rebuild the Temple preceding the one sponsored by themselves. There also came to light elements of contradiction and confusion in the Chronicler's account of events, sufficient to make one cautious in depending upon his accuracy. Certainly the impression he conveyed of a Judah that hardly existed any longer as a community until the return of the exiles could not be accepted, nor could his black-and-white contrast between the "people of the land" and the returnees. The Chronicler himself does not hesitate to speak of "the faithlessness of the returned exiles" in Ezra 9:4, and the representation of the priest Joshua in Zech. 3:3 as clothed in filthy garments suggests that the guilt of dabbling in pagan practices did not belong exclusively to the "people of the land." The least that this says to us is that The Book of Ezra should be used with extreme caution in reconstructing the historical situation in the sixth century that forms the background of the activity of Second Isaiah. The writings of Second Isaiah must take precedence as the primary record, originating in the period itself, whereas The Book of Ezra is part of a history written more than a century later which, although containing much valuable historical material, must be read with a full recognition of the strong biases that shape the story from beginning to end. Yet only too often Ezra has been used as though it were the primary historical record, and the writings of Second Isaiah have been interpreted to fit the historical pattern based on The Book of Ezra.

One instance of this subjection of Second Isaiah to the authority of the Chronicler appears in the approach of some scholars to chs. 56 to 66. They assume, like George Adam Smith, that the "post-exilic" Jerusalem community, especially in the period immediately following the return, must have been morally and spiritually on a very high level. Therefore, it becomes impossible for them to identify that community with the one attacked by the prophet in chs. 57 to 59 and chs. 65 and 66 for mingling pagan practices with the worship of Israel's God and for its callous heedlessness of the hungry, naked, and homeless poor. Duhm was so certain that no true prophet could have opposed the rebuilding of the Jerusalem Temple or condemned the sacrifices offered there that he identified the Temple in ch. 66:1 ff. as a rival Samaritan temple. Yet there are a number of indications that the actual order of life in the late sixth-century Jerusalem community may have been more authentically reflected in Isa., chs. 56 to 66, than in the later work of the Chronicler. If it be granted that a considerable population continued in Judah and in the midst of the ruins of Jerusalem after 587 b.c., we would expect to find a continuation of the general religious conditions and problems that are exposed by Jeremiah and Ezekiel in the early years of the century: priests and people combining an ostensible zeal for the worship of Yahweh with a devotion to pagan practices; ritual observances substituted for obedience to the will of God in everyday life; murderous resentment of any prophetic voice that would challenge the existing order.[10] On this score the suggestion has sometimes been made that chs. 56 to 66 are preexilic. Only the false conception of Judah's history in the sixth century prevents the recognition that, so far as Judah was concerned, "preexilic" conditions continued far into that century. Additional support comes from the Elephantine papyri, which disclose a Jewish community in southern Egypt in the fifth century b.c. in close contact with the Judean community and with a temple where the worship of Yahweh was combined with the worship of a goddess. Religious syncretism may well have been persistent also in Judah. But if unfaithfulness and hypocrisy persisted, so also may the prophetic tradition established by Jeremiah and his predecessors have persisted. Again, therefore, we are warned against assuming the validity of the Chronicler's picture of Judah in the sixth century and making our interpretation of Second Isaiah conform to that picture. We must let the text of the prophet's writings tell its own story and then face the problems that

---

[10] W. S. McCullough, "A Reexamination of Isaiah 56–66" (*JBL*, 1948, p. 27), finds the general religious and political conditions reflected in the chapters to be appropriate to the years between 587 b.c. and 562 b.c. in Palestine. He names five cities in Judah where archaeology has discovered evidence of occupation during that period. He therefore assigns the chapters to a prophet who preceded Second Isaiah. But there is no reason to think that these conditions terminated in 562 b.c. or to dismiss the possibility that Second Isaiah delivered these oracles in Palestine not long after 562 b.c.

it creates in relation to other records such as the books of Ezra, Haggai, and Zechariah.

If the plea for restraint on all these points is heeded, it means approaching the book in almost complete uncertainty about the historical situation—at least so far as chs. 40 to 55 are concerned. We do not know where the prophet was when he wrote those chapters. We do not know whether or not he paid any heed to the Persian conqueror Cyrus. We know that he hoped for a return of exiles from the four corners of the earth, but we find no trace of any close association with a specific group of exiles. Historical scholarship that regards its primary task as the placing of each Old Testament document in its historical setting meets at least a preliminary frustration here. An honest recognition of the meagerness of the evidence demands of us a suspension of judgment. Yet one commentator after another has proceeded to base his interpretation upon assumptions that have rested on the flimsiest of foundations. It should have been plain that, although the prophet in chs. 40 to 55 discloses little about his historical situation, he is much more generous in disclosing his mind and spirit and his theology to us, and that a sound method of approach, dictated by the character of the records themselves, should begin not with the uncertain but with the certain, not with the obscure but with what stands forth in the utmost clarity, namely, with his proclamation of the word that God has entrusted to him for the Israel of his day.

Like all expositions, the present one has its own asumptions, but they are of the simplest character. The first is a prejudice in favor of the unity of the chapters 35 and 40 to 66 rather than an assumption that they are a unity. It would be a most unusual phenomenon for two or three different prophets in Israel to be so nearly identical not only in their thought and attitudes but also in the details of their language and forms of poetic expression. It belongs to the nature of a prophet that, in spite of his unity with his predecessors, he speaks to his own time in his own distinctive way. Just as Paul could not copy the language of Jesus, so Second Isaiah could not copy the language of Jeremiah. I do not hear in chs. 56 to 66 the voice of a slavish imitator, but rather, of a true prophet equal in courage and insight to the author of chs. 40 to 55, and like him, persecuted for his faithful witness! Were there two such prophets or only one? There are passages in the text which set the unity in question and they must be dealt with faithfully, but it dare not be lost from view for a moment that the abandonment of the unity leaves us with the problem of two great prophets who were almost identical!

A second assumption I make is that we have to do here with a prophet and theologian of the greatest integrity, an integrity and also a clarity of thought comparable to that of Amos or Jeremiah, and therefore that he would be unlikely to talk nonsense or to be uncertain in his mind concerning the manner of God's dealings with his people. In a chapter such as ch. 40 he speaks with such distinctness and uniqueness that his voice is unlikely ever to be confused with that of any other prophet. Let us hear it then in its own right, not in a context contrived from other sources, and let us allow it to create for us chapter by chapter the context in which we read each following chapter. Perhaps by adopting this cumulative procedure we shall at least come close to letting the prophet himself create for us the context in which to interpret his writings. Perhaps also we shall find the theology illuminating the historical situation. The assumption of integrity is one that we make with any author who commands our respect. Suddenly to come upon a passage in The Book of Jeremiah in which the prophet was represented as encouraging the popular enthusiasm for the Temple and its cult would at once stir our suspicions (in the light of Jer. 7:1-15) that someone had tampered with the text. It would be impossible for us to believe that John the Baptist at one time expected the dawn of a new day through the advent of the Messiah, but at another time was convinced that it would come through the instrumentality of the Roman emperor, Augustus. Surely it is not assuming too much to attribute a similar integrity to Second Isaiah. With these minimal assumptions we approach the task of exegesis. Their validity can only be vindicated by the text itself.

The tentativeness that has been called for on such matters as the locale of the prophet and the significance of Cyrus for him has the effect of leaving him hanging in the air chronologically. This is unnecessary. The general period of his activity can be fixed within fairly definite limits. Such conclusions, however, depend in some degree upon the exegesis of particular passages, which is yet to be established.

That Second Isaiah addresses a nation scattered to the four winds places him after 587 B.C. and one would be inclined to say, some time after. Directly after 587 B.C. he would have been likely to have his mind primarily on the community which was most immediately at hand. Sufficient time has passed since 587 B.C. for him to say that the nation has been punished twice over for its sin. Yet the memory of Jerusalem's disaster seems still to be fresh in passages such as chs. 51:17-20; 60:15; and 64:10-11, almost as though the prophet himself had lived through the tragic experience. He could have been a child in 587 B.C. if he came to the height of his activity in the mid-century. Also the syncretistic religion of the community addressed by him, particularly in chs. 56 to 66, suggests that it was the direct continuation of the Judean community familiar to Jeremiah and Ezekiel.

A terminus for his ministry is suggested by ch. 66, where he opposes the rebuilding of the Temple and with his followers suffers expulsion from the community. There is no reason to identify the project with that which was sponsored by Haggai and Zechariah in 520 B.C., but the Chronicler preserves a tradition of an earlier attempt to rebuild the Temple in 538 B.C. that came to a stop because of opposition by Palestinians. The Chronicler, with his theory that only in Babylonia had the pure tradition of Israel's faith been preserved, describes the opponents as paganized "people of the land" who considered themselves entitled to a place in the activities and worship of the reconstituted community. May there not be in this a vague memory of the hostility of Second Isaiah and his followers to the first attempt to rebuild the Temple? If so, we may with fair assurance place the close of his ministry somewhere in the neighborhood of 538 B.C. The fact that the great redemption which he anticipates is consistently future, and that there is no clear reference to any restoration that has already taken place, would lend support to this conclusion.

Second Isaiah would thus be placed squarely in the midst of the international upheavals generated by the exploits of King Cyrus. The speed with which kings fell before Cyrus may well have formed the background of his conviction that all earthly power is insecure and transitory. It may also have helped to create his mood of urgency and expectancy: in a world so shaken God might be preparing the way for a new and greater exodus. But the very fact that Second Isaiah belonged in the period of King Cyrus made it almost inevitable that readers of his book in later generations would see none other than King Cyrus in the mysterious conqueror of the nations who would inaugurate a new day for Israel.

3. THE CHARACTER OF THE WRITING

A NUMBER of scholars in recent years have noted a peculiarity of the writings of Second Isaiah, that many of them seem to have been written for circulation rather than delivered orally to an immediate audience. A. Lods[1] says that "nothing in his work suggests that he tried, like the prophets who went before him, to influence by *word of mouth* a definite circle of *listeners*. He is a man of letters, endowed with magnificent lyrical gifts. . . . We must think of him, no doubt, as the editor of leaflets or tracts of which copies were anonymously and secretly circulated among the Jewish settlements scattered about the empire." Torrey[2] sees a poet-prophet writing for a scattered Israel and also for the cultivated circles of "a cosmopolitan city in whose upper stratum there was a prevailing atmosphere of urbanity, aesthetic appreciation, and intellectual freedom." Volz[3] thinks that the oracles were delivered publicly but were later circulated as broadsheets or pamphlets, a view expressed earlier by Budde. Muilenburg[4] considers the poems to be "so elaborate in their composition and in the detail of technical devices that they must have been written rather than spoken." Von Rad[5] finds it hard to conceive

---

[1] A. Lods, *The Prophets and the Rise of Judaism* (E. P. Dutton and Company, Inc., 1937), p. 241.
[2] Torrey, *op. cit.,* p. 204.
[3] Volz, *op. cit.,* p. xxv.
[4] Muilenburg, *loc. cit.,* p. 386.
[5] G. von Rad, *Theologie des A. T.,* Vol. II, p. 256.

of the prophet speaking publicly and terms him a religious writer rather than a typical prophet. There must be caution, however, in generalizing concerning the form of the oracles, especially when chs. 56 to 66 are included.

Certainly it is difficult to think of the chapters that have the most highly developed dramatic structure as having been delivered orally. There are sudden changes of speaker in them which would be confusing to listeners. The fact that there are six changes of dramatis personae in ch. 42 without breaking the thread of continuity in the thought makes it as essential for the reader to note who is speaking and who is being addressed as it is in reading a play. It is surprising how few commentators have drawn attention to this, and some who fail to recognize it have made the mistake of thinking each speech or scene to be a separate oracle.[6] The effect of this error is as though one were to expect each speech in a Shakespeare play to stand by itself.

A review of ch. 42 will illustrate the point. In vs. 1-4 God announces to the nations the glorious destiny of his Servant. In vs. 5-9 he addresses the Servant himself concerning his task. In vs. 10-12 the prophet bursts into a song of praise at the great new work that God is about to do. In v. 13 he announces God's advent to begin his work of deliverance, which in turn introduces a speech by God himself in vs. 14-17, concerning his intention. In vs. 18-20 God speaks about the blindness and deafness of his Servant, that is, the seeming unfitness of the Servant Israel for such a great task, and so the chapter closes in vs. 21-25 with a speech of the prophet himself that deals with the depressed condition of the Israelites, suffering as they have for years under the judgment of God, yet not recognizing in their deprivations the hand of God. It is hard to conceive of Second Isaiah making these rapid dramatic changes in direct oral address, but they are highly effective in a written form.

More than any other single factor, what distinguishes chs. 56 to 66 from chs. 40 to 55 is the frequency of passages in which the prophet is addressing a concrete community directly. No one would say of chs. 56:8 to 59:21 or of chs. 65 and 66 that they show a writ-

---

[6] Köhler, Begrich, and others who dissolve the chapters into fragments and apply form criticism to the fragments.

ten rather than an oral style. They are infused with the same passionate and dramatic quality as the written chapters, but we are conscious of the community to which they are spoken in a way that is not true of most of the earlier chapters. Where chs. 40 to 55 in the main seem to be a written appeal to an Israel that is scattered across the earth—north, south, east, and west, in chs. 56 to 66 the prophet seems to be standing in the midst of the Judean community, proclaiming his message of hope and striking out at the religious hypocrisies and vicious pagan perversions that obstruct the fulfillment of God's purpose. It is significant that whereas the text in chs. 40 to 55 is in a remarkably sound state of preservation, in chs. 56 to 66 it is frequently confused and difficult to translate. If chs. 40 to 55 were written by the prophet himself for circulation among his people in different lands, whereas chs. 56 to 66 represent a collection of his spoken sermons and prayers preserved by his disciples, this difference would be readily explained.

It would be wrong, however, to overstress the contrast between chs. 40 to 55 and 56 to 66. The strong similarities between chs. 60 to 62 and the earlier chapters have often been pointed out. But there is need also to recognize that in chs. 40 to 55, in spite of the writing being directed in general to a scattered Israel, there are times when the prophet seems to be arguing, not with distant exiles, but with persons close at hand, rebuking the attitudes and conduct of members of his immediate community. In chs. 40:12 ff. and 45:9-11 he ridicules people who think they know better than God does how the future of Israel can be shaped. The vividness of the persecution depicted in ch. 50:6-8 suggests events that have been observed by the prophet himself, rather than an imaginative representation of past experiences of a prophetic Israel. In chs. 50:10-11 and 51:1-8 it is difficult to think that those who are so directly addressed are other than close familiars of the prophet. This need not contradict the suggestion that chs. 40 to 55 constituted a document written for wide circulation. It would go not only to exiles in distant regions but also to members of the community close at hand, and it is only to be expected that the dialogue of the prophet with those immediately about him would find some expression in the more elaborate and general presentation.

Another distinctive feature of the prophet's writing is his weaving together of themes that gradually become familiar. Repetition is integral to his method. Single statements are sometimes repeated three or four times over in varying phrases and there is no limit to the frequency with which he may bring back a single theme. The chapters are knit together by this repetition of themes. For instance, in ch. 42:7 the Servant is to bring sight and light to the blind of the nations who sit in darkness; in v. 10 God in his new day leads these blind in a way they know not; and in vs. 18-19 he points out to them how blind the Servant is who is to bring them sight; then in ch. 43:8 all the blind in the day of restoration have eyes to see. Or again, in ch. 40:6-8 the perishability of all things human is stated; in v. 15 the nothingness of the power of the nations in comparison with the power of God begins to be emphasized; in v. 24 the rulers of the earth are the grass that withers when God blows upon it; again, in ch. 41:2, 11, 16, 25, the nations become dust as God deals with them through his Servant of the future. Rarely are the themes repeated exactly as before. Combined with new themes, they take on new nuances and gradually the full message of the prophet unfolds.

An introductory word also needs to be said about the eschatology of the prophet, since it has such a profound influence upon his writing, and the frequent failure of interpreters to allow it its full weight has led to serious misunderstandings. Duhm, Smith, and other earlier commentators regarded the eschatological language as though it were a kind of poetic hyperbole, fantastic in its imagery, but actually intended to refer to prosaic historical occurrences. Thus, the "highway for our God" in ch. 40:3-5, in whose preparation the mountains were melted down and the valleys filled up and on which in chs. 35:8-10 and 49:11-13 the exiles from *all* lands stream home when once the day of redemption has dawned, became for them the road from Babylon to Palestine that was to be traveled by a little group of exiles in 538 B.C. The fact that ch. 40:3-5, 9-11, describes a theophany, a return of God to his people, was simply ignored.

Beginning in ch. 41:22 the prophet uses the terms "former things" and "things to come" to refer to God's acts in past history and his new action anticipated in the future. Again and again he announces the impending action that is to bring salvation and a glorious new day not only to Israel but to the whole world. God's universal sovereignty is to be recognized by all nations and established as a just order everywhere. It is to be nothing less than a new heavens and a new earth. Israel will be expanded by converts from the nations so that its population will overflow a reconstructed Jerusalem and it will be God's instrument in both his judgment and his liberation of the nations. But this picture of the future seemed too fantastic for most commentators. In their confidence that the prophet was among the exiles in Babylon, they made his eschatology little more than an exuberant idealization of what was going to happen when once the Babylonian exiles got back to Palestine.

Perhaps what has been most misleading in the eschatological passages is that the future events are frequently described as though they had already taken place or were happening in the present moment. But by the rapid transitions that he makes between past, present, and future, and by the repeated assertions that the great day has not yet come, the prophet makes abundantly clear that he is projecting himself into the future to describe vividly the anticipated events. The consequence, however, has been that interpreters have tried to identify some of the "things to come" with historical events already taking place. This is a source of confusion in Volz's commentary. He, more than any earlier interpreter, has an appreciation of the eschatological language of Second Isaiah, but he is so certain that the movements of Cyrus were the source of the prophet's inspiration that he persistently turns eschatological into historical events. Muilenburg, who alone sees that ch. 40:3-11 describes a theophany and not a return of exiles and who goes far beyond Volz in recognizing the dimensions of the eschatology, nevertheless falls into the same confusion as Volz at some points.

The hopes of Second Isaiah are focused upon a future intervention of God in the history of his people and of the world. This great turning point is imminent, so imminent that he announces it as already present. It is a day of judgment for the nations and also for the unfaithful in Israel, but even more, a day of transformation. In a moment, Israel, the blind and helpless worm, is to become a mighty nation. Kings and princes of the earth will stand in awe at the sight. The prophet's assurance of this future is based upon the word that

God has spoken in Israel from the beginning of its history. In it he revealed his purpose both for Israel and for all mankind. Israel's past history validates the faith that what God says he does. His word has shaped history in the past and reveals the future course of history. The word of God has power in itself to bring God's purpose to its fulfillment (ch. 55:10-11). But the sin of Israel has power to delay—but only to delay, not to defeat—the coming of the redemption (chs. 48:18-19; 58:6-12; 59:2).

This eschatology has to be understood as an expression of the prophet's faith in God's sovereignty. If it is interpreted merely as a prediction of future events, then it becomes evidence of his inability to form a sober judgment concerning the future possibilities of his nation. The events that he heralded did not happen, just as the events heralded in the eschatological expectation of the early Christian church did not happen. But just as the latter does not detract from the church's confidence that the future belongs to God and to his Christ, so the former casts no shadow on the prophet's judgment. His faith in a sovereignty of God over the world and its history was rooted and grounded in the revelation of God, which was the very source of Israel's life and destiny. In the present God's purpose might seem to have been eclipsed, but this was only because it was the hour of judgment and a time of darkness. In the past Israel had experienced the seemingly impossible, and in the future nothing would be impossible for God. He must vindicate his sovereignty and fulfill his purpose. Therefore, the believer who puts all his trust in God's word can rejoice in the present darkness and go forward with confidence knowing that God's victory is certain. The eschatology is thus the expression of an unconquerable faith in God's power to bring his purpose to its fulfillment in history. It has also an ethical significance, for all of man's life in the present is seen in its antithesis to the true order that God intends should be realized and toward which the believer must be hastening.

II

Commentary on Isaiah, Chs. 40-66, 35

CHAPTER 40/ There can be little doubt that ch. 40 is the intended introduction to the chapters that follow. The only serious rival[1] is ch. 35, which has the same rounded completeness as ch. 40 and contains what reads like a summary of Second Isaiah's message. Chapter 55 has a similar character and forms a fitting conclusion to the sixteen chapters that seem to have been put together by the prophet himself for circulation to a scattered Israel. Chapter 40 is like the first sustained blast of a great trumpet heralding the coming of the King. It opens with a thrice-repeated call for messengers to take the news of God's coming to a broken and despairing nation. It lays the foundation for hope in the word that has been heard in Israel from the beginning of its life. It challenges the power of the nations that seems to make the fulfillment of God's promises impossible. Concluding with a passionate appeal for faith, it leads on into the following chapters, which are to spell out in more detail the future that awaits Israel and mankind.

The repetition of the verb "comfort" sounds a note of urgency, as though God were waiting impatiently for his stricken people to receive word of his forgiveness and to put behind them the dark

---

[1] Torrey, *op. cit.,* regards chs. 34, 35, and 40 to 66 as a literary unit with each chapter exactly where the prophet placed it. For him ch. 34 is thus the opening chapter. He insists that chs. 34 and 35 are inseparable, like two sides of a coin, expressing the twin themes of judgment on God's enemies and blessedness for the righteous. He is justified in his contention that these themes belong together in Second Isaiah, but that does not necessarily validate the attributing of ch. 34 to Second Isaiah. It is remarkably similar in its unrelieved proclamation of doom on Edom to oracles in Amos 1:11-12; Obadiah; Mal. 1:2-5; Jer. 49:7-22; Ezek. 25:12-14, which shows its theme to have been extremely common and popular, hardly the one that Second Isaiah would place in the forefront of his writings.

years of disciplinary judgment. Forgiveness means not just the end of judgment, but the restoration of the covenant relation which has in it the promise of life and the beginning of a new day in which God's purpose for Israel will move toward its fulfillment. In ch. 42:14 this new day is likened to a child with which God is already in labor that he may bring it forth. The announcement of God's return to his people conveys the message of forgiveness in a vivid fashion. Israel in its ruin and dispersion had seemed like a wife abandoned by her husband, but now, as promised by Hosea, the husband is returning. Different images are used by Second Isaiah to portray the condition of a people without God: an abandoned wife, a barren desert, shepherdless sheep, people without food, people who are blind and deaf, prisoners. The comfort offered, therefore, is simply the coming of God, which may be described as forgiveness of sin, the restoration of the marriage relation, the return of the shepherd, water in the desert, food for the hungry, sight and hearing for the blind and deaf, freedom for the prisoners. All are ways of saying that one word—God. What the prophet offers his people is the living, present God. One thing he knows for certain: if they have God, they will have a future no matter how great the obstacles may be.

The assurance with which the prophet offers his people God's forgiveness and God's presence with them is based solely on the word that God has spoken in the midst of Israel through the centuries. What that word promised is stated very succinctly in ch. 45:23: "To me every knee shall bow." History is not meaningless but has a goal, the bringing of all nations under the gracious rule of the one true God, and God's chosen agent to accomplish that goal has been Israel. This is what Israel has been told from the beginning (v. 21), and how a nation with such a God and such a destiny can destroy itself and its future by giving its worship to idols is incomprehensible. The years of judgment were intended to refine the nation and turn it back to God. But judgment cannot be a final word. Beyond such heavy judgment as the nation has suffered must be a time of restoration and fulfillment.

The resistance of the community to this message of hope was based on the strength of the nations among whom Israel was scattered.

The prophet was confronted with realists who measured future possibilities by what they could see. They complained how unjustly God had used them, but they refused to believe that he had the power to create a new future for his people. The gods of the nations seemed to them more powerful than Israel's God, so they were inclined to pay some homage to them in hope that they might be helpful. Hence the prophet's repeated emphasis upon the infinite power of God and his scorn and ridicule of the worship of idols. Only by an unconditional openness and trust toward the everlasting God who has revealed himself and his purpose for the world in their midst can Israelites keep their souls alive in the time of darkness.

The chapter is a magnificent unity. Joyful proclamation of the new day is followed by a biting indictment of those who forget their heritage and resist the prophet's message. The power of God is contrasted with the powerlessness of idols, and the nation is called to remember the incomparable nature of the God with whom they have had to do through the centuries. No one who trusts the word of such a God and waits in confidence for what he is yet to do can ever despair.

Various voices are heard throughout the chapter. In vs. 1-2 the prophet reports what he hears God saying. In vs. 3-5 another voice, not God's, since in v. 5 it speaks of God in the third person, commands the preparation of a road for God's return. In vs. 6-8 another unidentified voice commands the prophet to preach. Then, in vs. 9-11, the prophet calls upon Jerusalem to carry the good news to the cities of Judah. In vs. 12-24 the prophet contends with his opponents, but in v. 25 it is God who speaks, giving way again, however, in vs. 26-31 to the prophet. Volz and Muilenburg have both contended that the vaguely identified voices in vs. 3-11 are those of supernatural beings in a heavenly council. Second Isaiah has, like Isaiah in ch. 6, been given ears to hear the deliberations in the council of heaven (cf. Job, ch. 1; I Kings, ch. 22; Dan. 7:9 ff.). Volz makes it an ecstatic experience of the prophet. Muilenburg thinks that "the sublime background of the heavenly council accounts for the atmosphere and mood of the poems." There may be an element of truth in the suggestion, but it is by no means certain. It is characteristic of the prophet's dramatic style to let different voices speak for him. Why not angelic voices out of the unseen? But there is a difference be-tween the ecstatic experience of Isaiah and the use of such voices as a dramatic device. The one voice that really counts for Second Isaiah is the voice of God (cf. ch. 50:4).

Vs. 1-2. The focal point of these verses is not primarily comfort, but rather, forgiveness. A great decision has been made in heaven that at any moment will be reflected in events upon earth. God has forgiven Israel! Israel has been restored to its unique place within the world as God's covenant people. The closest parallel to this is in Paul's announcement in Rom. 8:1: "There is no more doom for those who are in Christ Jesus." The sentence of death has been lifted and there is now the promise of life. A people that had sep-arated itself from God by its sins has now been restored to God's fel-lowship by his forgiveness. Therefore, the comfort being offered to Israel is this great, life-encompassing comfort, that whereas they have been dying daily in the futility of their Godforsakenness, they now can live and lay hold upon a meaningful future as a people whose God is with them.

This good news could, and can, be understood only by people who have taken seriously the reality of God's judgment, that to rup-ture one's relation with God by sinning against his love and truth and justice is to set oneself upon the dark side of God and to bring darkness and disorder into all of life's experiences. Only an Israel that had learned from its prophets and priests to interpret the dis-asters of 722, 597, and 587 B.C. and the deprivations of the exile as the consequences of the broken covenant was prepared to receive and rejoice at Second Isaiah's message. Perhaps the unwillingness of most of the prophet's hearers to respond to his preaching (ch. 50:2) was rooted in this, that they could not know themselves forgiven with-out confessing themselves sinners. Judgment and forgiveness are inseparable, and the broad-minded man who has got rid of the dis-tressing and disturbing concept of judgment has also abandoned the possibility of forgiveness.

The word translated "warfare" or "time of service" signifies a compulsory service rendered in wartime, and it is this element of servitude that is meant to be predominant here. Forgiveness means freedom to live and to have a future, but to be not yet forgiven is to be in subjection.

The representation of God as eager for the moment to come when Israel can know his forgiveness suggests a limitation upon the freedom of God to forgive. Why did Israel have to wait so long for God's forgiveness? We ask this question because we have come to think of God's forgiveness as automatic and instantaneous upon man's profession of repentance. It ceases to be a personal act of God in which he restores us to a living relationship with himself, and becomes a ritual of repentance and forgiveness by which we give ourselves good consciences for bad. We have ceased to take sin seriously as the rupture of a nation's relation with God that could bring it into ruin and subjection for fifty years, or as the rupture of our own relation with God that can make us walk in darkness for weeks and months and perhaps even years on end. It is not because God is not free to forgive that the years of subjection continue, but because Israel is not yet ready to be forgiven.

It is worth noting in v. 2 that in the final phrase the prophet slips over from reporting the divine proclamation into speaking of God in the third person, a shift that occurs more than once (cf. ch. 51:1-3). The phrase, "that she has received from the Lord's hand double for all her sins," has been variously interpreted: as one half for Israel's own sins and the other for the sins of mankind in general, or as a complaint by the prophet that God has been unjust in laying upon Israel more punishment than its sins deserved. But elsewhere the prophet sees Israel's hard experiences as the just deserts of sin. Perhaps like Amos (Amos 3:2), he held Israel to be doubly responsible. Or it may be only a forceful expression of his conviction that the time of judgment is definitely over and that both in judgment and in mercy God gives full measure flowing over.

Vs. 3-5. Most commentators have seen in these verses a reference to the return of exiles from Babylon. Volz says that vs. 3-11 describe the return, vs. 3-5 the highway on which the exiles are to return, and vs. 9-11 the entrance of the exiles into Palestine. But he shows a consciousness of the remoteness of exiles from the scene when he adds that, whereas elsewhere the highway is made pleasant for the exiles, here the return "is a religious experience and the significance of the miracle is a tremendous, world-encompassing theophany of Yahweh." The highway through the desert in chs. 35:8 and 49:11 is certainly the road on which exiles return home, but three facts con-

cerning it must be noted with care: (1) it is symbolic of all the roads
by which exiles are to come from the four corners of the earth (note
especially ch. 49:11-12) and is not only through the desert but also
through the seas (ch. 43:2, 16), the way of the exodus from Egypt
contributing strongly to the imagery; (2) the ingathering of exiles is
just one feature of the great day in which God will reveal his power
and glory to the whole world; (3) in ch. 40:3-5 the emphasis is so
completely on the glorious return of God to his people that *nothing*
is said clearly about exiles returning. The miraculous road in the
wilderness for which mountains are leveled and valleys filled up is
before all else "a highway *for our God.*" (The imagery may be influenced by the Babylonian triumphal road for Marduk.) What all
mankind sees is "the glory *of the Lord.*" The news that Jerusalem
is to take to the cities of Judah is not "Behold the returning exiles,"
but "Behold your God!" This is so obvious in the text that when
once it is grasped, it becomes ludicrous that anyone should describe
the messengers in vs. 9-11 as mounting the hills of Palestine to catch
a first glimpse of the procession of exiles![2] Even in v. 10 the focus of
interest is wholly upon God's coming and upon the power with
which he will establish his rule. Moreover, in v. 11 where God is
pictured shepherding his flock and dealing gently with the young
lambs, this is the flock *to which he has returned,* the "Jerusalem"
and "my people" of vs. 1-2, and there is nothing to suggest that they
too are on the highway. The shepherdless sheep have had their great
shepherd restored to them. Only a failure to grasp the importance
of Second Isaiah's eschatological hope permits the thrusting of a
horde of returning Babylonian exiles into the forefront of the picture. It has not seemed possible that the prophet would base all his
hopes upon *a coming of God* to his people! Thus Marti sees in the
passage Babylonian exiles and behind them Cyrus' act of liberation
and concludes that the prophet's hopes and convictions took the particular form they did from the earthshaking success of the Persian
conqueror Cyrus! The prophet's eschatological conceptions then become merely a poetic and decorative way of announcing impending
historical events. That God has forgiven his people is deduced by
the prophet from Cyrus' liberation of the exiles, and the return of

[2] Volz and Marti do this.

God to his people is really only the return of a handful of his people to their former homes in Palestine. A similar demythologizing of New Testament eschatology would turn the early church's expectation of Christ's return in triumph into a poetic way of saying that they expected churches to be established in his name in all lands.

That the highway is through the wilderness and the desert has several levels of significance. For Second Isaiah the desert is symbolic of what man's life has become and must ever become when he is without God. The desert is barren of life, although seeds are hidden in it that will spring into life at the touch of water. Its dryness is the dryness of death. But the coming of God is like the coming of rain or snow from heaven (chs. 44:3; 45:8; 55:10), or the opening of springs (chs. 35:6; 41:18; 43:19; 48:21; 49:10) from which rivers flow through the land, transforming it from a desert or wilderness unfit for habitation into an Eden of fruitfulness (ch. 51:3-12). Therefore, the desert is not just a region between the place of exile and Palestine that has to be traversed, but rather, is a representation of the very life of this scattered people (and of the world) into whose midst God is about to come.

The leveling of the mountains and filling up of the valleys is not to make a pleasant road for the feet of the exiles, but is the melting of the earth at the fiery presence of God (Ps. 46:6; Isa. 51:6) and is closely connected with the appearance of God in glory in v. 5. Duhm is so unaware of Second Isaiah's eschatological orientation that he dismisses v. 5 as a marginal gloss that has crept into the text and joins v. 4 directly with v. 9 in order not to interrupt the trek of the exiles! But v. 5 is the crux of the entire chapter. The revealing of the glory of God is the appearance of God in glory, the dispersal of the darkness that as yet hides God's majestic, universal sovereignty from the eyes of men so that they at last will know who is master in the midst of the creation. God's glory is the radiance of his presence, which fills the whole earth (Isa. 6:3) and which traditionally in Israel was represented as a blinding fire or light. Where his glory appears, his sovereignty is recognized not just as a future possibility but as the present reality on which everything in the life of man depends. "God reigns; let the earth rejoice." "God reigns; let the unrighteous tremble." Man's blindness, about which Second Isaiah has much to say, is blindness to this fundamental basis of all existence, the rule of God. The disorder and confusion of life in the midst of which man finds himself is then mistaken by him for the whole of reality. God seems to do nothing in the face of rampant injustice and evil. There seems to be no possible future for Israel. Why then should one pay heed to Israel's God? The facts of history seem to say that he has no power. But these are the thoughts of blind men who have forgotten what men in Israel have seen of God when their eyes were opened to know him in his glory and majesty and holiness. Men have to be prepared to walk in darkness, remembering what God has been to his people in the past and trusting that what he has been he will again show himself to be, since he must be faithful to his own nature. Israel must ever live in the remembrance of past revelations and in the hope of future revelations.

The new revelation of God's glory anticipated by the prophet differs from the ancient one in the breadth of its scope. In the exodus God revealed himself to Israel, but in this new manifestation he will be revealed to all mankind. "All flesh shall see it together." Here at the very beginning the universal note is struck that is sustained throughout the writings of Second Isaiah. The fact that he emphasizes so strongly the unique destiny of Israel as the instrument of God's purpose and promises to Israel such power and wealth that the kings of the nations are to stand astonished at the unexpected sight has tended to conceal the radical universality of his vision. God is for him the Creator of the ends of the earth who has all mankind under his care. He is not content that Israel should be gathered home to dwell in his light (ch. 49:6), but sets this restored Israel the task of being a light to the nations (chs. 42:6; 49:6). The covenant relation of God with Israel is to be widened to take in all mankind through Israel (ch. 42:6). God's concern is not only for an Israel that has been robbed and plundered, trapped in holes, and hidden in prisons (ch. 42:22), but for all the blind, brokenhearted, despairing, hungry, and thirsty captives in the world (chs. 42:7; 61:1).

Volz has been so impressed with this universal element in Second Isaiah that he has developed a theory, on very slender evidence, that the prophet returned with the exiles from Babylon to Palestine, but was so filled with zeal for the coming of the day when every knee would bow to Israel's God (ch. 45:23) that he left Palestine to become the first missionary to the Gentiles. To this missionary period in the prophet's activity he assigns the four so-called "Servant Songs." But it should be observed that the mission of Israel to the nations and the extension of the covenant relation to include the Gentiles lie beyond the day of God's appearing, a day that throughout the book has not yet come. The prophet lives in constant and eager expectation of it, the great new turning point in the life of Israel and in the destiny of man. First will come the ingathering and the transformation of Israel and then the establishment of God's reign over the life of all mankind. But nowhere is there any indication that he considered the initial transformation to have already taken place. On the contrary, as the book proceeds, the sins of the people seem to rise up to prevent the coming of the day of renewal (chs. 57, 58). One thing is certain, the day of salvation is ever future for Second Isaiah, except in ch. 53, where the decisive intervention of God is seen to have already taken place, not in any return of exiles from Babylon, but in the suffering and death of the faithful Servant. Yet even here the day of universal triumph is still future. It is this consistent outreach toward a future day of God's revealing of his glory that casts the first suspicion upon all interpretations that identify Cyrus' edict of liberation for the subject peoples in Babylon with the day of deliverance on which the prophet sets his hope. That for which he hoped was not fulfilled in any external way within his lifetime. If a return from Babylon took place during his ministry, which is of course possible, it was not the transformation for which he looked but, what seems more likely, an accentuation of the distress. The mission to the Gentiles had to wait much longer for fulfillment than Volz assumes.

The concluding phrase of v. 5, "for the mouth of the Lord has spoken," is not to be passed over as merely a prophetic form, but rather, together with v. 8, points us to the source of the prophet's astounding confidence. God's coming in power and glory to fulfill his purpose of redemption and to vindicate his sovereignty is certain because God has spoken. He has put his words in the mouth of Israel from the beginning (chs. 49:2; 51:16; 59:21). It is this that has given Israel its unique destiny among the nations, not any qualities or virtues that Israelites have possessed to make them superior to other men, but simply God's choice of them to be the Servant of his word. In this word entrusted to them God has revealed himself, his holiness, his justice, his mercy, his intention that there should be order and not chaos in his world (ch. 45:19), his purpose that in covenant fellowship with him all men should one day find their true blessing. But the word in which all of this is revealed has in it the creative and re-creative power of God himself (ch. 55:11), so that where it is present, God is at work, and though his working may not be visible at present, the outcome is as certain as the coming of the harvest in fertile soil that has been well watered (ch. 55:11). Second Isaiah, more than any other prophet, has a comprehensive conception of God's activity in the whole history of Israel. He sees the present in the light of the past. His incitement of his people to "look to the rock whence you were hewn, and to the quarry from which you were digged. Look to Abraham, your father, and to Sarah who bore you" (ch. 51:1-2) is an appeal to history. So also are his many references to the exodus. God has spoken in Israel's past, revealing his inmost mind and will, and this word of revelation is the one point of absolute security in the whole creation.

When this is recognized, it will be seen at once how closely linked vs. 6-8 are with v. 5, and the suggestion of some commentators that vs. 6-8 should be transposed to follow v. 11 will be rejected. The prophet has begun to lay bare the very ground of his hope and of the hope of Israel, the basis of his certainty that a new day is at hand, the authority of his declaration that God has forgiven Israel.

Vs. 6-8 have rightly been recognized (Muilenburg) as reflecting an experience of the prophet in which he heard his call to take up his mission. He heard a voice out of the unseen saying, "Preach." The usual translation "Cry" is both colorless and misleading. The voice is one of command as in v. 1, but what was then a general command to speak to the heart of Jerusalem becomes now a specific command to the prophet to proclaim the good news that has come to him. The RSV translation "And I said" has been confirmed by the Qumran text of Isaiah, making clear that this is no conversation between two heavenly beings that is merely overheard by the prophet (Volz), but is a direct call to Second Isaiah. His response, "What shall I preach?"

shows him in a state of uncertainty and spiritual emptiness, with no good news to proclaim. This points perhaps to a period prior to his time of confidence and hope, when he himself needed to be rescued from the despair that he shared with his people and to find solid ground for his confidence. This interpretation is confirmed by vs. 6 and 7, wherein he expresses the futility of a life from which God is absent. "All flesh is grass, and all its grace is like the flower of the field." "All flesh" means "all human life." It takes in the life of nations, families, and individuals. It comprehends all history and all culture, all the constructions and achievements of men. To liken man's life to grass and to the flower of the field is not to deny to it beauty and value of a kind, but the devastating accusation against life is that there is nothing in it that endures. It adds up finally to nothing. It goes nowhere. It moves toward no goal. The grace that it possesses for the moment is shadowed by the knowledge that it must die, leaving nothing behind. But this nihilism was singularly painful to an Israelite whose nation had drawn its very life breath from the conviction that it had been brought into being by God to serve a glorious purpose and that all its history had been undergirded by the forward thrust of that purpose toward a hidden goal. After so many years of broken life and disappointed hopes, it must have seemed as though there were nothing more enduring in the life of Israel than in any other nation. It was possible to read the earlier prophets in such a way as to deduce from them that God had cast his people off completely because of their sins, so that they no longer had anything to hope for from him. This is the standpoint of the Israelites whom the prophet addresses in v. 27. They say, "My way is hid from the Lord, and my right is disregarded by my God." They do not abandon faith in their God entirely, but rather, like the prophet himself before he heard God's word, retain their belief in a God of Israel, finding in it, however, a source of bitterness and complaint because of what seems to be the injustice of God's dealings with them. But again the prophet's view is universal. It is not just the purposelessness of Israel's life that burdens him but the futility of life in general. "Surely the people is grass."

Verse 8 is the answer to the prophet's question in v. 6, "What shall I preach?" It is tempting to read it as a further utterance of the voice out of the unseen, but perhaps the absence of any indication of the identity of the speaker is best explained by the assumption that whereas the command to preach came to the prophet in a time of acute distress as he saw the deadly effects of despair in his people's life, his answer to despair came to him as he was driven to search more deeply into the traditions concerning God's dealings with Israel and into the earlier prophetic writings. All that we can say, however, is that at some one moment his whole being was laid open to the word from beyond that had been heard through the centuries by the prophets. This word had ever set the life of Israel completely in question and yet at the same time had been Israel's only enduring source of confidence and strength. The history of Israel was the history of Israel's response in faithfulness or in stubborn resistance to this word from God. In the past, when Israel truly lived it drew its life from this word, and when it died, its death was the consequence of a refusal to hear and obey. Let one man such as Abraham cling to this word in spite of every obstacle, and from him a nation could be born, but let a proud and powerful nation scorn this word, and it had no hope of a future. In a perishing world only God endures—and that which God brings into the life of man when man is bound to him in a covenant of love and faithfulness. God's word is his chosen means of opening to man the possibility of covenant fellowship with himself. God speaks and man answers, but God's speaking is God's giving of himself, and man's answer must be man's giving of himself completely in return. God's self-giving may be described as God's coming to man, and man's self-giving as man's coming to God. The word that endures forever is the word in which God comes and gives himself to man that man, responding in faith and obedience, may live and not die.

Vs. 9-11. The way in which the individual poems interlock with each other to build up the larger unity has already begun to be evident. The theme "the call to proclaim the good news" runs through all of these first four poems. The announcement of God's coming follows directly upon the proclamation of his forgiveness and as we have seen, the two express the same reality. Then the concluding phrase of v. 5 prepares the way for vs. 6-8. Now in v. 9 there is a repetition of the theme in a new form, or perhaps one should say, a gathering up of what has been said thus far before proceeding to the final description of what God will be to his people when he comes —mighty sovereign and loving shepherd. In v. 9 the call to preach is directed to Jerusalem, which is commanded to mount the highest hill and shout to all the cities of Judah the good news of God's coming. "Jerusalem-Zion" is in apposition to "bearer of glad tidings" and is not the receiver of the tidings as is evident in "Say to the cities of Judah." Duhm found the image of Jerusalem mounting a hill ridiculous, but it is perfectly in keeping with the poetic language of Second Isaiah. It should be noted also that both "Jerusalem" and "cities of Judah" may be symbolic of the whole widely scattered people of Israel and not just the Palestinian localities (though it would be strange if it were to exclude the Judean population), and that here distinctly the nation is called to discharge a mission *to the nation* (just as today one calls upon the church as minister of Christ to carry out a mission to the church as a body of people in need of a new grasp of the gospel of Christ). This becomes specially important in chs. 45:4-5 and 49:1-7 where it has frequently been argued that, since the Servant has a mission to Israel, he cannot possibly be Israel.

It is significant that in his description of the God who comes in vs. 10-11, the prophet combines the images of the conquering king and the gentle shepherd. The two are not as far apart in the ancient mind as they are in ours, for "shepherd of his people" was frequently one of the titles of the king in the ancient East. Sovereignty both in the human sphere and in God had two aspects, one that called for strength to maintain order against divisive forces from within and against enemies from without, and the other that required the gentleness and skill of the shepherd in securing the welfare of all the members of his flock. Therefore, not only God but also the human representative of God, through whom he establishes his rule among men, must be both strong and gentle. Frequently in the interpretation of Second Isaiah these attributes of kingship have been set in contradiction to each other, especially in the portrayal of God's Servant. The assertion that the Servant is gentle has been held to exclude his use of force (Duhm, Volz, etc.). He must win his way by persuasion alone; above all he must not deal violently with his enemies. He can only suffer for them in order to overcome their resistance. Perhaps it is the unconscious tendency to identify the figure of the Servant with the figure of Jesus that has made it seem to many interpreters a demeaning of the Servant to suggest that he could use force as well as gentle persuasion. What is evident to us in vs. 9-10 is that for the prophet there was no contradiction between the two attributes. He can even represent God as a man of war (chs. 42:13; 63:3) marching out against the forces that stand against him and crushing them utterly.

The emphasis in v. 10 upon God's power and his personal rule ("His arm shall rule for him") is to be understood against the background of the present complaint of the Israelites that the events which determine their lives are without plan or direction. God seems to have abdicated his place of rule. The world is like a driverless car careening to its ruin. But when their eyes are opened to the true order of things, they will see that God has not abandoned his world to chaos. God rules. So also the shepherd image reflects a time in which the Israelites have felt themselves to be sheep without a shepherd, helpless to defend themselves against their enemies. In Palestine sheep without a shepherd have no prospect of life. To men who saw in the life of the sheep the closest likeness of their own predicament there could be no better news than that they had a shepherd in the unseen.

One difficulty with the eschatological language that speaks of God "coming" is that it can be taken to mean that God is *not now* sovereign and that in the dark years of judgment he has *not* been the Shepherd of Israel, in short, that God has been absent from his people and not just hidden from them. That this is not the prophet's meaning is evident in various ways, but particularly when he speaks of God's self-revealing, not as his coming, but as the giving of sight to blind eyes and hearing to deaf ears. God is unchanging and is at work in every moment, but eyes and ears have to be open to him for his presence and action to be recognized.

It is puzzling why in v. 9 the prophet, in calling upon Jerusalem to lift up her voice, says, "Fear not." Why should anyone be afraid to declare such good news? This warns us that the proclamation of God's nearness and of the imminence of a confrontation with him is not good news for everyone. It is unrealistic sentimentality to assume that this was what all men in the Israel of the sixth century, or in any other nation in any other age, have wanted to hear. The nearness of God has in it not only promise for man but also menace. It sets the whole existing structure of his life in question. The establishment of God's sovereignty is the end of man's beloved self-sovereignty. This explains why the prophet expected his words of consolation and encouragement to rouse such bitter and violent opposition (ch. 50:4-6). An Israel in which God was actually sovereign and shepherd would have to undergo a far-reaching revolution in its life, and many established practices and ways of thinking would have to be abandoned. Here we glimpse the radical ethical implications of a thoroughgoing eschatological faith. Those who think that eschatology encourages an ethical irresponsibility by directing the vision away from present realities to focus it merely on a distant future day need to examine more closely the nature of Biblical eschatology. It is the expression of a faith that is concerned not only that God should be sovereign in the day of consummation but that he should be recognized as sovereign now in all regions of human life, and that an ethic of obedience to him should be spelled out uncompromisingly.

Vs. 12-31. With v. 12 the form of the prophet's address changes from joyful proclamation to sharp and penetrating argument. We become aware that among those to whom he speaks he anticipates opposition and skepticism. The early appearance of this polemical note is important. He cannot sweep his opponents along with him by the very exuberance of his faith. They too have convictions that they have formed in the years of misfortune and they will not be easily moved from them. Predominant in their minds seems to be the irresistableness of the power of the nations that stand in the way of any new day for Israel. The historical situation is not favorable. The obstacles are too great. We can imagine the ridicule they would heap on the prophet's seemingly hysterical conviction that deliverance and restoration are at hand. They were the realists who looked squarely at the facts and made their plans accordingly. They had no intention of building on any such fantastic hope as that which he offered them. Yet they were perishing in their realism, and many of

them in their despair were turning even to the crude and superstitious forms of worship of their neighbors. There was an emptiness
in them where their God had been that they tried to fill with
all manner of rubbish. The change from proclamation to argument does not indicate a new oracle. The unity with the preceding
verses is in the continuity of theme. The power of God to create a
new day for Israel has been proclaimed, but now it must be defended
and pressed home upon minds that have lost all confidence in God's
power.

There are two ways in which v. 12 can be read. Most expositors
have imagined that the prophet is extolling God's greatness by picturing him measuring out the waters of the sea in handfuls, marking
off the heavens with a yardstick (a heavenly one of large dimensions
surely!), and weighing the mountains in scales. The fact that there
are ancient documents in which Marduk does these very things has
seemed to support this view. But the tone of the prophet in the
whole passage must be grasped. Volz recognizes rightly that the
"who" in v. 12 must refer to the same person as the "who" in v. 13.
Verses 12 and 13 belong very closely together, both ridiculing the
man who thinks he knows what God can and cannot do. For him to
measure the mind of God is as impossible as though he were to
attempt to measure out the waters of the sea in little handfuls, or to
mark off the heavens with a yardstick, or to weigh out the mountains on a tiny pair of balances. There is biting humor in the attack
that the prophet here begins against his skeptical opponents. They
know too much. They think they know the mind of God with such
certainty that they are not open to any new word from God to man.
The attitude suggested by this is not an abandonment of faith, but
rather, a form of orthodoxy, not an unwillingness to know anything
of God, but a cocksureness, a certainty that they know all that there
is to know of God's mind. They have lost all perspective concerning
the relation between God and man. They have forgotten that God's
thoughts are not their thoughts, nor his ways their ways (ch. 55:9).
Therefore, their ears are closed against the possibility of hearing a
word from God that would set before them a totally new future.
Second Isaiah accuses them of acting as though they had the Spirit
of God under their private direction, as though they were God's
privy councilors to whom God must constantly turn for advice, as

though God needed to be enlightened by them and taught the meaning of justice. They understand what justice is better than God does! It is important to note how biting this attack is and that those who are the butt of it are undoubtedly men of considerable religious pretensions. Here we get our first glimpse of the religious community with which the prophet was most intimately confronted.

Where do the prophet's opponents find the starting point for their realistic thinking? They begin with "the realities of the present situation" and do not even notice that they have taken no account of the reality of God in the present situation. They see only the power of the nations. Therefore, in *v. 15* Second Isaiah turns from attacking their pretensions to belittling the political forces to which so much deference is being paid. What is the power of any nation in comparison with the power of God? Its king gives orders; its army marches; it may even hold other nations under its authority for a time. But how long does this endure? Men and nations alike are born, live out their day, and die. The breath of God blows upon them and they wither like the grass. But God does not die. To his sovereignty there is no end. Men have their day and then God has his day. It takes time for God's sovereignty in the affairs of men to be revealed in its true dimensions, but it will surely be revealed, and when it is, the power of all the nations massed together will seem no greater than one drop of water in a whole rain cloud[3] in comparison with the infinite power of God.

The sudden reference to sacrifice in *v. 16,* when seen in the light of the religious character of the prophet's opponents, suggests that they are setting their confidence upon the efficacy of sacrifices to secure a more favorable disposition of God toward themselves (cf. chs. 58:2-4; 66:3-4). In chs. 58 and 66 it is worth noting that those who occupy themselves with sacrifices and fasting turn a deaf ear to the prophet's word. Here in v. 16 the prophet taunts them that if they knew the greatness of God, they would know that all the forests of Lebanon for wood and all the wild animals in the forests of Lebanon for sacrifices would not be a sufficient offering to the Creator of heaven and earth. The only sufficient offering is a humble and responsive spirit (chs. 58:5 f.; 66:2) and an ear open unconditionally

---

[3] I am indebted to Prof. G. Landes for the information that Ugaritic studies have shown "bucket" to be an impossible translation and "rain cloud" to be more likely.

to God's bidding. (Volz excises v. 16 as a gloss! Muilenburg tends to agree.) Some expositors, concerned that Second Isaiah seems to be suggesting an offering of wild beasts, a thing forbidden specifically in the laws of sacrifice, miss the point of the verse. The contention that he was not unfriendly to sacrificial rites is also invalid. One point, however, that should be noted is the prophet's scorn for the power of *all* the nations, declaring that they are to be accounted less than nothing and emptiness. This surely makes us ask whether he would be likely to build his hopes for the future, at least in some measure, upon the power and worldly success of a Persian king. This dilemma is particularly acute for those who make Cyrus' exploits the primary source of the prophet's inspiration and of his wild hopes for a new day in the life of the world.

The concluding section of the chapter falls into two clear-cut divisions, each introduced by the question: "What do you think God is like?" which is another way of putting the searching question "Who is your God? Whom do you really worship?" After an initial suggestion of where perhaps his people tend to look for God, first, in crude and helpless idols and second, in the movements of the stars, the prophet asks if they have forgotten what has been known in Israel concerning God from the beginning of its life, and then proceeds to tell them the nature of the God of Israel. Again, in the light of the religious character of his opponents, we are reminded here of the persistent tendency of cult officials in preexilic times to mingle idol worship and astral worship with the worship of Israel's God. It would not be surprising to find this tendency persisting into the middle years of the sixth century. It is not necessary to assign the idol manufacture pictured in *vs. 19-20* to non-Israelites or to think that it could have taken place only in Babylonia. The description of the making of idols is shot through with prophetic scorn. A god is fashioned with such care by men! How beautifully they make him bright with gold and deck him with silver chains! Or if one cannot afford gold and silver, a piece of wood will be sufficient so long as it will not rot! The important thing finally is to have the image fastened firmly in place so that it will not move! If one is not careful, the poor god may fall over!

V. 21. "Have you not known? Have you not heard? Has it not been told you from the beginning? Have you not understood from the foundation of the earth?" refers to the revelatory word that has been entrusted to Israel from the beginning of its life as a nation (chs. 51:16; 59:21). How can a nation in whose midst God has so definitely and continuously revealed himself forget the nature of God and confuse him with a helpless idol? He is not to be confused with anything in the creation, for he sits in transcendent glory upon his throne above the firmament of the heavens and all that he sees below him is the work of his hands. The free use of anthropomorphic images by Second Isaiah to represent God is not inconsistent with the loftiness of his conception. God sits upon the circle of the earth, that is, at the high point of the semicircular firmament that arches over the earth, and as he looks down from such a height, human beings are reduced to the size of grasshoppers. The heavens are a curtain that he has spread out to make a tent for himself. But this God, who is so naïvely represented, is the Creator of the heavens and the earth and the Lord of history in whose hand are all the destinies of men and nations. It is he who humbles the proud power of earthly monarchs (v. 23). The recurrence of this theme (vs. 15, 17) shows how important it was in the prophet's mind. It is one that is constantly associated with the character of Israel's God, but which is usually balanced with a second thought, the exaltation of the weak. "The bows of the mighty are broken, but the feeble gird on strength." (I Sam. 2:4.) "He has put down the mighty from their thrones, and exalted those of low degree." (Luke 1:52.) The balancing theme, that the weak by God's present help shall become strong, is understood here, having been suggested in vs. 1-11 and coming fully to expression in vs. 29-31. Why should an Israelite be overawed by earthly powers, when they are of so little account in the sight of God, and why should he despair at Israel's weakness, when he knows that human weakness is no obstacle to God in the accomplishment of his purpose? Believers in a God who is Lord of history have a perspective with which to approach the events of life wholly different from that of unbelievers. They are not overwhelmed and destroyed by reverses and discouraging prospects because their confidence in God's control of all the issues makes them willing to wait for God to accomplish his purpose. The swift changes of dynasty in many kingdoms in the East would serve to illustrate v. 24. The all-powerful ruler of today before whom men tremble is dust tomorrow. But the God of Israel remains sovereign ever.

V. 25. A second time the prophet asks what his hearers think God is like. In imagination he is standing with them in the open with the starry skies above them. To many in the East the stars were gods and the movements of the stars revealed what the gods were about to do with men. There is no direct suggestion in *v.* 26 that the Israelites were confusing their God with the astral deities, but in the light of the parallel with vs. 19-20 this could be the background of the prophet's words. Some people may worship the stars as gods, but Israel's God is the Creator and Ruler of the stars. He gives to each its name, and it appears each night in orderly procession at his command. That so many stars come forth each night in an unchanging order with never one missing shows the power of the hand that in the unseen controls their movements. In v. 26 Volz sees a use of the stars and of nature by the prophet as an incitement to faith in God,[4] inferring that the laws of nature and the course of history are alike a revelation of God's will. But it is not from the contemplation of nature and history that the prophet expects Israel to know and acknowledge the one and only true God but, rather, from the re-membering of the word in which God has revealed himself uniquely. The generalizing of revelation as a manifestation of God in nature, history, conscience, music, art, and only climactically, in the witness of the prophets and apostles finds so little support anywhere in Scripture that it is forced to seize upon verses such as these to give itself a measure of Biblical legitimation. Second Isaiah does not expect his people to recognize their Creator merely by gazing at the stars. Stargazers are more likely to become star worshipers, unless in their past they have had revealed to them who it is that rules the stars from the unseen.

In *v.* 27 we meet again the Israelites who know better than God what justice is (v. 14) and who now complain that God has dealt unjustly with them. In fairness to them we must recognize that their years of banishment and humiliation had continued far beyond all

---

[4] Cf. Smith, *op. cit.,* p. 99. "It was upon the stars that the prophet bade his people feed their hearts."

that would seem reasonable to any man. Hosea had spoken of a period of discipline when Israel would be without king or prince, sacrifice or pillar, ephod or teraphim (Hos. 3:4), after which there would be a restoration. But how long should such a period of discipline last? It was just that Israel should be punished for its sins, but was it just that its national existence should be forever destroyed, that it should continue to exist brokenly in many lands, and that after so many years the beloved center of the nation's life in Jerusalem should still be largely in ruins? "Jacob" and "Israel," like "Jerusalem" and "Zion," and "cities of Judah," are used indiscriminately to denote the nation as a whole, so that the complaining and self-pitying attitude is attributed to Israelites in general. "My right is disregarded" expresses a legalistic way of thinking, perhaps a legalistic conception of the covenant relation. God has rights, but Israel also has rights in relation to God and by the fulfillment of the legal conditions, can even put God under obligation. This is the same demanding spirit that is evident in ch. 58:3, where the people concerned have performed certain religious rites such as fasting and cannot understand why God does not reward them for it. They have done their part—why does not God do his part? The faith of Second Isaiah is a protest against all such legalism. Man is in no position to make demands upon God. If God's face is turned away from him, it is because of his sins, and no amount of fasting or sacrifices will be of any avail to secure God's favor. The only sacrifice God asks is a humble and contrite heart, a willingness to trust his word even in the darkness and to hold fast to the certainty that his justice and faithfulness will eventually be vindicated by the events. And what God will eventually do for his people Israel will be far beyond their expectations and their deserving—not a careful measuring out to them of what they should have by legal right. The legal conception of the covenant reduces God to the stature of a supernatural partner in the unseen, whereas for Second Isaiah, God is a majestic sovereign and Israel his slave, bound to him and able to attain great honor in his service, but in no position to make demands upon him.

With *v. 28* begins one of the greatest and most moving confessions of faith in all the Scriptures. The prophet repeats only the first two of the questions of v. 21, pointing backward to what Israel has known of God in the past, and then launches into his confident confession: "The Lord is the everlasting God, the Creator of the ends of the earth." "Your God is too small," he says to his countrymen. "You have forgotten the dimensions of the God of Israel." "Everlasting" broadens out the viewpoint to take in the whole of time from the beginning to the end; it takes the whole of time for God to unfold his purpose, so that at any one point in time it can be seen only brokenly. Wherever man stands in time, God is hidden from him, but when God's work is complete, then the perfectness of what he has been doing will be revealed. "Creator of the ends of the earth" broadens the scope of God's rule so that all nations are seen as his creatures and come under his sovereignty. Again the prophet strikes the note of God's power. There are no limits to his power, no point beyond which it will not reach, and no man can fathom the depths of his understanding. That God's mind is unsearchable clearly does not mean that his mind is wholly hidden from man, for the word God speaks reveals sufficient of his mind to satisfy the needs of men. Rather, the emphasis upon "unsearchable" is a warning to religious men never to think that they have compassed the mind of God but to live daily in humility and openness, waiting for new light and life to break forth upon them from God's presence.

The testimony in *vs. 29-31* to what God can be to the weak who really set their hopes upon him and hold fast to him comes undoubtedly with directness from the prophet's own experience and from what he has discovered in ministering to the weary (ch. 50:4). He tasted in himself the death and darkness that are the fruit of despair and then he tasted the strength and renewal that are the evidence of God's presence with those who trust themselves to him. God's word was bread and milk and wine to him (ch. 55:2), and because he could feed upon it daily he had strength to go on each day in spite of every difficulty and every burden. But this was not a special privilege reserved for him, a religious experience for which he alone had the temperament and capacity. Whoever would eat of the same food could have the same strength. It was available to all who were hungry and thirsty, all who were fainthearted and weary. What was this word that was the bread of life for every Israelite? It is utter bathos to suggest, as so many commentators do, that the word of God from which Second Isaiah drew all his confidence was actually the report that Cyrus had conquered, or was about to conquer, Babylon and had released the Jewish exiles to return to Palestine. According to Volz, Cyrus' appearance and victorious advance was for Second Isaiah a revelation of God! It must surely be admitted that this is not the Second Isaiah who meets us in ch. 40, if we let the text speak for itself without forcing it into the mold of questionable historical assumptions. The transformation of life promised to the weak and weary in vs. 30 and 31 is not based on anything so transitory or unstable as the movements of a foreign king, but upon the reality of God's power and purpose at work in the life of Israel and of mankind. Faith is a "waiting for God," which may be translated "hoping in God." The eschatological character of faith comes clearly in sight again here. The time of waiting may be short or long. The prophet is certain that it will be short. But short or long, man can live and breathe and rejoice even in the time of waiting, in the time between the present and the day of God's victory, if he has come to know God through his word. God is hidden now in the events of history; but then he will be revealed in them. He is ruling now even though his hand is hidden and he is preparing a glorious future for his people. Therefore they taste in the present something of the joy and triumph that is still future. They no longer drag through the days in despair, but mount up with wings like eagles, which suggests the heights to which the prophet's spirit soared. But more important than any times of exaltation was the power to run and not be weary, to walk and not faint. George Adam Smith is right in pointing out that the latter is not an anticlimax psychologically because in the life of man with God, soaring and running are less difficult than the steady pace that is required in the ordinary situations of life. It is the capacity to *walk* that is the final test of faith.

CHAPTER 41 / The background against which to read

ch. 41 is that which has been created for the reader by ch. 40. If we follow this principle, we permit the prophet himself to be the primary interpreter of his own thought, and instead of prejudging the historical situation, we let it emerge bit by bit as the chapters open out the one from the other. The manner in which these early chapters are interlocked, each being closely linked with the preceding one and yet introducing some new feature of the prophet's thought, makes this method of approach a particularly suitable one.

The nations who in ch. 40 were so greatly feared by Israel and who were declared to be nothing and less than nothing in the sight of God are, in ch. 41, called into court by God to hear his judgment upon them. They may count themselves mighty and think Israel weak and helpless, but they do not know the mind of God. The hour is about to strike when the tables will be turned; they themselves will be exposed as weak and helpless, and Israel will be mighty. This impending eschatological transformation of Israel is in many ways the key to the understanding of the book that has been missing for many commentators. How can Israel be spoken of at one time as weak and at another as so powerful that the nations tremble at the sight, at one time as persistently sinful and blind and deaf to God and at another as a nation of priests and prophets bringing enlightenment to all mankind, at one time as suffering abuse and persecution and dying in utter neglect and at another as marching in triumph through the world? There are always two Israels in the prophet's mind, Israel now in the time of darkness and Israel beyond the day of transformation when God's glory has been revealed. The two are one, but only by the grace and power of God. The expectation of such a transformation is unreasonable, and there is evidence that it remained unbelievable to all except a few of the prophet's countrymen. It sounded like the wild dream of a crazy man. The prophet himself believed it because he had already experienced the miracle of a transformed world in his own life. For him the desert had already blossomed and become fruitful. If God could accomplish so much through man's hope and trust in his coming, what would he accomplish through his actual coming?[1]

---

[1] Muilenburg, in spite of his appreciation of the part that eschatology plays in the writings of Second Isaiah, fails to see that the great turning point in history on which the prophet's faith is focused is a future day of divine intervention. Convinced that the victories of Cyrus are for the prophet the most vivid demonstration of the power of God at work in history, he attributes to the prophet an awareness that "it was the end of the Semitic era and the rise of the Persian age" (loc. cit., pp. 445, 448). But this involves the prophet in the curious judgment that the

It is a serious mistake to read ch. 41 as though it were actually addressed to the nations. This is merely the dramatic form. Those who are being addressed by the prophet in this dramatic form are the same stubborn-minded, religious Israelites who were so distrustful of God's power and critical of his justice in ch. 40. Many interpretations of the chapter proceed as though the prophet were trying to convince non-Israelites that the God of Israel is the one true God and their own gods are false gods by showing them that the God of Israel predicted the rise of Cyrus, whereas their gods did not. But can anyone seriously suggest that the prophet was in fact addressing himself to pagan non-Israelites? Was his argument with them, or as in ch. 40, with his own people? Yet another question that must be faced is, Where are we to find this prediction of Cyrus' triumph to which it is supposed that reference is being made in ch. 41? It would have to be in the writings of earlier prophets. It will not do to say that the predictions are in Second Isaiah's own prophecies in chs. 44:28 and 45:1, first, because in vs. 4 and 26 of ch. 41 the triumph of the mysterious conqueror is said to have been revealed "from the beginning," and second, because these two specific references to Cyrus are interpreted, when they are accepted as genuine, as predictions based *not* on divine revelation but on knowledge of Cyrus' movements. Surely it would be trickery on the part of the prophet to make predictions concerning Cyrus on the basis of reports of the Persian king's character and triumphs, and then to represent these very triumphs as proof of the power of Israel's God to reveal and control the future! This interpretation also supposes that for Second Isaiah the superiority of Israel's God over the gods of the nations

---

transfer of world power from Semites to Persians is to usher in a glorious day of enlightenment and justice in which all nations will bow in humility before the God of Israel! On p. 452, Muilenburg quotes Volz, "The end of the age is the twilight of the gods," but he does not explain how the rise of Persia is to destroy idolatry; he then goes on to say, "It is the hour of the God of Israel and of his coming into history," but again he does not spell out how Cyrus can attain this crucial theological significance. On p. 530, he speaks of "an imminent eschatological event to which the campaigns of Cyrus are but the prelude," thereby attempting to minimize the part played by Cyrus in the inauguration of the new era in which the whole world is to be transformed, but if Cyrus remains in ch. 45:1, there is no way of attributing to him less than central significance in bringing the world to a knowledge of the one true God.

depended upon the power of his prophets to predict the success of a world conqueror such as Cyrus. But surely what is achieved thereby is merely to enroll this great Israelite prophet in the ranks of those cultic diviners of various nations who issued high-flown predictions of Cyrus' success in order to enlist his favor for themselves and their cult.

But let us read the chapter with only ch. 40 as background and in continuity with ch. 40. The prophet's aim was not to convince the foreign nations of the superiority of Yahweh, but to drive home upon the minds of his skeptical countrymen in dramatic form the nature of the transformation in their situation and destiny that he expected. First he called the nations to assemble and hear what God's justice had in store for them. Then he portrayed the movements of an unnamed conqueror who at God's call was to march in triumph across the world, kings going down before him as though they were nothing. He was to be so powerful that all the nations would be helpless before him. He would move quickly on from one to the other, through regions he had never seen before, establishing his sovereignty everywhere.

Two questions require an answer here: the identity of this mysterious conqueror and why upon his first appearance he remains unnamed. Perhaps what has most misled interpretation is the tense of the verbs in v. 4 when God asks the nations, "Who has performed and done this?" which gives the impression that the events described have already taken place. But if the events are not those of present history, but are the eschatological events anticipated by the prophet, events that are to reverse the balance of power between Israel and the nations, in short, the miraculous and unbelievable transformation on which his eyes were already focused in ch. 40, then the drama projects us forward into Israel's day of triumph. God is unveiling to the nations what is soon to happen to them when his purpose is fulfilled and in v. 4 he is looking back upon his people's triumph, which is at the same time the triumph of his own cause. This identity of God's victory with Israel's is found throughout the book. Sometimes God is represented as marching to victory alone, and then again he achieves his purpose through the instrumentality of his Servant Israel. But always it is the same victory, and both God and

Israel exhibit the same qualities. The Israel of this great day is powerful as God is powerful, so that no nation can stand against God's servant, and yet gentle toward a weak humanity as God is gentle in establishing his rule. That it is God's universal kingdom that is being established is evident particularly in vs. 1 and 5 where clearly all nations of the earth are comprehended in the scope of the victory. And that Israel is the victor on God's behalf becomes clear when vs. 8 ff. are seen in their direct continuity with vs. 1-7. The parallels are impressive and convincing. They can be evaded only by abandoning the unity of the chapter. In v. 2 the unnamed conqueror is roused by God from the east and in v. 25 he is said to come from the north and east, whereas in v. 9 Israel is taken by God from the ends of the earth and called from the farthest corners. In v. 2 the nations become as nothing before the conqueror, and in v. 25 he tramples on the rulers of the earth; in v. 11 the powerful enemies of Israel who stand in the way of her restoration are destined to crumble before her and become as nothing at all. Israel may be weak now, a mere worm (v. 14), but God will transform this puny, scattered people into a threshing sledge with which he will thresh the mountains and make the hills like chaff (v. 15). The mountains that become chaff before Israel are symbols of the kings who become dust and driven stubble before the sword and bow of the unnamed conqueror in v. 2. A parallel also to v. 3 is to be found in ch. 42:16, where the people that are led by God "in paths that they have not known before" is undeniably Israel. In short, there is no feature of the conqueror in vs. 2-3 that is not to be matched in the same chapter or in the immediately neighboring one by features that are clearly attributed to Israel.

Why, then, is the conqueror left mysteriously unnamed at the opening of ch. 41? This belongs to the superb dramatic sense of the prophet, what we might call his sense of timing. He has already said in ch. 40 that the nations who are so feared by his people are as nothing to God. Now he conjures up a scene in which the nations are summoned by God to learn their future fate. A conqueror is seen marching out of the east (or the north), and the nations go down before him as though they have no strength at all. Who is this conqueror before whom the whole earth trembles? In v. 9 the mystery is revealed. In the Hebrew the pronoun "you" with which the sentence begins is the point of emphasis, "You, Israel, my servant" are to be the conqueror! Once this is recognized, the whole chapter becomes a perfect unity and stands in continuity with ch. 40, developing a theme that was already introduced there.

V. 1. Various attempts have been made to find a substitute reading for "renew their strength," first, because it seemed inappropriate that God should encourage nations to renew their strength when he was destining them for subjection, and second, because the phrase, being identical with one in ch. 40:29, was thought to have slipped into ch. 41:1 by a copyist's mistake. Torrey is perhaps right, however, that the repetition of the phrase is intentional and is a product of the prophet's ironic humor that we have observed in ch. 40 and which appears again in chs. 41:5-7 and 41:23. God, as he calls the nations to judgment, tells them to renew their strength if they can, because they are going to need all of it. The repetition also forges an additional link between chs. 40 and 41.

V. 2. Torrey, who recognizes that the unity of the chapter is shattered when the conqueror in vs. 2, 11, 15, and 25 is identified with Cyrus, believes that the prophet is here developing a "great argument from history." The figure in v. 2, he (similar to the ancient Jewish exegetes and Calvin) says, is Abraham roused up from the east (Ur), and from the north in v. 25 (Haran). What Yahweh began in Abraham he will carry to its fulfillment in the Israel of the future, since he alone is a God who can achieve his purpose in history. This points in the right direction, because Israel for Second Isaiah comprehends not only the scattered Israelites of the present but God's people past, present, and future. But that he would represent Abraham as marching victoriously across the earth, beating down the kings of the nations, is hard to believe. Torrey, both here and elsewhere, fails to grasp the radical eschatological orientation of the prophet's mind. Duhm, Marti, Volz, Muilenburg, etc., consider it so obvious that Cyrus is the conqueror that they do not pay any serious regard to phenomena in the text that point in a different direction. They *assume* that it is Cyrus, just as they assume that Israel could not possibly be portrayed by Second Isaiah as destroying its enemies. Confronted by ch. 41:15 in which God makes Israel to be a threshing sledge to thresh the mountains, Volz first quotes a text of Tiglath-pileser II in which threshing is used as a vivid metaphor of an army's destruction of its foe and then curiously insists that, since Israel for Second Isaiah is God's implement only for turning the nations to himself, the mountains threshed in v. 15 must be merely the difficulties in the way of the exiles. He finds a parallel in the New Testament saying of Jesus about faith moving mountains, and ignores the parallel in v. 2 where the unnamed conqueror beats his enemies into dust and chaff. Marti recognizes that the mountains represent enemies, but then denies vs. 11-16 to Second Isaiah. For Volz, Cyrus is nothing less than a revealer of God to the prophet. He can say: "World events are for Deutero-Isaiah religious experiences; the turning point in history (Cyrus' victory) is an act of God." The prophet "greets Cyrus not so much as the liberator of Israel as the human instrument through whom the hidden God becomes visible and makes his voice audible." If God reveals himself in Cyrus, why not also in some modern self-appointed world conqueror? What one makes of Cyrus can have primary theological and practical significance.

The translation of the second phrase of v. 2 is very uncertain. The RSV "whom victory meets at every step" depends upon an emendation of the verb, proposed by Duhm, and the unusual translation "victory" for a noun whose primary meaning in Second Isaiah is "righteousness" or "salvation." Torrey proposes to read "who aroused from the East a righteous one, summoning him to his service," which is less strained. Verse 3b should read "he treads no road with his feet," which suggests hardly the swift movements of an ordinary conqueror with his army, but rather, the somewhat supernatural character of an eschatological one.

V. 4. That God "calls the generations from the beginning" and that he is "the first and the last" means that he is the Lord of history who assigns its destiny to each generation and that from beginning to end his will is the primary factor in history. This does not entail everything happening directly at his bidding, which would reduce history to a puppet show in which God holds all the strings in his hands. History for the prophets and for the Bible in general is no puppet show, but rather, a stage on which a drama constantly unfolds in which both God and man are confronted with decisions and have to act in freedom. But throughout the drama God has the initiative, and man's actions are responses to God's actions. The uniqueness of the Biblical conception of history is not that in it God alone acts and man is nothing, but that it is the story of the interacting of God and man, a story of which the more important and decisive part lies always in the unseen. The modern approach to history has often reduced it to a purely human play of forces in which every event is explicable in human terms. The dialogue of man with God, the very existence of a relation of man with God, is largely ignored as a factor in the shaping of events. The attempt is even made to explain the faith of Israel and the existence of the Christian church in terms of the interplay of purely human factors. If the Biblical faith is true, that man is truly himself only in a relation with God in which God has always the sovereign initiative and man finds his freedom by finding his rightful place in the world as God's covenant partner, then history that takes account of all the realities that determine man's life cannot ignore this relation on which man's very moment-by-moment existence depends. The Israelites of the sixth century, having experienced so much suffering and so many disappointments, had lost all confidence that God might have anything to do with the course of events.

Vs. 5-7. God describes the reaction of the assembled nations to his portrayal of their future destiny. First, they are overwhelmed with fear and each tries to bolster the other's courage. Perhaps what they need is a new god! So they put their craftsmen to work to fashion one of metal, and when it is ready they fix it in its place with nails so that it will not move! The contrast is powerful here between the living God whose action in history determines the destinies of men and nations and the idol that is a creature of men's hands and has to be protected lest it move or fall. The force of the contrast is lost upon us until we realize that many of those to whom the words were directed had exchanged the living God of their fathers for pagan idols such as this.

V. 8. God now turns from the nations to Israel, though later at v. 21 he will turn back to address the nations again in continuation of vs. 1-7. Into this verse is poured the same love for Israel that was evident at the beginning of ch. 40. Israel is "the offspring of Abraham, my friend," a title that recalls not only the intimate relation between God and Abraham but also the glorious destiny promised to Abraham in the traditions of Israel (Gen. 12:1 ff.), that through him and his descendants great blessings would flow out to all mankind. Second Isaiah's familiarity with these early traditions is of the greatest importance. To God, Israel is "my people" (chs. 40:1; 51:16, 22; 52:4, 6, 9), "my sons and daughters" (ch. 43:6), "my exiles" (ch. 45:13), and "wife" (chs. 50:1; 54:5-6). But this relation of the nation with its God is not conceived as one existing by nature, as it was in the surrounding nations, a relation in which God would be bound to Israel so that Israel could make demands upon him. The covenant relation belongs, not in the order of nature, but in the order of grace. God has chosen Israel to stand in a special relation to him in which he is Lord and Israel is Servant. Here in v. 8, Second Isaiah calls Israel Servant for the first time. The context shows it to be a title of honor, though it can mean "my slave" as well as "my servant." It carries here a double meaning, on the one hand the utter subjection of man's will to God's will in the covenant relation, and on the other hand, the high privilege and responsibility of being the one through whom God carries out his purposes in the world. "Servant of God" is used widely in the Old Testament for persons who stand in an intimate relation with God: the patriarchs, Moses (40 times), David, the prophets, Job, Israelites in general. By Jeremiah it is applied to Nebuchadnezzar as one appointed to rule by God (Jer. 27:6). Its application to Israel by Second Isaiah reflects, first, his emphasis upon the absolute sovereignty of Israel's God and second, his remarkable development of the doctrine of Israel's election to be the instrument of God's redemptive purpose.

The election of Israel in the Old Testament is best understood if it is seen in its parallel with the calling and election of the church in the New Testament. No one is likely to suggest that the existence of the church as a body of people called by God into communion with himself and to be the human instrumentality by which he extends the knowledge of his gospel ever more widely in the world contradicts God's universal fatherhood or is the expression of a divine favoritism. And yet the election of Israel has frequently been subject to both these accusations. Israelites frequently left themselves open to misunderstanding by forgetting the true meaning of the covenant and making it the basis of privilege and of claims to superiority rather than of opportunity and responsibility, and Christians constantly do the same. Second Isaiah's doctrine of the Servant Israel withstands such misconceptions and is a foreshadowing at many points of the Christian doctrine of the church. His vision reaches to the ends of the earth. The goal of history is a reign of God's truth and justice over all mankind. This cannot come until God himself has broken the power of the nations that stand in the way. But if God's rule is truly to be established, not as one of outward compulsion, but as one in which men freely and joyfully give themselves in obedience to him, there must be a human instrumentality that will be put at his service so that he may make himself known to the world as the God that he is. For the knowledge of God to make its way in Israel there had had to be special servants of God in the past —prophets, priests, and kings. So now it is the destiny of Israel to be a nation that will perform a similar service for the rest of the world. It is an error in the interpretation of the Servant in Second Isaiah to focus exclusively on the prophetic and priestly functions and to omit the kingly. The kingly element is so strong in some parts of the portrayal of the Servant that scholars have at times been inclined to identify him with a past or future king. Why this royal element should be considered impossible to combine with the prophetic and priestly is hard to see, particularly when we consider what an important place it has in the New Testament in the conception of the Servant Christ and his Servant church. Christ is both suffering Servant and Servant King, and his people are called both to suffer with him and to reign with him.

V. 9. The tense of the verbs here and in v. 10b (where they are invariably translated as future) is puzzling until we remember the dramatic framework established in vs. 1-7 in which God stands beyond the day of transformation and looks back upon it. Elsewhere (chs. 42:22 f.; 43:5-6; etc.), the ingathering of the exiles is still future. It is highly significant that this first clear reference to a return from exile makes no mention of a particular Babylonian *gōlāh,* but on the contrary sees the exiles coming "from the ends of the earth" and "from its farthest corners." It would be strange for the prophet to use such language if he was really thinking of a little group of Jews in Babylonia of which he himself was a member, that had just received permission from Cyrus to return to Palestine and was making ready for the journey. If his purpose was to encourage the sponsors of the project, he would hardly use such general terms. *This* return is not to be identified with any historical return, since it is one of the features of the miraculous transformation that is to take place when God comes. Israel will be restored by an ingathering of her children from the four corners of the earth and will become a nation of such strength that her enemies will tremble before her.

The denial that Israel has been cast off by God (cf. ch. 50:1-3) picks up the complaint that was heard in ch. 40:27. There were Israelites who held that God was finished with Israel. Whether this was said by persons who maintained both a semblance of belief and a participation in the forms of Israelite worship while charging God with unfaithfulness to his covenantal obligations, or by some who justified their apostasy from their ancestral faith to the worship of alien gods by the argument that the covenant was dissolved, is not wholly clear. The former is the more likely because as we have seen in ch. 40 and shall see elsewhere, the Israelites who are the most stubborn opponents of the prophet show a concern for cultic observances that were traditional in Israel. It is possible that both are included. The shaking of men's faith in God has varied consequences even today: unhappy despair, passionate absorption in some form of modern idolatry, militant atheism or agnosticism, or a confused and superstitious engrossment in the forms of religion, combined with radical skepticism about some of its central tenets.

V. 10 gathers up in summary form what has been said thus far. The time of rejection past, God has forgiven his people and they can face the future without fear, knowing that God is with them and that by his strength and help they will be kept from faltering or falling. This is repeated in v. 13, and vs. 11-12, which come between, show the dimensions of God's strengthening and helping of Israel. Poor, weak, fearful Israel is to be so strong that all her enemies will be confounded and put to shame. They will be so completely destroyed that when Israel seeks them she will not be able to find them. The same theme continues in vs. 14-17, where the contrast between the Israel of the present and the Israel of the future is expressed in its most extreme form. Israel now is a mere worm. If we accept Ewald's emendation in the second half of the line (*rimmat* for *m^etē;* cf. Isa. 14:11; Job 25:6, where the two words for "worm" are parallel), we read, "Fear not, you maggot, Jacob, and you worm, Israel." The insignificance of the empirical Israel could not be more emphasized. But Israel is not to remain insignificant. She has a *gō'ēl,* redeemer, in her God. The *gō'ēl* in Israel was the protector of the freedom of the family, whose duty it was, when any member was in danger of being sold into slavery or actually became a slave, to buy for him his freedom. God will perform this function for a captive and oppressed Israel and he will lift his people from the stature of a worm to a position of power in which they will thresh their enemies as grain is threshed with a threshing sledge. Threshing is not a symbol of wholesale annihilation, as we are reminded in John the Baptist's use of it to describe the Day of Judgment that he anticipated (Matt. 3:12; Luke 3:17). Only the worthless chaff is blown away by the wind and scattered. The grain remains to be gathered into God's storehouse. An indiscriminate destruction of the nations is not to be read into these verses. Only the enemies of God, who are also the enemies of Israel, are to be destroyed and some of these will be found within Israel itself, just as God's people will be found to include non-Israelites as well as Israelites (ch. 44:5). The term "vengefulness" has frequently been used to describe the spirit manifest in v. 15, but it is no more appropriate here than in reference to the last judgment in the New Testament. The prophet does not represent Israel as repaying the nations for the injuries they have inflicted on her, but rather, God through Israel is breaking down the forces in the world's life that stand in the way of the fulfillment of his purpose.

Vs. 17-20 describe the impending transformation from another standpoint. A people that is at present perishing in a bare desert will find itself in a fruitful Eden. Marti and Volz both insist that there is nothing figurative in the language of these verses, no eschatological reference. The desert is the desert between Babylon and Palestine, and the streams of water and the trees that are suddenly found in this dry and barren region are to provide drink and shade for the returning exiles. Frankly, if we are to take this suggestion seriously and assume that the prophet is here encouraging certain Jews in Babylon to set out for Palestine, promising them that they will find water and shade miraculously provided for them in the desert, we must conclude that he was a muddleheaded prophet who gave men bad advice. An expedition that trusted his promise and set out without adequate supplies for the long journey would have come to a bad end. The desert, however, is frequently for Second Isaiah a symbol of the life of men who are cut off from the sources of strength and understanding and joy in God. Life without God is a barren wasteland, but with the coming of God it wakens into an abundant fruitfulness. The poor and needy, whose tongues are parched with thirst, are the Israelites of the present, the worm Jacob. But when God answers them, that is, speaks to them his transforming word of pardon, rivers will break forth in the barren land, and trees of all kinds will spring up everywhere. What has been a desert will be a fruitful land to dwell in. The climax of the transformation, the desert becoming a forest, would be singularly irrelevant to the expediting of the journey of exiles from Babylon to Palestine. Verse 20 confirms the eschatological character of the events. The glory of God is manifest in them to all mankind even as in the events of chs. 40:5 and 41:4. The end of it all is not that Israel should be exalted, but that God should be acknowledged and known through all the earth as the God that he is. The use of the verb bārā' for God's creative act is also significant. Its frequent use by Second Isaiah in describing what God is about to do shows that the events are part of a new creation parallel with the first creation (Gen. 1:1). Not only a new Israel but a new heaven and earth are to come out of the chaos of the present. Only when this is seen clearly do we grasp the full magnitude of the transformation that is imminent.

Vs. 21-24. God takes up again his controversy with the nations, but this time he addresses himself, not to their kings, but to their gods (as becomes evident in vs. 22 ff.), the gods that he had mocked in vs. 6-7 for their helplessness! God has just finished his "case" against them, having set forth, as though it were already accomplished, the plan for Israel's destiny that has been revealed in Israel from the time that he first chose her and set his word in her heart. The whole of Israel's history up to the present represents just one stage in the unfolding of that plan. Looking only at the present moment, one might think the plan were at an end. But looking backward and forward, one is able to see that even the humiliations of the present and of the recent past are a part of the unfolding purpose (cf. ch. 48:10). The way leads through darkness to light. Israel has only to remember the way by which she had been led. God has shown his power to make a great nation out of one man, Abraham. To the friend of God all things are possible. And the uniqueness of Israel's God is that he has revealed to them his purpose for man in history. He can do this because he is the Lord of history, the living God. This understanding of the chapter puts an end to the embarrassing search for a prediction of Cyrus to which the prophet could be referring and to the idea that for Second Isaiah the proof of divinity was the power to foretell future events. The knowledge of the future that Israel possesses has nothing in common with mantic prediction. Her prophets have visions of what is to come, not by peering into the future, but by peering into the nature of God and by remembering what God has revealed of his mind and purposes in his dealings with Israel in the past.

God now calls upon the idols to make their case. They are to tell first the "former things" and then "the things to come." The division here is clearly between what has happened up to the present and what is to happen in the future, which corresponds to Second Isaiah's appeal to history and his eschatological vision of the future. First, what have they achieved among the nations which worship them that they can set alongside Israel's record of what God has done in her midst? What promises did the gods make that were fulfilled? What purposes did they ever conceive for men that were actually carried out? Second Isaiah's frequent references to "the former things" (which might be freely translated "history") as witness to God's living presence and power suggests, as do his references to Abraham, the exodus, and David, that he had pondered long on the historical records and traditions of his people. It should be remembered that the Deuteronomic history was most likely being written contemporaneously with Second Isaiah. May it not have been in the very circle to which he belonged? The interrelation of the two is worthy of careful investigation. But the gods have nothing to compare with what Yahweh possesses in the historical traditions of his people. Then the prophet turns to the question of the future. What have these gods to say to man about his future? What hope do they offer for him to move out of the present chaos of injustice and slavery and defilement into a world where there will be justice and peace and joy? The God of Israel has a plan for the future and he has already prepared the means for carrying it into execution. His purpose through the years has moved steadily toward its fulfillment. And now a great new stage in its development is at hand. What have the gods to say for themselves in comparison with this? They are silent. They have done nothing in the past and they are able to do nothing about the future. In v. 23 the prophet's scorn breaks out in the mocking exclamation, "Do good, or do harm, [but at least do *something*] that we may be dismayed and terrified." No one needs ever to be afraid of gods who are so powerless. They are "nothing" and to choose them or to worship them is to set one's heart on "nothing." Here again, as in the image of the desert, the essence of godlessness is nothingness, emptiness, vacancy. God alone is the source of a life that has in it meaning, purpose, and movement toward a goal. It is in line with this that John's Gospel limits the term "life" to describe, not any mere existing, but life in God in which the very life of God becomes the source of life for man, and portrays all other existence as an imprisonment in death and darkness.

Vs. 25-27 return to the theme of vs. 2, 11, and 15, and again there is the same air of mystery about the conqueror as in v. 2. Again the past tense is used because God is describing the day of triumph as though it had already come. This time the conqueror is said to come from both the north and the east. That he calls upon God's name naturally gives trouble to those who identify him with Cyrus, because, as Marti recognizes, the phrase signifies a recognition of Yahweh as God and a participation in the worship of his cult, which is more than anyone would like to attribute to Cyrus. Therefore, they have to amend it to have God call the conqueror by his name. No emendation is necessary when he is recognized as the restored and transformed Israel that has been drawn from the ends of the earth (v. 9). Verse 26 again taunts the nations that none of their diviners have been able to tell them what is about to happen to them. The first half of v. 27 is obscure, but the second half makes clear the continuity: the gods are unable to warn the nations of what awaits them, but Yahweh has given to Israel the good news of the coming victory. "First . . . to Zion, behold, behold them" makes no sense. The RSV emends it to read, "I first have declared it to Zion." Since *ri'šonōt* in v. 22 refers to oracles already fulfilled, we would expect it to have the same meaning here, which would create a perfect balance in the line, "The former things I have declared to Zion and to Jerusalem I give a messenger of good news for time to come" (cf. ch. 42:9). Verse 28 again describes the silence of the gods, the silence that demonstrates their nothingness, and on this note the chapter concludes.

CHAPTER 42 / Chapters 40, 41, and 42 build out the
message of Second Isaiah in three clear-cut steps, yet each chapter rests solidly on the one before it and requires it for background in order to be rightly understood. Chapter 40 proclaimed the forgiveness of God that was about to set Israel at the beginning of a new day and encouraged even the most fearful and skeptical to believe in it by contrasting the power of the nations who stood in Israel's way with the infinite power of God. In ch. 41, God drew back the curtain that still hid the new day to reveal an Israel that, gathered from the four corners of the earth and endowed by God with his own strength, would bring the power of the nations to a decisive end. He contrasted the gods of the nations, who neither in the past nor in relation to the future have been able to reveal to their people anything of the meaning or goal of history, with himself, the God of Israel, who from the beginning has shown his people what he is preparing for them. The prophet himself may have been quite conscious that his emphasis in ch. 41 upon the power of Israel to destroy her enemies could create a misapprehension concerning God's intention for the nations. Therefore, in ch. 42 he unfolds the

mission of his Servant Israel to the nations. The goal of God's purpose in history is the establishment of his sovereignty over all mankind, for only under his sovereignty can men know an order of justice, peace, and freedom. The destruction of the power of the nations is not intended to make room for a new power structure, with Israel lording it over the nations, but is a clearing of the ground to permit the establishment of God's perfect rule. And even as Israel is to be the instrument of God's purpose in executing wrath against his enemies, so now the same order is to continue in God's work of grace, and Israel is to be his Servant, who, with a gentleness like that of God himself (cf. ch. 40:11), will bring the brightness and joy of God's rule into the darkness and slavishness of the world's life.

The close relation between God and the instrument of his purpose is essential to the thought of Second Isaiah. The Servant is, in the human scene, a reflection of the very nature of God, but as with God himself, so with the Servant: his true nature is hidden until the day of its glorious revealing. Men looking at him would never suspect that this poor, weak specimen of humanity is the one in whom the destinies of all men are being determined. But from the beginning God has hidden in Israel's heart a word in which not only is the purpose of God revealed but God himself is present. This is Israel's destiny, to be the nation in whom God is hidden in order that eventually it may be the nation in whom God is revealed to the whole world. But what makes this Servant task so difficult is that the God hidden in his word in Israel is the God of justice as well as the God of mercy. As the God of mercy, he forgives his people, loves them, and sets before them a great future, but as the God of justice and holiness, he requires of them in their relation with him a justice, purity, and mercy like his own in their dealings with their fellowmen. In relation to the nations Israel must be the instrument of God's crushing judgment upon their proud and insolent rulers and also the agent of his mercy toward all those among the nations who await their liberation.

The failure to hold together these two elements in the nature of God and in the Servant's task has been responsible for the prolonged confusion in the interpretation of ch. 42 that has disrupted not only the unity of the chapter but also the continuity and development of the thought through the three chapters. Interpreters have been blind to the sharp contrast that the prophet constantly sets between the empirical Israel of the present and the glorified Israel of the time of fulfillment. The prophet moves back and forth between the two, showing that he was fully conscious of all the weaknesses and sins of the Israel in the midst of which he lived and yet fully confident that when God revealed his hand, a new Israel would stand forth before the eyes of men, an Israel that would be the culmination of all that God had been shaping in its midst through the centuries. A third source of confusion, as was indicated in the introduction, has been an inadequate appreciation of the dramatic style of the prophet. It is characteristic of him to bring his thought to expression in brief dramatic scenes in which God addresses the nations, or God addresses Israel, or Israel speaks, or Israel sings a song of praise, scenes that are sharply divided from one another by the change in dramatis personae, and yet maintain the continuity of the thought. Chapters 40 to 45 are a mosaic of these scenes, a number of themes being skillfully woven together in each chapter, old ones being repeated, and new ones being introduced.

Since Duhm has been responsible for destroying the unity of ch. 42 with his misleading conception of a series of "Servant Songs" that must be lifted out of their context and considered by themselves, and since his theory has held all European scholars and most English and American ones in some measure captive for seventy years, a careful consideration of the bases of his exegesis is in order. He holds that ch. 42:1-4 has a distinctive style of its own which is recognizably not that of Second Isaiah. But he is vague about what constitutes the distinctiveness of the style (e.g., *"die ruhige Sprache,"* as though Second Isaiah were incapable of speaking softly!), and many who agree with him in separating the "Servant Songs" from their present context assign them merely to a different period in Second Isaiah's own ministry because of the identity (!) of language and style (Volz). The argument on the basis of style is also disrupted when scholars find it necessary to extend this first "Song" to take in vs. 5-7 or vs. 5-9 (Volz). This latter revision speaks strongly against Duhm's assertion that vs. 1-4 have so little relation to their context that they can be lifted out without leaving any vacancy; they draw vs. 5-7 with them because of the continuity of theme. Whether or not they leave a vacancy depends upon how one understands the message and spirit of Second Isaiah. In his exegesis of chs. 40 and 41 Duhm has already so reduced the stature of the prophet that if one agrees with him in his interpretation of those chapters, then it *is* inconceivable that the author of ch. 42:1-4 is the same prophet. In fact, any passage that shows deep insight or universal vision would have to be denied to Second Isaiah. Also Duhm has failed to notice that, since the six chapters are a mosaic of dramatic scenes, each scene is marked off from its context and seems separable, but when more closely examined, is seen to be part of a closely woven texture of interlocking scenes. Now comes Duhm's primary argument, that the Servant of the "Songs" is different in character from the Servant of the remainder of the book. Elsewhere than in the "Songs," he says, Israel is the Servant, chosen, protected, and destined for a glorious future, though at present blind, deaf, imprisoned, insignificant, sinful, despised by the nations. But the Servant of the "Songs" has a mission to Israel and to the nations, is righteous, a disciple of God who daily hearkens to his voice, and fulfills his mission in utter quietness, never speaking publicly, in contrast to Second Isaiah himself, who shouts his message and calls on others to shout it. His sufferings, like those of Jeremiah, are at the hands of unbelievers, and not, like those of Israel, at the hands of foreign nations. It can be seen at once that Duhm is misled and confused by the contrast between the Israel of the present and the Israel of the future. He has no room in his interpretation for the prophet's eschatology. Everything must be historical. The day on which the prophet sets his hopes can only be the day of Cyrus' triumph and of Cyrus' liberation of a band of exiles to return to Palestine, and of course, there can be no essential difference between the Israel of the present and Israel beyond the day of liberation— except a change of locale. That a blind Israel should be given eyes, that a sinful Israel should be cleansed by God's forgiveness, that a poor, weak, captive Israel should become strong and free by God's grace, that a despised Israel should become the wonder of the nations, seems never to have entered Duhm's mind, although it is central to the thought of Second Isaiah. The antithesis between the noisy publicity of Second Isaiah, of the Servant Israel, and, for that matter, of all the earlier prophets, and the quietness of the Servant of the "Songs" rests upon a misreading of v. 2. Duhm assumes that the figure who appears here is being contrasted with all who formerly have undertaken to speak publicly for God, but this is because he cuts ch. 42 completely apart from ch. 41. When we see it against the background of ch. 41 where Israel, the Servant, appears as the conqueror of the nations, we realize that the purpose of vs. 2 and 3 is to define more clearly what kind of conqueror Israel will be, severe in judgment indeed, but not the kind of conqueror whom the nations have seen in the past, who noisily tramps across the earth crushing without discrimination all who stand in his way. He will have power to break the resistance of God's enemies, but his rule as conqueror will be quiet and gentle, encouraging the poor and weak among the nations and establishing a just order everywhere. Duhm, in order to find a "quiet" teacher of the nations, in distinction from a noisy, prophetic one, was forced to the assumption that the Servant of the "Songs" was conceived in the image of a teacher of the Torah in postexilic Judaism! It can be seen, thus, that the theory that has most influenced the interpretation of ch. 42 owed its origin to a complex of false assumptions.

As ch. 42 opens, God is speaking as in ch. 41 and is disclosing events that he has in store for man. He has just portrayed the nations and their gods as objects of utter futility and emptiness. Now he takes up the theme of the Servant and proceeds to show the character of his endowment and his rule. *V. 1a* repeats what has been said already in ch. 41:8-10, breathing the same warm love of God for Israel, but *v. 1b* adds two new features to the portrait: God's spirit rests upon the Servant (cf. ch. 61:1), and he brings forth justice to the nations. Endowment with the spirit may be either prophetic or kingly and here it may be a blending of both, even as in the past both prophets and kings were called servants of God. The prophet spoke for God, and the king ruled for God, but in such figures of the past as Abraham, Moses, and Samuel, there is a mingling of the prophetic and royal functions. They both speak for God and rule for him. It is not surprising, therefore, that a prophet whose conception of Israel and its destiny gathered up into it the whole of Israel's past should incorporate both elements in the Servant of the future. God's Spirit resting upon him indicates the intimacy of his relation with God, the identity of the purpose he fulfills with the purpose of God, and the presence of God's power in him to ensure the fulfillment. He will not ever stand alone, but always with God's immediate support and guidance. What the *mishpāṭ* is that he brings forth to the nations has been variously interpreted. Duhm translates it "religion," since his rabbinic teacher of the law will be chiefly interested in communicating to the nations the laws of the Jewish religion. Volz favors "religion," but finally chooses the broader term "truth," since the Servant is for him Second Isaiah himself, and ch. 42:1-9 is a description of the prophet's own missionary project to take the truth to the Gentiles. The repetition of the word three times in vs. 1-4 shows how important it is. The clue to its meaning here is the fact that Second Isaiah uses it directly parallel to "righteousness" and "salvation" in his depiction of the coming age. "Justice," as in the RSV, or "a just order" is more likely its meaning, and by this the prophet intends to describe the order of life that will prevail when God's universal rule is established through the instrumentality of his Servant Israel. It is parallel, therefore, to what in the New Testament is called the Kingdom of God. There is a vast difference between this and Duhm's universal propagation of the laws of religion or Volz's teaching the truth. The essential point missed by both is that God's universal sovereignty is no longer to be hidden but is to be visible to all as he rules in the person of the Servant. Also, Torrey fails to grasp this when he says that "the terrible might of the Servant, and his work as an avenger, are here entirely out of sight." It is true that the destructive task emphasized in ch. 41 receives no notice here, but there is no suggestion that the Servant is other than the conqueror. The force of vs. 2 and 3 depends upon his being a world conqueror, but not the kind with which the world is familiar. When God comes to reign through his Servant, the total order of things will be different from what man has ever known. Justice will prevail everywhere, not in a limited fashion for Jews alone, but for all men regardless of race.

V. 3. The bruised reed and the dimly burning wick on which the Servant has compassion are for the prophet symbols of a humanity that is bruised and almost broken, whose spirit is so quenched by the injustices and burdens of life that it is on the point of expiring. Not only in Israel but also among the nations are men and women who are weary (ch. 50:4) for lack of the word that God alone can speak to them, who have weak hands and feeble knees (ch. 35:3) that unfit them for life. They are blind (ch. 42:7) and so are in darkness because the light of life has never shone for them. They are like prisoners in a dungeon with no hope of ever being free (ch. 42:7). But when the Servant of God rules among the nations, the poor of the earth will find that their day has come. God's own compassion for the poor, the oppressed, the naked, the hungry, will fill the heart of his Servant. The breaking of the bruised reed and the quenching of the dimly burning wick was normal practice in the power state of the ancient world —and not only in the ancient world. To be weak and helpless was to be destined for destruction. But in God's new order there will be justice for all men alike, whether weak or strong. In ch. 41 the strong have heard what justice God has in store for them. Now in ch. 42 the weak of the earth hear what God's justice will mean for them. It is typical of the prophet's style that he picks up the two adjectives "bruised" and "dimly burning" and uses them in v. 4 in their verbal forms to describe what the Servant will not be. Israel itself may be like a bruised reed or a dimly burning wick now, but in the day of triumph it will not be so. Israel will have from God the strength to establish justice in the earth. "The coastlands wait for his law." His law is God's law. The coastlands or islands represent the remotest parts of the earth's surface. They acknowledge God as their sovereign, with Israel as his vicegerent, and await his commands as the words of instruction by which alone their life is to be rightly governed.

Vs. 5-9. In v. 5 the prophet himself speaks, introducing another speech of God, this time to his Servant Israel. The eschatological character of the theme is heralded by the way in which God's activity as Creator is set in the foreground. In both testaments the themes of creation and new creation always belong together. The thought of God's creative power that called the world into being leads over into the thought of how the same creative power can bring a new world into being. He who made heaven and earth can make a new heavens and a new earth. The God who conquered chaos in the beginning will conquer the chaos of man's life in the present era.

The first half of *v. 6* repeats what has already been said about the Servant in ch. 41; the second half brings something new that is really an elaboration of the new element in vs. 1-4. This pattern is characteristic, binding the two chapters together and attempting to prevent the very misunderstanding that has befallen the book. We can detect a number of links between chs. 41 and 42. "I have called thee in righteousness," repeats what was said of Israel in ch. 41:2. "I have taken you by the hand" was said in other words in ch. 41:10. "And have kept you" is paralleled over and over in ch. 41. Then comes the daring new assertion: "I have given you as a covenant of mankind, a light to the nations." The phrase "a covenant to the people" (RSV) is obscure, but the parallel phrase makes clear what is intended. "People" signifies the whole of mankind. That Israel is a covenant of mankind can only mean that through Israel a covenant relation is to be established between God and all mankind. The relation with God that has been the one sure source of light and life for Israel is to be extended through the agency of Israel to be a fountain of life for all men. Here all narrowness in the interpretation of Israel's relation with God is destroyed. The covenant between Yahweh and Israel is recognized as having been Israel's only that his people might one day reach out and draw all men into the relationship. It would be surprising if some of Second Isaiah's contemporaries had not revolted at such a revolutionary conception, accusing him of destroying Israel's choicest treasure, the very basis of its superiority among the nations, and of casting Israel's pearls before swine.

Volz has drawn attention to the fact that Israel does not merely establish a covenant relation for the nations but *is* a covenant of mankind, even as it *is* a light to the nations, i.e., incarnate truth. This aspect of the Servant will become increasingly significant for us. It is not sufficient that there should be a *bearer* of the truth, an *instrument* of the divine salvation; but because the truth to be

conveyed is the reality of God himself, and the salvation is the coming of God to be with man, the Servant of *this* truth and *this* salvation must have his total existence compassed by God so that the
light of God shines in and through him, and the truth of God is
manifest not just in his words but in his being. The truth in which
the salvation lies is a personal relation between God and man in
which alone is life. Therefore, it is to be known in the world only
when there is a man or a community of men who are willing to
have their entire life unconditionally open and wholly determined
by this relation with God. They bear *witness* to the God whom
they have known, and their words are of the highest importance,
but the words receive their meaning from the reality of the life
relationship to which they point and are understood only when they
are the means of opening the same covenantal life relationship to
others. The word in which God establishes and maintains the
covenantal relation with man can never have its true power when
it is no more than a word of witness recorded in a sacred tradition
or in a book. It lives only when there are human ears hearing it
as the word of life and responding to it in faith and obedience;
therefore, it lives only in a people and demands for its service in
the world a people who, like Second Isaiah, will have their ears
opened to it morning by morning and will follow its bidding no
matter how great may be the cost (ch. 50:4 ff.). Thus the nature of
God's truth and God's salvation called for a people such as Israel
to be its servant, that the truth which resided in the covenant relation should be embodied in them. But the resistance of human flesh
to God was such that the embodiment remained ever partial and
incomplete until in the fullness of time it was complete in Jesus
Christ, an incarnation. We cannot speak of an incarnation in the
Old Testament, and it is open to misunderstanding to use the term
"incarnate truth" in relation to Second Isaiah, but we *can* speak of
a foreshadowing of the incarnation or an outreach toward the incarnation which is the very essence of the Old Testament faith and
which comes to its most passionate expression in Second Isaiah.

The close relation between Second Isaiah and the earliest Christian developments is evident in Jesus' words to the disciples: "You
are the light of the world" (Matt. 5:14) and the representation of

Jesus in John's Gospel as saying: "I am the light of the world" (John 8:12). It is as though Jesus had said to the disciples, "In you the Servant's vision of the last days is being realized," and as though the church were confessing in the Gospel of John that Jesus alone was truly the Servant of God[1] and his disciples sharers in that fulfillment only insofar as by faith their lives were bound together with his.

The blind and the prisoners who sit in darkness in *v. 7* are certainly Gentiles and not Jews. It is much too strained to make Yahweh the subject of the infinitives and to assume (as Duhm does) that in midsentence the focus swings from Gentiles to Jews. Blindness and imprisonment are here, as elsewhere, a representation of the condition of men who are without God. He alone is the light, and in separation from him men are in darkness. He alone makes men free when he has bound them to him as his people. Outside the covenant relation with God there are only prisoners. This conception was to come to its most forceful expression in Paul's doctrine of man's imprisonment in a world of sin and death until liberated by the power of God in Jesus Christ into the freedom of the sons of God.

Vs. 8-9. Again we are reminded that the events just described belong to the day of the Lord that the prophet anticipates so eagerly. They are the revelation of the glory of God, events in which the purpose of God that has been at work in Israel through the centuries will come to its triumphant vindication. All nations will see at last that Yahweh alone is God and that their own gods are nothing. Verse 8, with its contrast between the true God and the idols, picks up again the theme of ch. 41, as does also v. 9, with its reference to the "former things" promised by God that have come to pass and the "new things" that are now foretold. In the past God's word fulfilled itself in history, and so will it in the future. The former things and the new things are just two stages in the unfolding of one continuous plan and purpose of God for the world. Volz finds vs. 8 and 9 inappropriate as the conclusion to what he calls the first "Servant Song," since he identifies the Servant in vs. 1-7 as the prophet himself. When the Servant is identified with Israel and the full scope of Israel's historical and eschatological

[1] See Appendix.

destiny is seen, vs. 8-9 become the perfect conclusion to the passage.

Vs. 10-12. Second Isaiah is like Paul in the way that from time to time he breaks out into a song of praise to God (cf. chs. 44:23; 49:13). It is as though the thought of the great things that God has in store for his people became so soul-filling that his joy at the prospect had to find expression. He calls on the whole world in this new day to sing a new song to God. Since God is the redeemer of all, all should join in his praise. He envisages the song rising up from the ends of the earth, from every nation. Also, the roaring (emending the text as in the RSV) of the sea is nature's participation in the praise of God. The inhabitants of the desert unite their voices, and even the Edomites in Sela, traditional enemies of Judah, are encouraged to sing for joy. It is the world's salvation that is in prospect, and how shall mankind greet such a day except with songs of thanksgiving?

Vs. 13-17. In a new scene the prophet pictures God himself going forth to visit wrath upon his enemies and to bring deliverance to the blind. It is important to note that although sometimes the destruction of God's enemies and the establishment of his justice are effected through the agency of the Servant, at other times God is represented as marching forth in person to achieve the same ends. In chs. 59:15 f. and 63:5 it is because the Servant Israel proves so unready that God goes forth alone to punish his enemies and to inaugurate the day of salvation. There is no suggestion of this in ch. 42:1-17, although in vs. 18-25 the blindness of the Israelites to what God has been doing with them comes to expression, showing that here too this may have been the reason for emphasizing God's personal intervention. Not even the sin and blindness of Israel will be able to hold back the great day. Later, in chs. 58 and 59, the prophet is to accuse his people of preventing the coming of God's salvation by the stubbornness of their sins. It is to be noted, however, that whether represented as God's personal act or as his action through his Servant Israel, it is one and the same day of judgment and salvation that is described, a day of sorrow for some and of joy for others. When the two sides of the representation are thus held together, it becomes apparent how impossible it is to separate the

Servant's task of judgment from his gentler and more gracious task of showing mercy. There is one Servant, just as there is one God, both in judgment and in mercy.

V. 13 is the prophet's descriptive introduction to the new scene before God speaks, similar to v. 5. The inclusion of v. 13 with vs. 10-12 is very unlikely, since the emphasis now is upon God's wrath against his enemies, whereas in vs. 10-12 the world was rejoicing at its deliverance. The prophet is inclined to vivid anthropomorphic representations of God (cf. ch. 40:22) and is likely to offend modern spiritual sensibilities when he portrays him as a mighty warrior going forth to destroy his enemies (cf. ch. 63:1-7). This being so, it is curious that so many commentators have been certain that he could not possibly have been describing his Servant in the victorious warrior of ch. 41. The assimilation of the Servant to the likeness of his Lord ought rather to make us expect that a warrior God could have a warrior Servant. It may help to overcome what most alienates us in this representation both of God and of the Servant if we remember that it is intended only to express the power of God and of his Servant to conquer the forces of evil and to clear away every obstacle to the establishment of God's rule.

God's speech in *v. 14* makes use of the most daring image to suggest the imminence of the new day. God is like a woman great with child, the child being the "new things" that are about to appear. God has been eager and impatient for the day when the child will be born, but like every child it has had to wait until its time would come. But now the time has come, and God will cry out, gasping and panting like a woman in the pangs of childbirth. Two things are perfectly clear here: the day for which the prophet hopes *has not yet come,* and he expects it to arrive at any moment. He lives in tense anticipation of God's decisive intervention in history to set men at the beginning of a wholly new era. For him the world is poised on the very threshold of the new day. The long period of God's stillness and restraint to which the verse refers points backward to the years in which God has seemed to Israel to do nothing, the years in which Israelites have thought themselves deserted by their God. But, says the prophet, God has been more impatient than we have been for the ending of this dark era and the beginning of a brighter one. It has pained God that his people should have had to suffer so long. But perhaps we should retain here the universal viewpoint: it has pained him that *humanity* has had to live so long in darkness and captivity. Now he is throwing off all restraint, and the coming of the new era is certain.

Again, in *vs. 15-16* the destructive aspect of the new day takes precedence over the redemptive. As in Jer. 1:10, there has to be a plucking up, a breaking down, an overthrowing and destroying of the old order before there can be a building and a planting of the new. God's judgment turns the fruitful earth into a desert, destroying all plant life and drying up the rivers, just as his mercy does the reverse, turning the desert into a garden. If v. 16 were intended to describe a return of exiles from Babylon (Duhm), v. 15 would be a very inappropriate introduction. But, since both judgment and mercy are in the prophet's mind, the two verses belong perfectly together. God's coming is always the terror of his enemies and the comfort and blessing of all who put their trust in him. The blind in v. 16 are the same blind ones as in v. 7 (note the parallel mention of darkness). Therefore, they are not just Israelites, but all who dwell in darkness waiting for the light. "A way that they know not" and "paths that they have not known" are meant to describe, not a road from Babylon to Palestine, but rather, the infinite new possibilities of life that will be open to men when once their eyes are opened and they have been brought forth out of the narrow and dark cells of life in which they have been imprisoned. In knowing God they will have a new world set before them. All things will be new to them. The ways in which God will lead them will be such as they have never known before. No longer will they walk in darkness, because God's presence with them will itself turn darkness into light (note again the parallel with v. 6). Since the blindness, darkness, and light have been figurative expressions, we may expect the same to be true of the rough places that are to be smoothed into level ground. God will remove the difficulties from the path of his people. At the close of the scene, in the last section of v. 16 and in v. 17, the same theme recurs as in v. 8: the coming day will vindicate the faithfulness and power of God and will expose the nothingness of idols. The way in which this theme is constantly repeated shows what a temptation idol worship was to the Israelites among whom the prophet lived. That they should turn from the living God of their fathers to worship helpless idols seemed inconceivable, and yet it was the reality of the situation that confronted Second Isaiah. To what man gives the worship of his heart is not determined by a consideration of the possible alternatives, with an intelligent weighing of the relative worthiness of the various objects of worship. He worships idols because they promise him more immediate satisfactions than does the worship of an unseen God. They are substantial. He can touch and handle them. He can shape them to his heart's desire. And besides, they do not seem to make inordinate demands upon him without giving anything definite in return. They are part of his world, the natural world to which he himself belongs, so that he is at home with them, whereas the imperious unseen God of Israel is ever shaking him loose from the natural world, forcing him out of the order that he has fashioned for his comfort to go in search of a new order, and making claims upon him that are wholly beyond all reason. Men worship idols because they are so constituted as men that they must worship someone or something beyond themselves, but when men who have heard the word of the living God turn to idols, it is because they are not prepared to yield the place of authority and rule over their lives to a God who expects of them a faithfulness, holiness, justice, and mercy like his own.

Vs. 18-20. There is now a sudden change of mood. God continues to speak, but no longer is he announcing the impending day of judgment and salvation. His eyes have turned to the Israel of the present and he describes a nation wholly unprepared for its future task. It is interesting that Duhm rightly grasped the contrast between the Servant of the present in vs. 18-25 and the Servant of the future in vs. 1-4, calling the one an empirical reality and the other an ideal reality. However, he thought the two were unrelated, for his inability to understand the prophet's eschatological faith kept him from seeing that the contrast between Israel present and Israel future lay at the very core of the prophet's message. Whom God is addressing here is not entirely clear. The blind and deaf of *v. 18* may be the blind of vs. 7 and 16 who represent the people of the world who wait for their redemption, or they may be the blind and deaf

Israelites. Since God speaks *about* Israel in vs. 18, 20, the former is the more likely. It maintains a continuity with the preceding scene and it would be in keeping with the prophet's style to use "blind" and "deaf" with diverse meanings in close proximity. He calls on the blind and deaf of the world, whose hope of redemption is through Israel, to witness how blind and deaf Israel now is! He makes his own prophecy of Israel's future destiny seem wholly unbelievable and impossible, but in ch. 43:1 ff. it will be seen that the emphasis upon Israel's unfitness only heightens the exaltation of God's power and love by which the seemingly impossible becomes possible and actual. It will not be through any virtue or strength of its own that Israel will inherit a glorious future. It will be entirely a work of God's grace. Its possibility lies, not in anything that can be observed in the present situation, either within Israel or in the world round about, but wholly in God. Without God there is no future. With God the future is a certainty.

Second Isaiah had no delusions about the people with whom he was dealing. His rhapsodies about Israel's future destiny did not cloud his vision in observing his fellow countrymen. That men are blind and deaf means that men are blind and deaf to God, unable to recognize the true nature of their God, unable to hear the word in which he is continually revealing himself to them, but more than that, unable to understand their own history as the story of God's faithful dealings with them. The Servant of the word is deaf to the word he is intended to serve! The Messenger of God does not know what the message is with which he has been sent! In *v. 19b "Meshullam"* ("my dedicated one" in the RSV) may be a name for Israel that is used only here, similar to *Jeshurun* in ch. 44:2. The parallels make abundantly clear what is intended. The alternation of "blind" and "deaf" in vs. 18 and 19a suggests that the second "blind" in v. 19b was written mistakenly for "deaf." But again the break in pattern and the repetition of "blind" may be the prophet's way of emphasizing Israel's lack of vision. Israel has lost the power of understanding what it sees and hears, i.e., of rightly interpreting its present experiences. The key to the experiences is the revealing word of God.

Vs. 21-25. These verses continue the theme begun in vs. 18-20, but the scene has changed. God is no longer speaking. The prophet himself now speaks of God's intention and Israel's unreadiness. This is a good example of how the theme may continue unbroken, although the speaker changes. Torrey fails to take account of the change of scene in v. 21. Duhm and Volz as usual are distressed by the change and doubt the genuineness of v. 21. Duhm feels that it is too legalistic, and Volz sees in it a scribal gloss to explain the dispersion of Israel through the world as having been, not a punishment for sin, but a means of glorifying the law. Actually what we have in vs. 21-25 is a recapitulation of the chapter by the prophet. *V. 21* summarizes vs. 1-9, "God has been pleased [cf. v. 1, where he is pleased with his Servant] to magnify his Torah and make it glorious." (Cf. v. 4, where the whole earth waits for his Torah.) It is God's pleasure to establish his rule over all mankind. "For the sake of his righteousness" could be translated "because of the justice that is intrinsic to his nature"; God must be faithful to his own nature; he cannot be untrue to himself; therefore, he must one day establish a just order. But how can such a people as the present Israel be useful for God's glorious purpose? the prophet asks (*v. 22*). The description that follows must not be taken as literally true of the scattered Israelites. They were not all robbed and plundered, trapped in holes, and hidden in prisons, as far as we can judge from references in Jeremiah and Ezekiel. Duhm, taking the description literally, based on it the conclusion that the prophet was unfamiliar with conditions in the exile and must have lived elsewhere than in Babylon. But as in vs. 7 and 16, the expressions are figurative, at least in part. Undoubtedly there were severe deprivations and oppressive conditions for many of the Jews both in Palestine and in other lands. Even though the exiles were free to earn their living, there would be discrimination against them as there was to be in later times. The Jewish colony at Elephantine in Lower Egypt in the fifth century B.C. was to suffer severely at the hands of its neighbors. Some of the psalms such as Ps. 42 and 137 reflect the mockery to which the exiles were exposed. Also Jerusalem without its defensive walls was exposed constantly to the inroads of hostile neighbors. The images used would apply best perhaps to conditions in Palestine in the sixth century. In fact, the language here and in ch. 64:10-11 would be most appropriate to the situation in Palestine not too long after the destruction of Jerusalem and its Temple in 587 B.C., at any rate, before the middle of the century. How much is literal description and how much merely figurative of a people that has lost its national existence and leads an uneasy and uncertain existence both in Palestine and in foreign lands is difficult to determine.

In *v. 23* the prophet turns directly upon his countrymen with the searching question: "Have you understood the meaning and purpose of all you have been enduring?" Again the distinction is made between the events of the past and the events of the future. "This" signifies what has happened and is happening, the whole painful era of Israel's discipline, what is called "the former things" in chs. 41:22 and 42:9, in contrast to the happier "things to come." An Israel that has no understanding of its past will have no right anticipation of its future. It must look backward to see what God has done if it is ever to look forward in faith and hope. Thus, listening to the word that explains the past is a "listening for the time to come," since the word that shaped the past will shape the future.

We are so familiar with the prophetic interpretation of Israel's disaster in the books of the great prophets and in the Deuteronomic history that we take for granted that every Israelite in the sixth century would be equally familiar with it. But there were, no doubt, wide circles of Israelites who as yet knew nothing of such teaching. Their only contact with religion had been their participation in national religious festivals or their presence at priestly ceremonies in the Temple. The destruction of their national life was to them an incomprehensible calamity that shook their faith in the power and justice of the God of Israel. Far from being driven to repentance by it, they felt themselves betrayed and deserted by their God. One has only to ask what the effect would be upon many American Christians if a corresponding disaster were to be suffered by their nation; then one realizes the confusion and the bitter sense of wrong that existed among the Israelites. "Why has this happened to us who worship God more truly than any other nation?" The answer of the prophets was that a nation that had broken its covenant with God and sinned against his holiness, justice, and truth could not expect anything other than an overwhelming disaster. Therefore (*v. 24*), it was the God of Israel himself who delivered his people into the hand of the spoiler, the God against whom they had sinned and whose law they would not obey. Two different expressions are used to represent God's judgment, "the heat of his anger" and "the fierceness of battle." To some commentators the latter has seemed out of keeping with the image of fire that is predominant in the verse, so that they have emended it to read "and his might like a flame" (Klostermann, Torrey). But if God's coming in judgment could be described as the advance of a warrior to battle in v. 13, it is not out of place for the judgment itself to be likened to a destructive battle. The Israel of these dark years has been like a man standing in the midst of a raging fire or a battle and not even noticing what is going on round about him. Blindness to God makes him unable to understand any of the events of his own history.

CHAPTERS 43 AND 44/ We have already ob-

served an interlocking of the themes of the first three chapters. Although ch. 40 and ch. 41 each has a unity in itself, ch. 41 builds on ch. 40 and embodies elements from it in its own construction, and ch. 42, although it makes a spectacular advance upon the theme of ch. 41, does not lose hold upon what has been developed there. It seems impossible, however (as Torrey and Muilenburg have recognized), that ch. 42 should end where it does, with Israel surrounded by the fires of judgment, and ch. 43:1-7 provides the next scene that we would expect. Torrey and Muilenburg, therefore, call ch. 43:1-7 the conclusion of ch. 42 and think the chapter ending wrongly placed. But ch. 43:8 f. can be equally defended as continuous with what has preceded, for the giving of eyes to the blind and ears to the deaf in ch. 43:8 is best understood in the light of ch. 42:19-20. Also ch. 43:28 has a chapter ending similar to ch. 42:25, and ch. 44:1 is a continuation almost identical with ch. 43:1. The fact is that chs. 43:1 to 44:27 consist of scenes that without exception repeat themes which have already been introduced in chs. 40 to 42, making no fresh advance in the thought, and as these scenes follow one upon the other, not in any chance order, but with the same alternation between the greatness of the future and the distress of the present, it is difficult to establish clear-cut unities. "And now" (chs. 43:1; 44:1) is certainly no way for *this* prophet to begin a chapter. His careful balancing of the former things and the things to come would lead us to expect "And now" to introduce the second half of an argument. Thus, no hard and fast chapter divisions between chs. 42, 43, and 44 can be drawn. The repetition of themes makes unnecessary any extensive commentary. Whoever has understood chs. 40 to 42 will find no great difficulties in chs. 43:1 to 44:27.

V. 1. God's power in creation is called to mind as the prophet points to the new creative act by which Israel is to be redeemed (cf. ch. 42:5). The past tense is used of the redemptive act as though it had already taken place. The certainty is so great that it can be announced as a fact. God speaks of it as though he stood beyond it. The decision has already been made in heaven, Israel has been forgiven (ch. 40:1-2), and so the change in the human situation must follow immediately. In spite of Israel's continued sin and incomprehension, God's purpose for the world in and through her must go forward to its fulfillment. God's calling his people by name signifies the intimate relation of the covenant that elsewhere is likened by the prophet to the relation of husband and wife. "You are mine" has in it the same warmth of love. God has no human instrument through which to accomplish his purpose other than this people to whom he has given himself through the centuries, but who have been so blind to his self-giving. He has disciplined them severely for their sin and blindness, but they must not misunderstand the discipline. They have tasted the bitterness of God's wrath against them, but hidden in it is the greatness of his love that will not let them go. The basis of Israel's confidence and hope is that God says to them, "You are mine."

The aspect of the day of redemption on which the prophet focuses in these verses is the ingathering of Israelites from the ends of the earth (cf. ch. 41:9). The waters and the fire through which God brings them safely are the dangers of the way. The waters call to mind the exodus from Egypt, which is certainly in the prophet's mind in vs. 16-17. The release of exiles from the four corners of the earth is to be like a new exodus that will begin a new era in the life of Israel.

Torrey is justified in his scorn for the clumsy interpretations of *v. 3* that take the figure of speech literally and have God paying Cyrus for the release of Israel by presenting him with three African nations (Duhm), or which protest against the injustice of a God who will sacrifice three nations for the sake of Israel (Cheyne). Torrey quotes a similar metaphor in Arabic poetry: "I and my father's house are thy ransom." It is love that speaks here and uses extravagant language that must not be pressed too closely as though it were a careful theological statement. God's beloved Israel is in bondage, but she has a *gō'ēl* who will pay any price, even the whole of Africa, to buy back her freedom. It is to be noted that all three countries named are in Africa, whereas in the repetition of the statement in *v. 4* the general terms "men" and "peoples" are used. That the prophet's mind lighted upon African nations suggests that he was, at least in imagination, in Palestine, as does also the fact that he sees the exiles coming from the four corners of the earth. It is strange that, when the prophet in his first two clear-cut references to the return of exiles (here and in ch. 41:9) envisages an ingathering from north, south, east, and west, even naming the four directions, interpreters have consistently assumed that in these chapters he is really talking about the return from Babylon that is narrated by the Chronicler in Ezra, ch. 1. This is extended by some into the assumption that Second Isaiah composed these jubilant oracles in Babylonia to encourage Sheshbazzar (or Zerubbabel) and his expedition to get on their way, which not only reduces his high-flown eschatological conceptions to banality but makes nonsense of his theology. The great turning point would thus lie, not in the future to be effected by a new and glorious coming of God to his people, but already in the past with Cyrus' edict of liberation and Sheshbazzar's expedition to Palestine!

Vs. 7 and 8 seem at first sight to refer only to Israel—called by God's name, created for his glory, yet in the past blind and deaf—but in the light of ch. 42 the possibility must be kept open that the prophet is here operating with an extended conception of who rightly belongs to God's people. He has sons and daughters who have been created for his glory among the nations also. There are blind in every nation (ch. 42:7, 16) who are waiting for the light.

But there is not sufficient basis to say with certainty that more than Israel is intended here. Torrey, surprisingly, takes v. 8 as the beginning of the next scene (also Muilenburg). But the assembling of the nations in v. 9 opens the new scene as in ch. 41:1. Volz is certain that v. 7 forms the conclusion of the preceding scene and therefore dismisses v. 8 as a scribal gloss that was introduced to create a connection between chs. 42:18-25 and 43:1-7. But when ch. 43:1 ff. is interpreted as the direct continuation of ch. 42, ch. 43:8 brings the section chs. 42:18 to 43:8 to its most forceful conclusion: the Servant Israel is blind and deaf and therefore unready for the great task; nevertheless, the powerful hand of the Creator will gather this uncomprehending people out of all the nations where they have been scattered, and lo, when they appear they will have eyes and ears; they will be transformed not only in their external situation but also in their inner vision and responsiveness to God. This is the great miracle that forms the turning point of all history. What use would a restored Israel be to God if it were still as blind and deaf as ever? Verse 8 is the climax of the transformation that makes the Servant ready for the task. To omit the verse or to separate it from vs. 1-7 is to obscure disastrously the thought of the prophet.

Vs. 9-13. Again as in chs. 41:1 and 41:21 God calls the nations into an assembly to compare the witness that they can bear to their gods with the witness that Israel can bear for him. The scene is like a court in which different parties give their testimony. The question is: who has shown himself Lord of history and therefore the one true God by his ability to disclose to those who trust in him the meaning of past, present, and future in the life of man? Who gave the true interpretation of the events of the past before they ever happened, and who is now able to draw the curtain aside and disclose to man how his life is to be brought to its fulfillment? Second Isaiah drives this argument home with full force again and again, challenging the priests and worshipers of false gods to show what their gods have ever revealed to man of the meaning of his life in the past or what hope they offer him for the future. He himself could lay Israel's witness on the table in the writings of the prophets and the historical traditions. Israel's past, even the most painful episodes in the past, made sense when understood as the story of the covenant relation between God and Israel. Israel had a key to the understanding of the past that was also a key to understanding the present and the future. It was no mechanical key, but rather, the light of God's revelation of himself in the midst of his people. What had the other nations with their gods to compare with this? It was simple fact that nothing to be found in these other religions threw any light upon the history of man or interpreted his future as movement toward a goal. They offered him mythological explanations of the origins of his world and his institutions, divination of the immediate future, cultic rites to control the events of life, and an exaltation of the natural processes of life in religious ceremonial, but polytheism by its nature splintered man's existence instead of drawing it into meaningful unity. Only where man's worship was given to one God, the Creator of all things and therefore the unseen center from which all events received their meaning, was man impelled to seek a unity in his and his people's total experience of life and therefore to see in events in time a continuous movement which was the unfolding of the purpose of the Creator. History and eschatology were born of the same faith, the unique faith of Israel in the sovereign purpose of a Creator God. The impulse to write history arose from the imperative need of such a faith to find God's purpose in the past, and the eschatological vision was the product of the confidence that God's purpose must ultimately reach its goal in the future. Second Isaiah, more than any other prophet, is the spokesman of an absolute monotheism, perhaps in part because he had experienced in the confused era of the sixth century the baneful effects of polytheism upon the life of his people. To worship a multiplicity of gods was to have life split into fragments and to have one's very being torn in different directions (as was to be vividly evident in the later phenomenon of demon possession). In polytheism the unity of life that is essential to man's health was impossible. Therefore, Second Isaiah presses his countrymen to a decision: to face the facts about the God of Israel and the gods of the nations, to listen honestly and fairly as one would in a court of justice to the evidence that each could produce in his own behalf, and then to choose whichever would show himself by the evidence to be the living God. The nations and the Israelites alike are witnesses presenting evidence in this court, but both are also judges of the truth of the evidence and are called upon to give an honest decision. (Let them hear and say, "It is true." V. 9.)

The concept of Israel as "witness" (*v. 10*) that is here introduced is important not only in the total thought of Second Isaiah but for the whole of the future. It is used in the plural, parallel with "Servant" in the singular, and expresses the primary function of the Servant as the human instrumentality through which the whole world is to be brought to a true faith in the one and only Creator God. The performance of the negative task of overcoming God's enemies merely clears the way for God's rule. The true sovereignty of God cannot be established by compulsion because it is the personal rule of God in justice, truth, and love, which is never established until there is a human response to it in faith and obedience. God has to be *revealed* to men as the God that he is if men are to respond. He has been revealed in Israel to certain chosen men such as Abraham, Moses, Samuel, and the great succession of the prophets, through a word that he has spoken in their ears. But the word spoken to them has not been an isolated, private, inner word, but the revelation of the meaning of what was happening to Israel in history. It was spoken to them by God in order to make plain to his people as a whole what he was doing with them and more than that, to open to them the covenant relationship with himself in which alone they could find their life in the world. God was revealed thus as maintaining a double relationship with his people that corresponded to the outer and inner aspects of life: through the events in which they found themselves involved in history and through their communion with him in genuine worship. History books and psalms are thus complementary to each other in the Scriptures, and in the prophets the word and the deed of God are inseparable. The prophet, through his inner relation with God in which he both hears God speaking and speaks to God, has his eyes opened to recognize God's acts in past, present, and future history. The idea that God was revealed in historical events apart from this inner word separates two essential and corresponding elements in the revelation and leads to the misconception that a revelation can be found directly in history. The witness, however, is the man whose ear is open to the word of God and whose eyes are open to what God is doing in the outer world because he has heard the word of God, and he makes faith possible for others by witnessing truthfully to what he has heard and seen. The term "witness" is taken from the lawcourts, as is evident from its context in Second Isaiah. The court, in arriving at a right decision, is dependent upon the faithful witness of those who have heard and seen the event concerned. The witness that Israel gives for God will therefore be the declaration of the word that it has heard from him (ch. 51:16) and the narration of the history that has been the validation of the word. But it will be more than a verbal witness. Because the word of God has to be heard, not just with the ears but with the whole of one's existence, and because the history is not just a narrative about Israel but is the very life of Israel with God, Israel's witness to the world is ultimately the reality of the life it lives in covenant fellowship with him. This is the miracle of Israel's life from beginning to end, that it lives and does not die, and when the source of the miracle is revealed, the living God is revealed.

Israel is the witness, but the first to benefit from the witness are Israelites themselves—"that you may know and believe me and understand that I am He." This is only what we would expect in Second Isaiah, knowing as we do how concerned he was that Israel as a whole had not yet opened its eyes and ears to the witness of its prophets and was not yet capable of taking up its task of witnessing to the world. Israel, the true witness, must first discharge a mission to the blind and deaf in Israel.

Vs. 10b-13. The God of Israel is the one and only God. He is the First and the Last and all things are in his hand. He alone can deliver man out of his distress, and from his judgment there is no escape. His power is such that what he purposes he will accomplish, since no human power can stand against him.

Vs. 14-21. The general significance of this passage is quite plain. It belongs perfectly in the context, describing, like vs. 1-8, the new exodus in which Israel will be gathered out of the nations, and uses language and images in vs. 16 and 17 that are reminiscent of the exodus from Egypt: the making of a way through the waters and the destruction of the Egyptian army with its horses and chariots.

The one problem that it presents is how v. 14 is to be reconstructed, for as the Hebrew text now stands it makes no sense. Confusion such as this in the Hebrew text of Isa., chs. 40 to 55, is so unusual that it is significant, and when we discover that two other verses in which the words "Babylon" and "Chaldea" occur, ch. 48:14 and 20, raise serious problems of interpretation, we become aware that we are confronted with a three-cornered puzzle. There will be advantages in considering the three passages together for the light that they throw on each other.

<h3>EXCURSUS ON THE BABYLON-CHALDEA PASSAGES</h3>

The last of the three passages, ch. 48:20, poses the problem in what is perhaps its simplest form. The verse begins with a command to Israelites to "go out from Babylon and flee from Chaldea," which at once calls up before us a picture of exiles in Babylon on the point of departure in order to return to Palestine. But as the verse continues, the command is to "declare this," and "this," we soon learn, is the news that "God has redeemed his servant Jacob." The flight from Babylon, it now appears, is, not in order to return to Palestine, but to carry news of the redemption to the ends of the earth. The problem with which the text confronts us, therefore, is that its first phrase points us in one direction, whereas the remainder points in another. Which had the author in mind: a return of exiles from Babylon to Palestine or the dispatch of messengers to the ends of the earth to announce the imminent deliverance of *all* Israel?

The context may be of help. There are definite parallels between ch. 48 and chs. 42 to 44:5. In chs. 42 and 43 we have already seen how the prophet swings abruptly between the two poles of ecstatic vision of a glorious future for Israel and severely realistic assessment of the present sin, blindness, and misery of the nation. In ch. 48 the same thing happens. The prophet begins with a severe denunciation of Israel's religious hypocrisy and agelong sinfulness and then goes over into a depiction of the better future that God will bring in spite of the sin. Had this people paid heed to God's commandments they would already be as numerous as the sands of the sea, and God's peace would be flowing through their life like a river.

Twice in ch. 48 the prophet makes the transition from realistic recognition of the present situation to glowing promise of the future,
first in vs. 12-13, where the reference to God's activity in creation
signals the approach of the theme of the new day. Then, after
vs. 18-19 have reverted to the theme of Israel's disobedience, in v. 20
the news of God's imminent redemption of his servant Jacob is sent
to the ends of the earth. These sharp transitions are similar to those
in chs. 42:18; 43:1; 43:22; 44:1. In ch. 43:1 ff. the deliverance is
described in the language of the exodus, just as it is in ch. 48:21, and
the sons and daughters are brought from the four corners of the
earth. In ch. 44:1 ff., Israel experiences a vast expansion; multitudes
from among the nations declare that they belong to Israel. Chapter
48:20, against this background, can hardly be made to refer to anything less than the same universal redemption. To narrow it to a
return from Babylon such as took place in 538 B.C. does violence
both to three quarters of the verse and to the context. At best, if the
words "Babylon" and "Chaldea" are retained, it is a call to Israel in
Babylon to become heralds of redemption to Israel at the ends of
the earth. As Torrey has shown, when the two words are removed,
the verse becomes a perfect unity: "Go forth, flee with a shout of
joy, proclaim this, make it known, send it forth to the end of the
earth." The piling up of verbs, giving a note of great urgency, is
typical of Second Isaiah.

The second passage, ch. 48:14, requires some form of emendation
to make it yield any clear meaning. The introductory phrase, "Assemble all of you and give ear; who among them (you) has declared
these things," suggests a gathering of Israelites to hear what God is
about to do. They are challenged by God to produce any among
them who has been able to unravel the future course of history.
Only in Israel is there such knowledge. There then follows the
cryptic phrase with which the prophet indicates the agent of God's
purpose, "The Lord loves him," using only the pronoun as in chs.
41:2 and 45:13. But now, where we would expect some indication
of the world-encompassing achievement of this agent, as in chs. 41
and 43, we read, "He shall do his pleasure against Babylon and his
arm Chaldea." To make sense of it at all the preposition "against"
has to be supplied before "Chaldea."

The context definitely suggests an achievement of much greater dimensions than the destruction of Babylon. In fact, it suggests not a destructive, but rather, a creative achievement. In vs. 12 and 13 God is portrayed as the Lord of history—"the first and the last"— the Creator and controller of the heavens and the earth, which for Second Isaiah is usually the background for the announcement of the creative events of the new day. Again in v. 16 the event is said to have been openly declared "from the beginning," the claim that Second Isaiah consistently makes for the future deliverance that he announces. This is reinforced when we go farther back in the chapter and find in vs. 6 and 7 that the anticipated event is called "new things" in contrast to the "former things." The "new things" include judgment upon God's enemies, such as Babylon, but they are primarily the transformation first of Israel, then of the nations. The context calls for something more than the fall of Babylon. Certainly, the original text of v. 14 may have included judgment upon Babylon, but every indication points to some more creative fulfillment of God's purpose. The broken condition of the text leaves us to surmise what it may originally have said. Torrey may well be right that the words "Babylon" and "Chaldea" have been intruded by a later editor, producing the present confusion and incompleteness.

We now approach the third occurrence of "Babylon" and "Chaldea" in ch. 43:14. Following the same procedure, we must establish the meaning of the passage as a whole within its context. The theme already introduced in vs. 1-8 is the redemption, ingathering, and transformation of Israel. The new exodus is about to take place, and God's people will be brought by him from the four corners of the earth. This will be the fulfillment of the purpose that God revealed long ago in Israel, and its accomplishment will manifest to all the world that he alone is God. No nation can stand against him. Then in v. 14 God announces himself as Israel's Redeemer, the Holy One of Israel, which we would expect to introduce a further description of the universal restoration of Israel. Leaving the corrupt text of v. 14 for the moment and continuing with vs. 15 ff., we hear God speaking of himself as Creator and King of Israel and calling to mind his mighty acts for Israel's deliverance in the exodus from

Egypt, the making of a way through the sea, and the overthrow of Pharaoh's army. But in vs. 18 and 19 God tells Israel to forget what he has done in the past and to fix its gaze upon the far greater things that he is about to do. So vividly does the prophet see these future events in his mind's eye that it is as though they were already happening, and he asks his audience, "Do you not see it?" The section concludes with a characteristic likening of the coming transformation to the turning of the barren desert into an Eden of fruitfulness, so that even the wild beasts will give praise to God and the returning Israelites will find a road to travel and abundant water to drink. Both these features are reminiscent of the exodus.

In this context, how shall we understand v. 14? It reads: "For your sake I have sent to Babylon and I will bring down fugitives all of them and Chaldea in ships their rejoicing." The three words "fugitives," "ships," and "rejoicing" suggest the character of the original sentence. The noun translated "fugitives" occurs in its verbal form in ch. 48:20, where it is the command to "flee" with the good news of redemption. "Ships" of Tarshish in ch. 60:9 bring the exiles home from the far west. The "rejoicing" would be that of the voyagers. The verb "bring down" can be used of embarking passengers in ships. Ships, however, are of no use to transport exiles home from Babylon. Most convincing of all is the fact that when the words "Babylon" and "Chaldea" are removed from the sentence, the confusion disappears. It then reads: "For your sake I will send and cause all the fugitives to embark with rejoicing in their ships."

Summing up, it is difficult to be as confident as Torrey that no reference to Babylon or Chaldea whatsoever was present in the original form of any of these three texts. It can be said definitely, however, that there is nothing in any of the three passages to connect them with Cyrus' liberation of Jews to return to Palestine as reported by the Chronicler. All three passages, read in their full context, are concerned with a broader and more profound deliverance, the eschatological event that the prophet anticipated in which not only Babylon but all the nations would have their power broken, and exiles would be gathered in, not only from Babylon but from the four corners of the earth. Torrey seems to be justified in his theory that a later hand has attempted by the insertion of the two words to make this universal ingathering refer to the specific return of exiles in 538 B.C.

Vs. 22-28. The focus shifts again from the Israel of the future to the Israel of the present, from Israel in the mind and intention of God to the empirical Israel that the prophet saw immediately before him. The severity of Second Isaiah's accusations against his contemporaries stems from the intensity of his consciousness of the high destiny to which Israel had been called by God. If we were transported into the communities with which he was familiar, we would not be likely to find the Jews of the time more corrupt, idolatrous, irreligious, or irresponsible than most men, even professing Christians, of our own time. There is evidence that those of whom Second Isaiah was most critical were quite religious: observing fasts, offering sacrifices, counting themselves faithful believers in the God of Israel, and even planning to build a Temple for him (ch. 66:1). But with their religion they pleased themselves, not God. They were not interested in hearing of a purpose of God to redeem mankind through his Servant Israel; they were content if their religious observances contributed to their own comfort and prosperity in the present moment. To Second Isaiah they were unbelievers, blind and deaf to God, and destroyers of the destiny of Israel.

V. 22. "Yet you did not call upon me" can be understood in two ways, that Israel had ceased to worship Yahweh and had given its worship and offered its sacrifices to other gods, or that in the worship and sacrifices that it had been ostensibly offering to Yahweh, it was not Yahweh who was really worshiped. That the latter is the true interpretation is suggested by ch. 48:1-2, where the Israelites are said to swear by the name of Yahweh, confess the God of Israel, and stay themselves on him, "but not in truth or right," and by ch. 58:2 where "they seek Yahweh daily as if they were a nation that did righteousness and did not forsake the ordinance of their God" and "they delight to draw near to God," but in actuality withhold themselves from God's service. The tone of these verses is one of biting sarcasm such as we find elsewhere in Second Isaiah: in all the sacrifices that Israel has heaped upon her altars God has received nothing of the sacrifice that he desires, the humble and obedient heart (ch. 66:2), but instead, has had loaded upon him the sins and follies of a disobedient people. "You have been weary of me." This is the verb that was used three times in ch. 40:28-31. God does not grow weary in his watchfulness over his purpose for Israel and mankind; Israel grows weary and faint under the pressures of life, but when Israel trusts God's word and sets all its hope upon him, it will no longer grow weary. The prophet now picks up this verb again to use it three times in a new way: Israel has been weary *of God*. It has not wearied him with frankincense, but with the burden of its sins. This is a play on words, a common occurrence in Second Isaiah, and one which gives a new turn to his thought while knitting it together with what he has said before. The emphasis in *v. 23* is upon "me." This emphasis is highly important, and without its recognition the force of the passage becomes confused, more so in the English translation than in the Hebrew. The first half of the verse could be read, and has been read, as a complaint of God that Israel has failed to offer sacrifices to him (Duhm), giving to other gods what should have been given to him, but the second half makes it abundantly clear that this is not the meaning. Second Isaiah stands directly in line with Amos 5:25; Isa. 29:13; and Jer. 7:21-23 in holding that what Israel's God has asked of his people is not primarily the offering of sacrifices. He has from the beginning, i.e., from the time of the Mosaic institution of the law, asked for the love and obedience of Israel, that Israel should be demonstrably his people in the total character of its life, reflecting his own justice, truth, and holiness in its life relationships. But Israel has persistently withheld this response and has offered its sacrifices as a substitute. Therefore, God does not recognize any of the sacrifices as offered to him. How Second Isaiah felt about sacrifices comes out even more vehemently in ch. 66:3 where he says that he who slaughters an ox for sacrifice is like someone who kills a man and he who sacrifices a lamb is like someone who breaks a dog's neck, a cereal offering is no better than swine's blood and a memorial offering of frankincense is like the blessing of an idol. Here it is indisputable that the offerings are made to Yahweh and are part of the traditional worship of the community, but the prophet condemns them as pagan institutions, no better than the idol worship with which Israel confuses itself in its relation with God.

We saw earlier in ch. 40:16 a suggestion that the community addressed most directly by the prophet was inclined to put its trust in sacrifices. But now, if *vs. 23-24* are not a complaint about the withholding of sacrifices, but as in ch. 66:3, a condemnation of sacrifices that are being offered, this could have important implications for identifying the community where the prophet lived. We know that in Jerusalem sacrifices continued to be made in the ruins of the Temple in the period after 587 B.C. In Jer. 41:4 we read of eighty men going from Shechem, Shiloh, and Samaria to Jerusalem on the day after the murder of Gedaliah to make sacrifices in the ruined Temple. Also, in Ezra 3:6 burnt offerings are made in the open before the walls of the Temple have been rebuilt, which suggests what may have been done for many years, although the Chronicler assumes that sacrifices ceased between 587 and 538 B.C. However, Jer. 41:4 shows this latter to be untrue, and since there was a large majority of the Jewish population remaining in Judah, it is likely that sacrificial worship continued throughout those years. Where sacrifices ceased was in exile. The position has been taken by some interpreters that the sacrifices referred to must be those of pre-exilic times. This, of course, is possible because vs. 27 and 28 make clear that the prophet has in mind the whole of Israel's sinful history from the time of "the first father." His concern, however, is not just with what Israel has been in the past but more directly with what Israel is in the present, and present sacrifices would point to Palestine.

In *v. 25* God's grace and mercy break through again. The forgiveness of God does not depend upon the worthiness of Israel. God forgives "for his own sake," i.e., because he is not willing that the sins of Israel should defeat his purpose for mankind. He acts in sovereign freedom. Israel was not chosen in the beginning because of its worthiness, its superior spiritual character, or its religious genius, nor does its future destiny as God's Servant depend upon its attainment of perfection. What is needful is Israel's humility, which will acknowledge its own persistent sinfulness and wait in faith and eager longing for God's forgiveness. Without forgiveness there can be no future for Israel. God's forgiveness is the miracle that liberates Israel from the bondage of its past, restores the covenant relation that is the source of its life, and so creates a new Israel with a new future. But in *vs. 26-28* the prophet's mind reverts to the theme of vs. 22-24. He conjures up a court scene again, this time with God and Israel as the adversaries. The appeal to Israel to "set forth your case, that you may be proved right" reminds us of the Israelites in ch. 40:27 who complained that God had been unjust in his dealings with them and who drew upon themselves the sarcasm of the prophet in ch. 40:14 by acting as though they could teach God a thing or two about justice. Like the nations in ch. 41:1 ff., the Israelites are silent, so God proceeds in vs. 27 and 28 to make *his* case against Israel. By "your first father," most likely Abraham is meant, who in ch. 41:8 is called "the friend of God," and who in ch. 51:1-3 seems to represent the Servant's point of origin. By "your mediators" we are to understand the succession of prophets, priests, and kings who have stood between God and Israel through the centuries. All have sinned. Second Isaiah was familiar with the traditions which, in all their honoring of the forefathers such as Abraham and David, concealed nothing of their human frailty and sinfulness. The prophet, like Paul, is determined to leave man, and particularly the religious man, the proud Israelite, nothing on which to base a confidence in his own righteousness, that he may be led to set all his confidence upon God. It seems best in v. 28, by the change of one letter, to read with Torrey, "I let my holy cities be profaned" (cf. ch. 64:10 where the same expression is used). But the prophet did not end on this somber note. Verse 25 has shown that this is no last word for him. Therefore, we must disregard the chapter division and read ch. 44:1 ff. as a direct continuation.

There is no break between chs. 43 and 44. Having just emphasized that Israel was a sinful nation from its beginning, Second Isaiah now builds out the other side of the truth, that Israel was God's chosen Servant from the beginning, formed in the womb to be the agent of God's purpose (cf. ch. 49:1). These are not two Israels any more than the sinful church is to be distinguished from the true church. The same body of people are at one and the same moment a church of sinners and the called of God through whom by the grace and mercy of God light shines out into the darkness of the world. The expressions "who formed you from the womb" and "called me from the womb" (ch. 49:1) seem to be an echo of Jer. 1:5, "Before I formed you in the womb I knew you, and before you were born I consecrated you." What Jeremiah says of his own destiny as a prophet, Second Isaiah says of Israel as God's prophet-people, most likely in direct dependence upon Jeremiah. God's choice of Israel and preparation of Israel for its task from its time of origin is like the calling and preparation of a prophet. In the figure of the Servant the prophet image predominates, although at times it is combined with the image of the priest or of the king who rules for God. The Servant is Israel according to God's intention, the Israel that knows itself called, sustained, and equipped by God to serve him in the world. The double image of his nation that the prophet sees when he looks into the past—Israel the sinner and Israel the Servant—is exactly what is set before us in the Deuteronomic history. The historian is unsparing in disclosing the stubborn and persistent sinfulness of his people and yet, at the same time, bears witness to the unique calling and destiny of Israel and to the fact that even in the darkest hour God has seven thousand who have remained faithful, though not even Elijah can see them. The Servant Israel has often been hidden, but he has ever been there. God does not let his witnessing people perish from the earth.

The parallel in *ch. 44:3* between "I will pour water on the thirsty land" and "I will pour my Spirit upon your descendants" is highly important in confirming the impression that in all passages where streams flow in the desert, the desert represents Israel in its barrenness and hopelessness and that the coming of water is the coming of God to transform all things. Thirsty land and men thirsty for God both represent the same reality. The outpouring of the Spirit is the outpouring of God and not just the conferring of certain spiritual benefits upon Israel. This must be kept clearly in mind because the references to the desert have so frequently been assumed to signify the desert between Babylon and Palestine.

The refusal to take Second Isaiah's words in earnest is responsible for a complete misunderstanding of his message. When he says that God is coming (ch. 40:3-5) or that God will pour out his Spirit upon Israel (chs. 42:1; 44:3) or that, filled with the Spirit of God, Israel will experience an astounding transformation, as though the desert had become an Eden, can it be that he merely means no more than that Cyrus is about to let a handful of exiles return from Babylon to Jerusalem? Did he really expect from this event a new beginning for Israel and mankind? (Duhm, Volz, Muilenburg.) This form of interpretation could be called a dekerygmatizing of Second Isaiah; it strips him of the very essence of his message. It may be urged that since no such transformation as Second Isaiah expected ever took place—the exiles were not gathered from north, south, east, and west; Israel remained insignificant for many centuries still; the enemies of Israel were not destroyed; the hour never arrived when the kings of the nations gazed in wonder at mighty Israel— perhaps his eschatological ravings were better forgotten. Could he have been so foolish as to expect these impossibilities? Was he not unconsciously deceiving and misleading his people with such promises? But identically the same objections can be made against the New Testament eschatological hopes. The Christians expected a day to come almost immediately when the Kingdom of God, in which all life's meanings are transformed and the will of God triumphs over the evil forces that afflict humanity, would be established universally. Christ would return to reign until he had put all things under his feet. The kingdoms of this world would become the kingdoms of our Lord and of his Christ. It is likely that not only the early Christians but Jesus himself cherished the expectation of such a day when God's will would actually triumph in the life of the world. We shall do well also to note that at the heart of the New Testament gospel is the proclamation of the coming of God to man. This is expressed in two ways: as the coming of God's kingdom, i.e., of God himself to establish his personal and immediate rule in men's lives, and as the outpouring of God's Spirit upon men, i.e., the indwelling of men by God himself in his Spirit so that they are immediately possessed, empowered, enlightened, and transformed by his presence in them. The conviction of the church, and the very basis of its life, was that this "impossible" expectation, that God should actually come to man and by his presence with man create a new world, had actually been fulfilled in Jesus Christ, and

112 HISTORY AND THEOLOGY IN SECOND ISAIAH

then in his church. In him God was with man, the rule of God was reality in the life of man, God's triumph over the forces of evil had begun, and a new world with a new humanity was being born. The intense expectation of a final triumph of God in the life of the world in a second coming of Christ was created by the experience of God's present triumph in Jesus of Nazareth and in the church. The Spirit of God, which transformed life for the Christians, was only the earnest or promise of a yet greater coming of God in the future. New Testament eschatology thus was not an unfortunate mistake and it is not to be interpreted as a poetic way of saying that the Christian religion is going to make some progress in the world!

The event on which Second Isaiah's eyes were fixed was the fantastic and seemingly impossible event that Christians claim took place in Jesus Christ and is to be consummated at the end of the age. It is this all-important fact that has been obscured by the focusing of attention on Cyrus. Drawing a line through all the points at which God had revealed his purpose for man in Israel and projecting this line into the future, Second Isaiah was certain what the outcome must eventually be. God would not be God if he were powerless to bring his purpose to its triumph in history. Moreover, the whole story of Israel was witness to the power of God's word to translate itself into earthly event. Would God begin a work with men and not complete it? Would God choose Israel, reveal himself in his word in Israel, guide, support, and chasten Israel in such a drastic fashion, and then abandon Israel as the instrument of his purpose? Would the sin of man be stronger than the grace and mercy of God? Second Isaiah's faith was a great resounding and joyous affirmation that God in faithfulness to his own nature and purpose would complete what he had already begun and that he would complete it by coming himself in a new and wonderful way to be with his people. But we need to go one step farther to explain the remarkable confidence of the prophet. He himself had been the first to hear with joy the word of God's forgiveness and, trusting God's faithfulness to his word, lived moment by moment in anticipation of God's coming. As we saw in ch. 40, he knew in himself that to await God's coming in faith was to experience already the transforming power of God and to have weakness changed into strength. To live in expectation of the day of God's triumph was to live now for that day and in the light and joy and strength of that day. This is evident in the exuberant joy with which Second Isaiah speaks of the day as though it were already present, although he at once reminds us that it is still future. Like the early Christians he was convinced that if a foretaste of God's coming could transport him into a new world and a new life, the actual coming of God would transform the entire creation and bring a new heaven and a new earth into being (chs. 51:6; 65:17; 66:22).

The miraculous multiplication of Israel's descendants in *ch. 44:4 and 5* breaks out beyond the ingathering described in chs. 43:1-8 and 43:14-21 to envisage the incorporation of non-Israelites in Israel (so also Muilenburg) in line with the universal vision of ch. 42. It would be pointless for the prophet to say that in the future Jews would call themselves by the name of Jacob, would write on their hands "The Lord's," and would surname themselves by the name of Israel. These are the poor, the blind, the prisoners from among the nations, who are to rejoice with Israel at God's triumph and wait humbly to be taught God's ways. Believing Israel's witness, they will acknowledge that the God of Israel is the only living and true God (ch. 45:14) and will join themselves to Israel as members of the people of God. They will be as many as the grass in a well-watered region and will make of Israel a great universal nation (cf. ch. 54:1-3). This feature of Second Isaiah's thought should be kept in mind in the interpretation of passages that speak of Israel "possessing" the nations. There is in this no narrow nationalistic lust for power, since God's rule in and through Israel is to be the source of blessing for all nations and the destruction only of tyrants who oppress mankind, and the doors are to be open for all who will come from among the nations to be incorporated into Israel.

A new section begins with *ch. 44:6*. The theme is familiar. Yahweh alone is God. He alone has spoken a word to man in which the course of events in history has been revealed. Israel has heard and cherished this word so that Israelites are God's witnesses among the nations. It is like Second Isaiah to introduce then a speech in which he mocks at the idols that workmen have created and that men worship as though they were gods. Many interpreters have regarded vs. 9-20 as an alien insertion breaking the continuity between vs. 8 and 21, but the parallels (chs. 40:18-20; 41:6-7) are too similar, particularly in tone, for us to deny these verses to Second Isaiah, and they are most appropriate following vs. 6-8. Idolatry was a singular temptation to Israelites in the seemingly hopeless situation of the mid-sixth century. But whereas among the nations men shaped gods, in Israel God shaped and formed a Servant people (v. 21). Israel must not despair, for it has not been forgotten by God. On the contrary God has already forgiven Israel's sins and prepared for her a day of redemption. In *v. 23* the prophet sees the day as though it had already come and calls upon the heavens and the earth, the mountains and the trees, to sing with joy at what God is doing. *V. 24* celebrates in typical fashion the Redeemer God as the Creator of all things. He who creates the new world is he who created the heavens and the earth in the beginning and brought Israel into being as a nation. The emphasis here is upon the fact that God was alone when he stretched out the heavens and when he spread out the earth. He needed no help. So also now in the day of redemption *he needs no one to assist him.* He can create the new day *alone.* This emphasis is notable in view of what is to come in chs. 44:28 and 45:1. *Vs. 25-26* set the omens of the diviners of the nations parallel with the word of God in Israel, maintaining the line of comparison between the one true God and the idols that was established in vs. 6-20. The diviners attempt to know the future and think themselves wise, but God exposes their wisdom as folly. How different it is with the word of God's own Servant people. Events have ever confirmed its truth. What God has promised in his word he has done. And now we reach the climax of the passage. What is the word of God for Israel's future? Jerusalem shall be inhabited and her cities shall be built! This is directly in line with the preceding unit, chs. 43:1 to 44:5, where the repopulation of Jerusalem by a great new expanded Israel was the joyous announcement, an Israel drawn from the four corners of the earth and enlarged by newcomers from among the nations. It is notable that in v. 26 there is no mention of a return of exiles from Babylon. We hear only of a wonderful restoration of Israel in Palestine which God is to effect *alone* as he sets his transformed people at the beginning of a new day.

EXCURSUS ON THE REFERENCES TO CYRUS

We now find ourselves before what is perhaps the thorniest problem in Second Isaiah—the references to Cyrus in chs. 44:28 and 45:1. Torrey has argued at length for the excision of both references to Cyrus as later insertions, but he has apparently convinced few who have written on Second Isaiah. More frequently Cyrus has been discovered far beyond these two verses in the book and has sometimes even attained a prominence that throws the prophet himself completely into the shade. Second Isaiah has been interpreted so extensively in the light of the career of Cyrus that he has not been permitted to deliver to a modern age the message entrusted to him by God and delivered by him faithfully to his own time.

Thus far we have found no reason to read Cyrus into the text (for he has to be read into it in passages such as ch. 41:2, since the text in its context makes perfectly good sense without him), and we have now to ask ourselves what kind of entrance Cyrus makes when finally he appears in ch. 44:28. First, we must be struck by the fact that so great a personage should seem to come in almost as an afterthought. The chapter is complete with v. 26, so far as the development of its thought is concerned. The day of salvation promised by God in his word is attained with the repopulation of Jerusalem and the cities of Judah. Beyond this restoration lies the mission to the nations, but frequently redemption and restoration are equated, and restoration forms the climax. But now in ch. 44:27-28 something is added: beyond the restoration of Jerusalem and the cities of Judah, God promises that Cyrus will be his shepherd to fulfill *all* his purpose and also that the foundation of the Temple will be laid. It cannot be excluded as impossible that Second Isaiah is here introducing two completely new ideas: that the Persian king Cyrus will be the "fulfiller of all God's purpose" and that foundations for the rebuilding of the Jerusalem Temple will shortly be laid, but it is strange that he has given no hint of any such intention earlier in the chapter. These are weighty themes to be dropped in suddenly at the end of a chapter, being tacked on at the end of a very long sentence that already has been rendered clumsy by an unusual succession of participles. The second half of v. 28 has long been suspected of being a later addition (see especially

Volz, but also Duhm, Klostermann, Marti, and Muilenburg) because of the repetition of the prediction concerning the rebuilding of
Jerusalem and the introduction of a reference to the refounding of
the Temple. But there is no excuse for separating the two halves of
v. 28. The depiction of Cyrus as the liberator of Israel who not only
sets the exiles free in Babylon but arranges for the rebuilding of the
Temple in Jerusalem was a fixed tradition in Israel in the time of
the Chronicler (Ezra, ch. 1) and was likely current much earlier.
It is no accident that the references to Cyrus and the Temple stand
together, and they should stand or fall together in our consideration
of the chapter. What is most remarkable is that the laying of the
foundations of the Temple should now suddenly become the climax
of the day of redemption. No mention has been made of the Temple
thus far by Second Isaiah. The redemption of Israel and of the world
has been described without the Temple ever coming into view. We
have heard Yahweh say that the sacrifices that formed such an
important part of the Temple worship were not really offered to
him (ch. 43:22-24), and they are later to be attacked with bitter
ferocity (ch. 66:3). It is surprising, therefore, that the prophet should
suddenly make the reconstruction of the Temple the crowning act
of God on behalf of his people. And equally remarkable is it that
the verse concerns itself only with *the laying of foundations* for
the Temple rather than with the total rebuilding of it. We hear of
such *foundation*-laying in Ezra, ch. 1 (also in Ezra 3:10 and Zech.
4:9) in a context where it is inseparable from the beneficence of
Cyrus. For the Chronicler it is an essential element of the great day
with which God brings the darkness of the exile to an end and
opens a new era before his people. But is it conceivable that the
prophet who in ch. 66:1 roundly condemns those who think to win
God's favor by building him a Temple would make this the climax
of his prophecy of restoration and universal redemption?

    There are difficulties of almost equal weight connected with the
reference to Cyrus. Unless the unity of ch. 44:6-26 is abandoned, the
promise of restoration for Jerusalem and the cities of Judah must be
understood as the content of the word of God's Servant, known in
Israel from of old (v. 7). This creates no difficulty, for there are
specific passages in Hosea and Jeremiah that envision a restoration

beyond the days of judgment, and the promise is inherent in God's covenant relation with Israel that there should be mercy as well as disciplinary justice in God's dealings with his people. But it is a very different matter to make the exploits of Cyrus the content of the word revealed long ago to Israel. How could a self-respecting prophet make the superiority and honor of Yahweh dependent upon the claim that the coming of Cyrus had been long ago foretold in Israel? The dilemma is not escaped by saying that God's word to Second Isaiah predicted the triumphal march of Cyrus. The argument in ch. 44, as in ch. 41, that God's power in history is demonstrated by the correspondence between the destiny promised in his word to Israel and the destiny actually realized in history, falls to the ground if the ability of God to foretell the coming of Cyrus is made the chief point at issue.

Also, if the reference to Cyrus is held to be genuine, the significance attributed to him dare not be watered down; "he shall fulfill *all* my purpose" is in this context a very comprehensive claim. It is striking how many commentaries ignore this important word "all." God's purpose is not just the release of a few Babylonian captives and the rebuilding of a Temple in Jerusalem. It is the redemption of mankind, with the destruction of God's enemies and the marvelous transformation of Israel as the first steps toward that goal. God's purpose is the establishment among men of an order of justice under his rule, but more than that, an order in which all men will freely acknowledge him as their God and he will take them under his protection as his people, in short, the fulfillment of his will for man in history. Thus far in history Israel has been the chosen instrument for that purpose and when the persistent sinfulness and the reluctance of Israel to serve rises up before the prophet's mind, he declares that God will himself bring the victory. He will do it alone, i.e., without a human instrument. Two things, then, are strange in the text of ch. 44:6-28: that having emphasized the power of God to create the heavens and the earth without any help from anyone (v. 24), he should suddenly name Cyrus as his helper in the great new creative act, and that he should expect of the foreign king, who was not even a worshiper of Yahweh, the work of universal redemption for which Israel had been so carefully prepared from the beginning of history. Attempts have been made in various ways to get around this latter dilemma. The function of Cyrus has been carefully limited to political and military measures, relieving him of all spiritual responsibilities (Duhm, Kittel, Mowinckel, Jenni, Von Rad). The Cyrus passages are sometimes quoted as an instance of God using an unbeliever to get his work done. But who would suggest that through an unbelieving foreign ruler God may establish his Kingdom on earth, fulfilling through him *all* his purpose?

V. 27 furnishes one further peculiarity of this unusual ending to ch. 44. The theme of vs. 6-26 is God's redemptive purpose, the restoration of Israel, and there is no word at any point concerning God's judgment. Yet v. 27 portrays God drying up the rivers of the earth in order to turn it into a barren desert, an imagery that in ch. 42:15 is coupled with a description of God coming in judgment upon his enemies as hot winds wither the grass (cf. ch. 40:7, where God's breath kills men as hot winds wither the grass). The opposite representation of God, making rivers flow in the desert, is the appropriate image of redemption. Are we to assume, then, that the prophet faltered in his choice of images in v. 27, or was it that someone who did not understand Second Isaiah too well seized upon this image to introduce a reference to Cyrus and the Temple?

We do not know how early to place the Chronicler's tradition that the Jerusalem community with its center in the Temple owed its restoration to the beneficence of King Cyrus of Persia. Torrey's abrupt and wholesale dismissal of the Chronicler and all his works has seemed to most scholars to be much too severe. That the Chronicler exercised great freedom in the use of his sources is evident to anyone who compares I and II Chronicles with I and II Samuel and I and II Kings. Also, like other ancient historians, he composed documents freely. But a comparison of the Cyrus edict in Ezra 1:2-4 with the version of it that is preserved in Ezra 6:2-5 suggests that he did not always proceed in the same fashion. In the former, Cyrus is represented as acknowledging Yahweh as the source of all his power, claiming that Yahweh has charged him to build a Temple in Jerusalem, and piously invoking the presence of Yahweh with all who volunteer to return to Jerusalem, transparently a free construction of the Chronicler. But in the latter, the tone is coldly matter-of-fact and much closer to what we would expect to be the form of an edict of Cyrus. What Torrey does not credit is the possibility that genuine traditions may lie behind the Chronicler's free compositions.

Historically it is credible that Cyrus gave Jews in Babylonia permission to return to Palestine and arranged for the rebuilding of the Temple, since he did the same for other exiled peoples. Such Jews as returned after 539 B.C. would remember Cyrus as their liberator. It increases the credibility of the tradition in The Book of Ezra that it reports the failure of the first attempt to rebuild the Temple and also the continuance of pagan practices among the returned exiles (Ezra 9:1-4).

We may therefore consider it possible that the Jerusalem community, early in the fifth century B.C., not only considered the purity of its faith and its traditions to have been preserved in Babylonia but also saw in Cyrus the instrument of God in the reconstruction of Jerusalem and its Temple, the transferring of the pure tradition to Palestine, and the opening of a new day for Israel beyond the exile. We must then ask ourselves the question how such a community would be likely to understand the writings of Second Isaiah. When he wrote of the ingathering of exiles they would quite naturally assume that he meant the return of exiles from Babylon. When he pictured a conqueror coming from the north or east to subdue the nations, who could this have been but Cyrus? That Israel was the conqueror referred to would be unbelievable in a poor, struggling Jewish community in Palestine that had lost the prophet's vision of the future. But if Cyrus was to be identified as the conqueror, then there had to be some recognition of what Cyrus had contributed toward the refounding of the Temple. The meaning of Second Isaiah's eschatological language had by that time been lost so that there would be no consciousness of doing violence to his thought or of producing confusion in it when two sentences were added to ch. 44 and one word to ch. 45:1 in order to make perfectly clear to everyone how the prophecies were to be interpreted. The same rather clumsy hand that made the additions can be recognized also in the

Babylon-Chaldea insertions in chs. 43:14; 48:14 and 20 (most likely also in chs. 56:1-7; 58:13, 14; and 66:15-24).

CHAPTER 45/ This chapter is a magnificent unity, blending together themes with which we have already become familiar. It begins with Israel's triumph over the nations and mounts scene by scene until it reaches its climax with the whole world acknowledging the God of Israel as the source of its salvation—but only when Cyrus has been recognized as an intruder in v. 1. It is impossible to hold the chapter together once he is identified as the conqueror. Interpreters who retain Cyrus in v. 1 must, unless they evade the plain meaning of the text, claim that Second Isaiah expected Cyrus' conquests to prove to all men that Yahweh was the only true God (v. 6), a strange expectation for a prophet of Israel and, in fact, a foolhardy one for any man. It would be like expecting the victories of Napoleon to put an end to the atheism of the French intellectuals of the time! Then v. 8, which is inseparable from vs. 1-7 and is a characteristic song of joy at the arrival of the great day of salvation, makes clear that the preceding verses have been describing not just the march of an earthly conqueror but the triumph of God's salvation in the midst of the nations. If Cyrus is the human agent here, then he is indeed the "anointed one" in whom God "fulfills all his purpose." Duhm, Kittel, Mowinckel, and most recently Jenni, recognizing how unlikely it is that any Israelite would identify a foreign king with the Messiah, have tried to establish a special use of the title in this one instance as merely a name to indicate the high rank of God's chosen instrument who performs a limited task, "perhaps a military-political expression for the high place of trust that Cyrus holds with Yahweh." "For purely historical reasons it cannot signify a transference of the national Messianic hope (to Cyrus)."[1] But unless v. 8 is ruthlessly chopped away from its context, it *does* signify such a transference. Further difficulty is experienced in vs. 9-13, where the pot that has just been created argues with its creator about what he is making. In vs. 1-7 the conqueror of the nations was described as God's creation (v. 7), so it

[1] Jenni, *loc. cit.*, p. 255.

should be Cyrus who in vs. 9-13 is protesting to God about what he is doing! But this is clearly impossible, so the text is twisted usually to mean that orthodox Israelites who were horrified that a foreign king should be called the Messiah were protesting to the prophet against his bold conception (Volz). Verses 14-17 are linked with vs. 1-7 by their parallel references to the conqueror's receiving wealth from the conquered nations, but it becomes embarrassing to those who support the Cyrus theory when these nations have to be represented not only as bowing down to Cyrus but as making supplication to him and saying, "God is with you only and there is no other, no god besides him." Here, as we have found elsewhere, is the identification of God with the agent of his victory, of God with his Servant who is his witness, so that the victory of the witness is the manifestation of God's own glory. But how could Second Isaiah identify Cyrus with God in exactly the same fashion as this and expect the nations to see God's glory manifested in a triumphant Cyrus? It is impossible to relate the remainder of the chapter in any way to Cyrus.

There is no mystery, then, why every interpreter who leaves Cyrus in the text is forced eventually to chop ch. 45 in pieces. (Volz even cuts vs. 5-8 apart from vs. 1-4!) But remove Cyrus, and the chapter becomes a splendid unity.

The weakness of Torrey's argument for the excision of Cyrus lay in his failure to deal adequately with the full context of the Cyrus verses. He tended to place his primary reliance upon metrical arguments, and where meter in Hebrew poetry is concerned, the judgments of scholars are very diverse. But the metrical argument in ch. 45 is not to be disregarded. The name of Cyrus, with its prepositional prefix, projects beyond the normal length of the line in this poem and destroys the symmetry. But the metrical consideration is only one element in the picture. A much more important one is the effect of Cyrus' presence both upon the unity of the chapter and upon our estimation of the theological integrity of the prophet. A prophet who could at one moment expect God to redeem the world through the power of his transforming word and Spirit in Israel and at another moment could transfer the same hope of redemption to a Persian king, using almost the same language concerning him that he had used concerning Israel, exhibits a serious confusion. Such a prophet would not merit the respect we pay to the integrity of the great preexilic prophets. It is no accident that Duhm places Second Isaiah on a much lower level than all the other prophets. It is also strange that a prophet who so emphasized the nothingness of the power of all earthly rulers in comparison with the power of God and portrayed their humiliation as the prelude to the establishment of God's rule on earth through his Servant should have made one exception and given to one such ruler a place of the highest power and glory! It is much more reasonable to see the hand of a later interpreter at work here, and when once we grasp how the later Jewish community regarded Cyrus as its great alien benefactor, we can appreciate how hard it would be for the community in reading these chapters not to see Cyrus as the mysterious stranger called by God to build his city and set his exiles free without price or reward (v. 13). No one noticed that in passages such as chs. 49:5 and 61:4 the Servant Israel has the task of gathering the scattered exiles and rebuilding the waste places of Palestine and that in ch. 55:1 it is God's redemption of Israel and of mankind that is said to be "without money and without price." It is free, not because Cyrus is generous, but because God is generous and gives both to Israel and to all men what they do not deserve. Cyrus has tramped across the text of Second Isaiah with his clumsy feet long enough, robbing the prophet of his integrity and confusing the character of his message. When he is finally allowed to depart, a prophet will be restored to Israel and to the Christian church who was with good reason the most intimate Old Testament companion of Jesus Christ. It has never been possible to conceal his message completely, for no matter how confused the interpretation has been at some points, the glorious music of Second Isaiah's good news has broken through in chapters such as chs. 40, 42, 49, 53, and 55. But vast areas of the remaining chapters, and some parts of these chosen few, have remained a shambles, and the magnificent unity of the prophet's thought and writing has been almost completely concealed.

It changes completely the significance of the victories in *vs. 1-3* when they are understood, not as a series of military conquests in the mid-sixth century, but as the subduing of the nations before God's anointed Servant in preparation for the establishment of God's universal kingdom. So interpreted, the victories of vs. 1-3 are the first act in a drama of judgment and salvation in whose final act (vs. 22-25) every knee is bowed before the God of all the earth. Here, as elsewhere, the Servant combines royal and prophetic characteristics (cf. ch. 55:4, where he is both witness to the peoples and a leader and commander for the peoples). "Anointed" is connected here with the kingly function of ruling, but in ch. 61:1 it is an anointing with the Spirit that equips the Servant for prophetic tasks. In chs. 41:13 and 42:6 God grasps Israel's right hand, a symbol of his solidarity with his Servant. What the Servant does is God's own action, just as when the Servant speaks it is God's own word. A parallel to this can be found in the Johannine concept of the words and actions of Jesus corresponding to the words and actions of God, and the words and actions of the apostles corresponding to the words and actions of Jesus. This is no carte blanche for Israel or the church to claim divine authority for their words and actions, but rather, points to the divine possibility of a covenant people—or a covenant person—being taken so completely into God's service that the concrete human existence becomes transparent to the grace, the holiness, and the power of God. Note how at every point in vs. 1-7 the Servant triumphs, and yet it is God who triumphs. The leveling of the mountains in v. 2 is reminiscent of ch. 40:4, where it is part of a theophany. The riches of the nations belong to Israel, as in chs. 45:14; 61:6; and notably in ch. 53:12. It is not often pointed out that the Servant who suffers and dies in ch. 53 has a day of justification when he "divides the spoil with the strong." The fact that this feature of the Servant's triumph is mentioned in ch. 53 suggests that, like so much else in Second Isaiah, it is figurative, signifying not an enrichment of Israel at the expense of all other nations, but rather, the transformation of the condition of Israel from poverty to abundance. We must not forget either that the poor of the nations are to share in this transformation. The rich and powerful are to lose their wealth and power, undoubtedly since they have used them unjustly. The new order is one in which God's justice prevails for Jew and Gentile alike.

God's triumph *in* the Servant will be the revelation to the Servant himself of the presence and power of God—"that you may know that it is I, the Lord, the God of Israel, who call you by your name"

(v. 3). Just as God revealed himself in his power and love in the deliverance of the exodus and so called Israel into being, so in the new deliverance he will reveal himself conclusively as the God of Israel and initiate a new era in her destiny. All confusion and uncertainty in Israel concerning her God will be removed. Name and nature, or destiny, are so closely bound together in the Hebrew mind that to be given one's name by God is to receive one's destiny from God. To be given a new name is to receive a new destiny (cf. ch. 65:15). The depth of Israel's blindness is that it no longer knows who named it in the beginning and gave it a unique destiny. The day of redemption will be a day of remembering the word hidden in its life through the centuries (cf. ch. 40:21), and with that remembrance will come a life-transforming knowledge of God.

V. 4 is a crux of interpretation. The anointed conqueror seems to be quite definitely distinguished from "my servant Jacob and Israel my chosen" for whose sake he has been called, just as in v. 13 he is distinguished from "my exiles." This point has been a bulwark of those who see in Cyrus the instrument of God's conquest of the nations. But a consideration of parallel phenomena should have made them cautious. In ch. 49:5 there is a similar passage in which the Servant seems, with equal definiteness, to be distinguished from Israel, since he is assigned a mission to Israel, and yet in ch. 49:3 the Servant is specifically named "Israel." Attempts have been made to get rid of this identification from the text, but they represent eisegesis of the worst kind, the changing of what is plainly a text that has the support of all the most dependable traditions in the interest of a theory.[2] Who is it that has been called from the womb and given his name by God (ch. 49:1) and has complained that all his efforts have been in vain (ch. 49:4; cf. ch. 40:27)? Who except Israel? The fact is that it belongs in the nature of things that from within Israel must come the voice that will recall Israel to its destiny —just as it is always from within the church that a servant is raised up to restore the church. Jerusalem is the messenger to the cities of

[2] J. A. Bewer, "Two Notes on Isaiah 49:1-6," *Jewish Studies in Memory of George A. Kohut,* ed. by Salo W. Baron and A. Marx (The Alexander Kohut Memorial Foundation, 1935), pp. 86–90. Bewer has shown the baselessness of the emendation conclusively.

Judah (ch. 40:9-11), Israel the messenger to Israel. The repetition of "though you do not know me" in *vs. 4 and 5* is Second Isaiah's familiar theme of Israel's blindness to God (ch. 42:18 ff.). The glorious Servant of the future is none other than the blind and helpless Servant of the present, but transformed by God's re-creative power.

"That you may know" in v. 3 is expanded in *v. 6* to *"that men may know, from the rising of the sun and from the west."* Neither Duhm, Volz, nor Muilenburg gives us any suggestion of how the triumphs of Cyrus were to convince the whole of humanity that the God of Israel was the one and only true God. They do not face squarely the dilemma that their interpretation creates: that a prophet who would set his sublimest hopes so confidently upon even the most benevolent foreign ruler would show himself more the victim of his own enthusiasm than a man of real discernment. The universal outlook of Second Isaiah, already so clearly expressed in chs. 42 and 44:1-5, and which forms the climax of ch. 45 in vs. 14-15 and vs. 22-25, is integral also to vs. 1-7. Israel has precedence. First comes the restoration and transformation of Israel, but this is only the prelude to the world's redemption. The manifestation of God's glory in Israel does not merely make the nations bow down in astonishment. It does that, but more than that, they recognize their own true God in the God of Israel, the only living God who is worthy of worship and obedience, and they unite themselves with Israel into one great universal people of God. The concluding verse of the scene (*v. 7*) recalls the first creation when God said "Let there be light" and divided the light from the darkness. Usually the prophet introduces a scene depicting the new work of God by pointing back to the first creation (cf. chs. 42:5; 44:24), but here he does it to conclude. In either position it warns us of the eschatological character of the scene. Creation heralds new creation. That the prophet here fastens upon the creation of light shows how central to the whole scene is the thought of light shining out through Israel into all the world (cf. chs. 42:6; 49:6). But he who creates light for some creates darkness for others, weal for some and woe for others. For those who stubbornly hold to their own way against God and use their power and wealth in contradiction to his purpose, the day of salvation is darkness and not light. But the prophet's mind is primarily upon light and salvation and in *v. 8* he breaks out into a psalm of praise in his joy at the prospect. "Righteousness," a favorite word of Second Isaiah's, does not always have the same force, although in all its uses it retains some aspect of its original reference to the righteous will of God. Here and in many other passages it is a synonym of "salvation," denoting the righteous order that will prevail on earth when God's will is sovereign. This throws light on its New Testament use. In this eschatological context the word has lost its juristic significance and is no longer suggestive of a lawcourt. To participate in the righteousness of God and to have one's life under God's rule or in his Kingdom are one and the same thing.

The woe of *v. 9* is directed against the same skeptical mind in Israel that we met in ch. 40:12 ff. Also the similarity in structure between chs. 45 and 40 is to be noted. Each begins with a proclamation of what God is about to do and then suddenly takes on an argumentative character, dealing with the objections of those who are quite certain that God cannot and will not do what Second Isaiah declares. In both passages the prophet uses biting sarcasm against his opponents. Here he likens them to a pot that, while being manufactured, begins to complain at the way in which the potter is shaping it. First it shouts impertinently, "What are you doing?" as though it must be perfectly clear to everyone that the potter does not know what he is doing. Then, "What you are making has no handles." The pot knows better than the potter how it should be shaped! In *v. 10* the image changes. A newborn child complains to its father and mother, asking if they know what they are bringing into being. The emendation of *v. 11* by the RSV, "Will you question me," is simple and gives the meaning that is obviously intended. It is also supported by the Dead Sea Isaiah Scroll. *God's* children, the works of his hands, are complaining at the destiny that he has in store for them and has already been shaping in their midst. They presume to give him orders concerning it, as though they knew better than he what it should be. There can be no mistaking the identification of the Israelites who are lampooned with those who in ch. 40:14 were undertaking to teach God the meaning of justice. In ch. 40 they had too much respect for the power of the nations and too small an estimate of the power of God, so that any radical change in their lot seemed to them impossible. They were realists who looked conditions in the eye and planned the future in the light of what was clearly possible. But Second Isaiah, with his reckless faith in the power of God, believed in the impossible and taught that if God were the God that he claimed to be in his revelation of himself to Israel, then the man of faith must live in each moment expecting that which, in the light of the so-called realities, seemed to be impossible. The Creator God, the living God, the God of justice and mercy, the God who holds in his hands life and death, weal and woe, is always the possibility of the impossible. It was impossible for Abraham to have descendants, but God gave them to him. It was impossible for slaves in Egypt to become a free nation with a unique destiny, but it happened. It is impossible for life to come out of death—unless there happens to be a God whose nature it is to raise the dead to life. Second Isaiah is certain that this is God's nature, not only from the history of his people but from the fact that he and those who with him "tremble at God's word" (ch. 66:5) and trust themselves wholly to God (chs. 40:31; 50:10; 51:7) have already known a transformation from paralyzing despair to jubilant confidence that is like passing from death to life.

Second Isaiah must have seemed like a crazy man to the sober realists whose religion had room only for the humanly possible and the humanly reasonable. Liturgical sacrifices were eminently reasonable. All nations knew that this was the way to influence the actions of deity in order to make them favorable to one's self or to one's nation. It was fantastic to talk of a future in which Israel as God's Servant would conquer the world for God—almost as fantastic as the later claim of Christians for one Israelite that he would conquer the world and lay it at God's feet! And this talk about the Gentiles being built into Israel to share in the future salvation and to be God's people together with the Israelites! What kind of treason was this against the proud prerogatives and exclusive rights of Israel as God's people? We know how persistent was a narrow interpretation of Israel's covenant relation with God in the time of Amos and in the time of Jeremiah, and there is no reason to expect that the national catastrophe would weaken the strength of nationalistic pride. More often such pride grows in intensity in a period of subjection. The book of Jonah indicates its stubborn persistence. It may be anticipated, therefore, that the daring universalism of Second Isaiah would be too much for many of the Israelites. A future triumph of Israel was robbed of its glory for them if it was to be merely the triumph of God's purpose in Israel, and Gentiles were to be allowed to share in it. Second Isaiah called for an Israel that would put itself unconditionally in God's hands, as clay in the hands of the potter, for him to shape it and use it as his instrument in the redemption of a dark and unhappy world. At more than one point he cried out that no one was responding to God's call (chs. 50:2; 51:18; 59:16; 63:5; 64:7; 65:1 ff.; 66:4), that all Israel was turning a deaf ear to the one true word of God. But in a number of passages we read of "servants" within Israel who hear in humility and respond in faithfulness (chs. 50:10; 51:7; 57:1; 63:16; 65:13 ff.; 66:5). The impression this leaves upon us is that the official community rejected the message of the prophet and that he received a hearing only from a remnant within the community. The sharpness with which Second Isaiah attacked his opponents and the ridicule with which he portrayed their attitude are sufficiently provocative to explain the harsh treatment of him of which we shall find evidence as we proceed.

Those who retain Cyrus in the chapter are forced to explain the complaints of Second Isaiah's compatriots as being against his designation of Cyrus as the Messianic deliverer of the Jews (Volz, Muilenburg, etc.). But would these Jewish realists be disturbed at bestowing honors, even the highest honors, on a foreign king who would forward the national interests of the Jews? We would expect the opposite. If Assyrian and Babylonian kings were the instruments of God's judgment upon Israel, why should not the Persian king be the instrument of liberation? The Chronicler, who represents the continuation of a Temple-centered, nationalistic, exclusive conception of Israel's religion, was not backward about recognizing Cyrus as God's servant. Quite plainly the objection of the pot against the potter and of the child against his parents is that God is doing the wrong thing, not with someone else, but with his own people, not with Cyrus, but with Israel. The discouraged Israelites will not believe that God by a new creative act can bring into being a new and transformed Israel. The reference to the first creation of the heavens and the earth in *v. 12* signals the coming announcement of the new creation in v. 13.

The air of mystery that is thrown round the conqueror by referring to him only by the personal pronoun "him" or "me" is deliberate (cf. chs. 41:2, 25; 46:11; 48:14; 49:1; 53:2), for this is the as yet uncreated Israel of the future. He exists in the intention of God as the miracle of miracles, the impossible possibility. The promise of his future existence in human form is already present in the history of God's faithful servants in Israel's past, but he is so much the embodiment of God's power, God's righteousness, God's truth, God's justice, and God's love for all mankind that he can be spoken of only with hesitation and in an atmosphere of mystery. He is the future mediator of God's salvation to the world. The prophet cannot set the Israel of the present in direct continuity with him as the historical entity out of which he is to be born without immediately setting him in a relation of discontinuity with the Israel of the present as the judgment of God upon all that Israel has been and is. In this it might seem that Second Isaiah was condemning his fellow countrymen unfairly for not being what they could never be or for what was no more than a common human sinfulness. But what must in fairness be recognized here is that the revelation of man's destiny in God is always a devastating judgment upon what he is. It must be remembered that although the prophet exposes the stubborn persistence of his people in their blindness and sin, the keynote of his message is joyful affirmation of the certainty of a world-encompassing salvation. How the Israel of the present was to become the triumphant mediator of man's salvation in the future was shrouded in mystery, as well it might be. But of the certainty of the event the prophet had not a doubt. The purpose of God was revealed in his word, and how would God be God if his purpose should eventually fail to triumph? The clue to the mystery of how the present Israel is to be transformed into the glorious Servant lies in the emphasis upon forgiveness with which ch. 40 opened and which breaks through again and again. Were there no possibility of forgiveness in God, there would be no future for Israel or for any man. All would be prisoners of the sins of the past. But where there is forgiveness, what is not possible?

The task of the Servant in *v. 13* is a limited one, the first act in the program of redemption: the restoration of Jerusalem and the liberation of the exiles. The order in the prophet's mind is not that of the book of Ezra where liberation comes first, then the attempt to rebuild the Temple, and finally the reconstruction of Jerusalem. He sees, rather, the rebuilding of the city first and then the ingathering of the exiles from the four corners of the earth. *The Temple is not mentioned.* The Cyrus interpretations show a remarkable inconsistency regarding v. 13, emphasizing the generosity of Cyrus in his liberation of the Babylonian Jews without receiving any "price or reward," but forgetting that they have already pictured Cyrus in vs. 1-3 as being richly rewarded by God. Volz even regards ch. 43:3 as saying that God paid to Cyrus as ransom for Israel the three lands, Egypt and Ethiopia in Africa and Seba in South Arabia! Parallel passages, however, such as chs. 52:3 and 55:1, in which Israel's redemption is "without money and without price," indicate that the prophet's mind is upon the freedom of *God's* gracious action. Israel does not have to earn or deserve or purchase its redemption, nor does mankind. It is God's love that offers the gift. Perhaps the phrase is meant as a warning to all Israelites that they cannot purchase a new day for Israel by lavish sacrificial offerings, thereby laying upon God the obligation to do something for them (cf. chs. 43:22-24; 58:3). All God asks is a humility, openness, and responsiveness toward him.

The second half of Israel's task, witnessing for God to the nations, comes to expression in *v. 14,* demonstrating again the close-knit unity of the chapter. Most interpreters see the African peoples being led past Jerusalem in chains by Cyrus on their way into captivity and confessing the presence of God in Israel as they pass, but this ignores the fact that they come *to* Israel and bow themselves down. Violent distortion of the text is necessary to retain Cyrus in it. Volz and Muilenburg escape the difficulty by cutting vs. 14 ff. away from the earlier part of the chapter, bringing Israel into the center of the picture, and ignoring the parallels. But the passage is the logical continuation of vs. 1-13. Israel restored receives the homage of the nations. The African peoples are merely representatives of mankind. The passage is directly parallel to ch. 44:1-5 where Gentiles join themselves to Israel. The one difficulty lies in the description of the

Africans as coming "in chains." Otherwise the impression of the verse is that they come because they have seen that in Israel alone is there a living God and they desire to share in his worship and service. Torrey eliminates "in chains" as an addition that is metrically superfluous. It may have been added by whoever saw only Cyrus' conquests in the chapter. If it remains, however, it is a symbol that the nations were first conquered by God and then, opening their eyes to his glory, responded to him in faith. What is clear is that not only Israel but nations from the ends of the earth know that there is no other God than the God of Israel (cf. vs. 3 and 6).

In *vs. 15 and 16* the prophet interrupts his vision of the future to offer a prayer of his own to God. It is as though he were overwhelmed from time to time by the wonder of what God has in store for Israel and mankind and has to break out into songs of joy or into prayers (cf. chs. 42:10-12; 44:23; 45:8). Here in v. 15 he marvels that God has so hidden himself and his purpose from the eyes of man, that is, that what God is now revealing to him has been so long hidden from mankind in general and even from Israel. To say, "Thou art a God who hidest thyself," is really only a negative way of saying, "Thou art a God whose revelation lifts man out of darkness into light." Standing in the light of the revelation and looking back into the world of darkness that he had known before, or looking out across the world at the darkness in which men live day by day, the prophet interprets this darkness which is the source of man's misery and weakness as God's hiding of himself from man. God's coming to man and being present with man is blessing and salvation, but God's withdrawal from man or absence from him brings darkness and death. It is as though the sun had withdrawn from the earth. God's hiding of himself is, not an arbitrary act, but the consequence of man's sin. The horror of sin is that it ruptures the relation with God from man's side so that where God has been there seems to be only emptiness, darkness, nothingness. God takes his Holy Spirit from us (Ps. 51:11). God is still present, but his presence is felt as wrath rather than love, as fire that burns (ch. 42:25) rather than as a fountain of life. Therefore, the prophet can speak either of Israel's, and mankind's, blindness and deafness or of God's hiddenness. The idea that God is hidden is not an agreeable one to the present generation. It seems almost an insult to human nature to deny it the capacity to know God and a narrowing of the conception of God. Surely God reveals himself to men everywhere through nature, conscience, and reason. It was spiritual arrogance in Israel, men say, to think that it was entrusted with a knowledge of God that the world could possess only through the witness of Israel. And it must also be spiritual arrogance in the Christian church for it to think that God is hidden from men until he is revealed in the church's witness to Jesus Christ. But strangely, or not so strangely, when Christians surrender to this way of thinking, they begin to lose their interest in and understanding of the unique and life-shaking revelation of God that was the wonder and despair of prophets and apostles, and they become content with the tame and comfortable revelation that is more easily available to them in nature and conscience. They no longer notice the darkness and emptiness. Only the prophet who has seen the world in the light of God's revelation knows how deep the darkness is, and only the apostle who has seen the world reconciled with God in the person of Jesus Christ knows how far his own world has fallen and how much it has lost in its alienation from God.

Vs. 16-17. The prophet speaks. The theme is a familiar one. The makers of idols will be utterly confounded in the day that God reveals himself to all the world as God alone, but Israel will be vindicated before the world as the one nation in which God is truly known.

Vs. 18-19. How can the prophet be so sure about what God will yet do? What is the basis of his confidence? The Creator of the world has spoken a word in Israel in which he has revealed his intention for his creation. There is no secret about this word. It is open for all to know. The prophet seems definitely to be referring to the stories of creation that belonged at the heart of Israel's traditions. Here God is no longer hidden, but is revealed, and there is no excuse for any Israelite to walk in darkness. God did not create the world to be a chaos; his creation was a victory over chaos. Nor did he say to Israel, "Seek me in chaos," but rather, by his revelation of himself to Israel he brought order and fruitfulness into the life of his people. Chaos is the condition of the world and man without God.

The coming of God is the end of chaos and the beginning of a new order. The word, therefore, on which Second Isaiah bases his hope for the future (ch. 40:8) is to be found not so much in specific predictions of future events as in the revelation of God's purpose for the world and man that permeated the writings of the prophets, the stories of creation, the sagas of the patriarchs, the history of the nation, and the songs of praise and prayer. God revealed *himself* in Israel and in revealing himself he revealed the future of his world. The prophet's trust is in the integrity of God's nature. He cannot be the God that he is and leave the future a chaos or man the helpless prey of ruthless and unscrupulous powers.

Vs. 20-23. A third time in this chapter the balance is preserved in the prophet's concern for both Israel and the nations. Each time he opens a bright prospect before Israel he expands it to take in the remainder of mankind. In *v. 20* God addresses the "fugitives" of the nations, that is, all who have survived the judgment, and calls them, as in earlier scenes, to assemble themselves, that the truth may be set clearly before them concerning their gods and the one true God. Let them say what they can for their gods, then let them listen while God speaks. The familiar argument from history is presented briefly: the God of Israel alone has revealed beforehand the meaning and purpose of events and so has shown himself to be the Lord of history. There is no hope for man except in him. There is no deliverance from the chaos of the world except by him. The appeal goes out to all mankind to turn to God and find salvation (*v.* 22), but this is more than an appeal and a pious hope for Second Isaiah. In *v. 23* he calls to mind again the word on which he based his confidence concerning Israel's future in vs. 18 and 19. In it God has revealed the goal of his purpose for the world, a world in which all men will be a people in covenant with him, giving to him their entire allegiance and receiving from him their own true life. The day must come when the completeness of God's rule on earth will be the measure of the fullness of man's joy. God says, "By myself I have sworn," that is, the integrity of his own being is the guarantee of his promise. If God's word be not true, then God himself is not true.

A word has gone forth from God's mouth never to return until it is fulfilled (cf. ch. 55:11). Such strong assertions by the prophet concerning the source of his confidence are robbed of their central and decisive significance when the facile and baseless theory is propounded that he received his first impulse to prophesy when he saw the great king Cyrus moving from triumph to triumph! He could not say more clearly to us than he does that his whole reliance is upon God's word.

CHAPTER 46/ The theme of ch. 46 is a favorite one with Second Isaiah: the contrast between the powerlessness of idols to do anything and the power of God long manifest in Israel's history. From this history Israel should draw a firm assurance that in spite of every obstacle God will open before his people a new future. Duhm, Volz, and others have broken the chapter into fragments because they have been so certain that the prophet has Cyrus and his capture of Babylon in mind that they have been unable to see what the chapter is about from beginning to end. It is a perfect unity and typical of the prophet's dramatic writing. First, a vivid picture is drawn of the two chief gods of the Babylonians being loaded on weary beasts to be carried helplessly into captivity, and in contrast to this is set the power and patience of the living God, who carries Israel as his burden from the beginning to the end of its history. The true God carries and the false gods have to be carried! Then, he repeats the contrast, depicting the process of making an idol and comparing with the helpless idol the revelation in Israel of God's power in the shaping of history. The false gods are shaped by the hands of men, but the lives of men are shaped by the hand of the one true God. There is a beautiful symmetry in the parallels and contrasts. The thought of God's power in history leads on to a depiction of the mysterious conqueror from a far country, the bird of prey, the Israel of the future in its office as the agent of God's judgment upon all the great powers of the world including Babylon. The chapter closes appropriately with God's announcement to an unbelieving Israel, not that the fall of Babylon or the coming of Cyrus is near, but that its salvation is near. The fall of Babylon is merely part of the preparatory clearing of the ground for the establishment of God's Kingdom.

The unity of the chapter is also evident in the consistently sharp tone of God's address to Israel. The emphasis upon God's carrying Israel throughout its history suggests not only God's unfailing support of his people but also the burdensomeness of Israel to God. Already in ch. 43:24 the prophet had spoken of Israel burdening God with its sins and wearying him with its iniquities. The same tone appears when Israel is addressed in v. 8 as "you transgressors" and in v. 12 as "you stubborn of heart who are far from salvation." These are the Israelites who in ch. 40 were so impressed with the power of such nations as Babylon and Egypt that they distrusted the power of the God of Israel to do anything for his people. Such belittling of their own God could easily lead to the tempting thought that the real power in the world lay in the hands of the gods of the powerful nations.

Torrey recognizes the unity of ch. 46, but unfortunately, in his zeal to erase every reference to Babylon from the book, refuses to tolerate the idea that the prophet was thinking of the fall of Babylon. Babylon, to him, is merely symbolic of a great world power, most likely Persia near the close of the fifth century. His evidence for this conclusion, and for his whole theory of a late fifth-century origin of the book, is almost completely nonexistent. Erratic features of this kind in Torrey's argument have helped to conceal the solid and enduring contribution of his commentary to the understanding of Second Isaiah. The mention of Babylon as one of the world powers that are soon to be destroyed gives no support to the theory of a Babylonian location of the prophet. He did not have to live in Babylon to know the names of its gods or to rejoice at the prospect of its humiliation as he does in chs. 46 and 47. In ch. 45, Egypt, Ethiopia, and Seba were singled out for mention; in chs. 46 and 47, Babylon. It would be surprising if a prophet writing for the whole of scattered Israel should make no particular mention of Babylonia, which was the overlord of Palestine in the sixth century and the locale of a substantial body of exiles. What he says of Babylon in chs. 46; 47 gives no indication whatever concerning his own location.

The prophet plainly enjoys depicting the helplessness of the idols, and the scenes where he does so are touched with humor and playfulness. He has just spoken in ch. 45:23 of every knee of man bowing down to the one true God. Now in *ch. 46:1* he uses the same verb of proud Bêl of Babylon whom the Babylonians delighted to enthrone as the king over all the earth, describing him as *bowing down* in utter humiliation in the day that Yahweh is enthroned. Nebo, the god of Borsippa, whose name is incorporated in the names of the kings, Nebuchadnezzar, and Nabopolassar, had become equally prominent in Babylon alongside Bêl. The great gods, from whom the Babylonians expected deliverance from every danger, are loaded on the backs of weary beasts as the attempt is made to "save the gods!" The attempt is fruitless. Men and gods alike are carried into captivity. The fact that these events did *not* happen when Babylon fell indicates that the oracle was earlier than 539 B.C.

This picture was being drawn for the instruction of foolish Israelites who had begun to think the Babylonian gods more powerful than the God of Israel. In *v. 3*, God addresses the Israelites directly. His name for them, "the remnant,"[1] is more fitting for those left behind in Palestine than for the exiles. Now they are bidden to compare their God with the pagan gods. From the beginning of their history God has faithfully and patiently borne with them, burdened by their sins and yet unceasingly carrying forward his creative purpose in their midst. And what he has ever been to them he will be through all time. They have forgotten what God has spoken to Israel, what God has done in Israel, what God has been to Israel. *V. 5* suggests that the Israelites were dragging their God down to the level of an idol. Perhaps some of them even went so far as to copy the pagan practice of fashioning an image of their god, and fashioned an image of Yahweh, thinking thereby to endow him with more power. Certainly here and in ch. 40:18-20 the suggestion is that Israelites are finding a likeness of their god in an image. This has usually been dismissed from consideration because of the long-standing prohibition in Israel of any form of material representation of Yahweh, but there is no reason to think that the paganizing tenden-

---

[1] Kosters, *op. cit.,* p. 17, points out that this name is used in Jer. 42:2, 15, 19; 43:5; 44:7; 44:12, 14 for those who remained in Palestine after the deportations.

cies of the eighth and seventh centuries suddenly ceased in the sixth century. Hosea complained of Israelites who worshiped Yahweh as though he were a Baal (Hos. 2:16; 8:4-5; 10:5), and Jeremiah in Egypt had to contend with exiles who were certain that they would get more help from the queen of heaven than from Yahweh (Jer. 44:17 ff.). Second Isaiah's repeated attacks on the making and worshiping of idols have much more point if chs. 40:18 and 46:5 are taken literally and are understood to mean that many Israelites had reduced their God to a stature no different from that of an idol, in short, had degenerated into polytheists. They did not cease to worship Yahweh, but they gave their worship also to other seemingly more powerful gods. This would explain why in later chapters the same people seem to be attacked for trusting in fasting and sacrifices to influence Yahweh and also for participation in crude pagan practices. We are reminded of Ezekiel's picture of the syncretistic religion of priests in the Jerusalem Temple early in the sixth century (Ezek. 8:9 ff.). Second Isaiah seems to have had their direct descendants as his opponents. Such syncretists would not take kindly the ridicule that Second Isaiah heaped upon them and they would have no scruples in trying to silence him.

In *vs. 8 ff.* the prophet makes his appeal to history as in vs. 3-4. The word of God that ruled the past will rule the future, and intrinsic to that word is the promise that God's purpose will prevail in the life of man. Again the agent of God's purpose is shrouded in mystery. He is "a bird of prey from the east, the man of my counsel from a far country." Those who insist that this must be Cyrus have never rightly explained either how the prophet found Cyrus in the word that God had declared "from the beginning" (v. 10), or how the "former things" (v. 9) in which Israel was the agent of God's purpose could reach their ultimate fulfillment in the "things not yet done" in which not Israel but Cyrus would fulfill "all God's purpose." Their theory necessitates that God should have cast aside Israel as his instrument and should have chosen Cyrus instead, but the prophet's constant insistence is that God has not cast Israel aside (ch. 50:1-3), but on the contrary, has expanded Israel's responsibility. There is no escape from this dilemma. "Bird of prey" and "man of my counsel" depict perfectly the double function of the future

Servant Israel, who will sit in judgment upon the nations and effect the establishment of God's rule in all the world.

"Hearken to me" in vs. 3, 12, has in it an admonitory tone. Those who are addressed are not disposed to hearken to God's word. They are "stubborn of heart" and "far from righteousness." The RSV translation "far from deliverance" misses the play on words. The same Hebrew word *sedaqah* is used here and in v. 13, but where in v. 13 it means "deliverance," as the parallel with "salvation" shows, in v. 12 it has another meaning, "righteousness," which is the quality lacking in the unbelieving Israelites. They are far from *sedaqah,* but God's *sedaqah* is closer to them than they know. Not even the sin and unbelief of Israel can hold back the fulfillment of God's purpose.

CHAPTER 47 / A chapter that from beginning to end

consists of one long oracle of doom upon Babylon necessarily stands by itself in the writings of Second Isaiah. There is nothing like it elsewhere in the book. The preceding and the following chapters are similar in character to chs. 40 to 45, being made up of scenes or passages each of which carries a theme, a number of such scenes being fitted together like a mosaic to create a larger pattern. As the chapters have advanced, many of these scenes have become familiar by repetition, but always a fresh element is introduced to carry the thought forward. But ch. 47 is not at all of this character. It contains one long unbroken scene in which God addresses a proud and confident Babylon and proclaims to her the certainty of her fall and humiliation. There are scenes of judgment elsewhere in Second Isaiah, but always the judgment is upon all the nations, never upon a single nation, and always it is a preparation of the world for the establishment of God's universal sovereignty. To find anything similar to ch. 47 one has to go outside the writings of Second Isaiah to those of other prophets, or at least to writings contained in the books that bear their names. Oracles of doom upon individual nations of an exactly similar kind exist in considerable number—on Egypt, Edom, Tyre, Nineveh, and Babylon. They show varied authorship, being written in different styles, but they have certain common features that occur again and again. What brings down God's destructive judgment is the unbridled egotism of the foreign nation in which it sets itself in place of God. None of the powers or achievements on which it has prided itself and in which it has seemed to be superior to other nations is able to save it. From the highest eminence it is brought down to the most wretched servitude. The site of the great city, which was thronged with people, becomes the habitation of wild beasts and birds. Oracles of doom of this nature on Babylon are found in Isa. 13:17-22; 14:4 ff.; Jer., chs. 50; 51:1-58, the examples in Jeremiah being of great length. The note appended to Jer. 51:1-58, whether historical or not, shows the purpose of these oracles. They were not merely the outcries of an oppressed people for God to punish the cruelty and pride of the oppressor. As words of God they were thought to have power in themselves, like the curse of the medicine man, to bring the destruction they predicted upon their victim. The oracle of doom, secretly transported to Babylon, attached to a stone, and flung into the Euphrates, would procure the destruction of Babylon. It is difficult to believe that a Jeremiah, or any other of the great prophets, would participate in a magical practice of this kind. It belongs on a lower level of prophecy in Israel, where prophet and medicine man were not so far apart and the prophet was conceived as controlling the power of God in some measure. Whether the oracles of doom on foreign cities are genuinely by Isaiah and Jeremiah is seriously open to question. Yet, strangely, no one except Torrey has ever questioned whether ch. 47 is original to Second Isaiah, and even Torrey merely raises the question and proceeds to interpret the chapter as original. Commentators who have been most zealous to separate the "genuine" Second Isaiah from a multitude of later additions have paid no heed to the solitary position of ch. 47 in the book and have assumed its genuineness, no doubt because it has to do with Babylon and because Second Isaiah was, in their minds, the Babylonian prophet.

The striking differences between ch. 47 and the surrounding chapters (e.g., an unusual number of words that are not found elsewhere in these writings) and its similarity to the oracles of doom on Babylon in other books, while not sufficient to deny it to Second Isaiah, should at least make the interpreter cautious about basing his theories concerning Second Isaiah on this particular chapter. It is highly questionable to attempt to prove Babylonian authorship for the whole book from the chapter's familiarity with various features of Babylonian life. No one would think of using chs. 50 and 51 of Jeremiah to prove that he had been in Babylon. Why then should ch. 47 be valid evidence that Second Isaiah was in Babylon? The character of Babylon and its people was very well known in the ancient world, especially in countries ruled by Babylon and among people who had some of their fellow countrymen living in Babylonia. It would be going beyond the evidence, however, to deny ch. 47 to Second Isaiah, because it was certainly written before the fall of Babylon when the Babylonians as yet suspected no threat to their power (vs. 8, 10), that is, in the period of Second Isaiah's activity, and it was an essential element in his thought that the arrogant power not only of Babylon but of all the nations would be broken with the coming of God to subdue the earth to his rule.

These oracles of doom on foreign nations, in spite of Jer. 51:59 ff. with its description of a superstitious use that was made of them, are not to be dismissed as unessential to the corpus of prophetic writings. Certainly a church that is only too much inclined to make a neat separation between the spiritual concerns of life where God has his interests and international politics with which its gospel has nothing to do, will do well to ponder their significance, particularly if the church concerned has its life in the midst of a great world power. From the beginning of time superiority over other nations in power and in cultural achievements seems to have had remarkably similar consequences for the character of the nation that possesses it. Whether the nation be called Egypt, Assyria, Babylonia, Tyre, or Rome, or in the modern world, Germany, Britain, Russia, or the United States, seems to make no difference. The same phenomena reproduce themselves in such a way that the Biblical description of ancient Tyre or Babylon, blinded by its consciousness of power and superiority, applies in an almost frightening manner to the modern state that knows a concentration of power of which the ancient world never dreamed. Power is the most dangerous poison to the soul of a nation, exalting its ego in such a fashion that it ceases even to be aware of what is happening when it is walking over the little people of the world. Power conjures up fears and suspicions that destroy human relationships both within the nation and without and eventually prepare its destruction. The prophets of Israel understood the inner process by which the human self, unbroken by the recognition of God's sovereignty and coveting an unlimited sovereignty, involves itself in conflict with all other selves, with the world and with God, choosing the way to death rather than the way to life (cf. Gen., ch. 3). What was true in the life of individuals was true also in the life of nations, and a church that acknowledges a responsibility toward the nation in which it finds itself and toward mankind in general should learn this lesson in the school of the prophets and never cease to warn its people of the peril from within.

There are few comments that need to be made on the details of the chapter. Babylon is likened to a queen who has been accustomed to sitting on a throne and to being treated with great respect, but now is to be reduced to the status of a slave, stripped of all her splendid clothing and in seminakedness set to the task of grinding grain. *V. 3* suggests that the royal garments have concealed a corrupt and shameful body. *V. 6* contains the only mention of Israel in the chapter, interpreting Israel's subjection to Babylon as God's punishment of its sin, but accusing Babylon of a mercilessness, particularly toward the aged among the exiles. Torrey questions the genuineness of this verse. In the remainder of the chapter the reason given for Babylon's fall is the arrogance of its pride in itself, rather than any maltreatment of Israel, but there is no reason why the lesser offense should not be included. What Babylon says of itself in *vs. 8 and 10* is identical with what God says of himself elsewhere in Second Isaiah: "I am, and there is no one besides me." The ultimate pretension of the power state is that it tries to set itself in the place of the sovereign God. In *v. 9* the inability of Babylon to save itself by its religious practices, sorceries, and enchantments—further defined in v. 13, is directly in line with Second Isaiah's constant emphasis upon the futility of the pagan religions. The judgment that is to overtake Babylon is likened to a great fire, which was the image of God's judgment on Israel in the exile in ch. 42:25, and the ironic comment, so like Second Isaiah, is added that it will be no comfortable fire before which one may sit and warm himself.

CHAPTER 48 / The severity with which Israel is arraigned for unfaithfulness in ch. 48 has made this chapter a stone of stumbling for Duhm and for those who have followed his lead. Duhm's comments are a perfect illustration of how a false assumption can carry the interpretation astray. Because Second Isaiah has proclaimed Israel's sin forgiven, its punishment complete, and the time of redemption at hand, Duhm concludes that the prophet has "only comfort, sympathy and encouragement for Israel; if he has anything to criticize concerning the nation, it is only its discouragement and slowness to believe." Therefore, he supposes that someone has worked over an original oracle of Second Isaiah to make it into the present grim denunciation. Volz proceeds with a similar assumption. The sharpness of the prophet's attack on Israel makes him suspicious of the chapter's genuineness. It is not like the prophet to speak in such a tone, he says, nor would it have been just on his part to address the Babylonian exiles in this way. Volz operates with two assumptions, the inability of Second Isaiah to speak with severity to the Israel of his time and the freedom of the exilic community from the corruptions that the prophet castigates. Volz states "that it is impossible for the exilic community to have practiced idol worship." This is set forth as a fact by him, but the fragmentariness of the evidence makes it an assumption. He resorts to diverse expedients to remove the sting from ch. 48. He cannot follow Duhm in denying its genuineness, because in language and style it is thoroughly characteristic of Second Isaiah. He cannot follow those who eliminate the harshest verses because the omissions destroy the meaning of the text. So he explains that Second Isaiah really had the sins of *preexilic* Israel in mind when he wrote, and besides, that he composed the chapter for use in a service of repentance, so that all the expressions are not to be taken literally. The only people in his audience with whom he could have been severe were those whose opposition to him is evident in chs. 45:9; 46:8; and 49:4.

The note of sharp criticism has been present in the prophet's words, however, from the very beginning. Already in ch. 40 he entered into controversy with Israelites who questioned God's justice and power and were inclined to confuse him with an idol. He used ridicule in his argument (ch. 40:14), and ridicule is a sharp weapon. In ch. 42:18-25 he lamented the blindness and deafness of Israel to God that made them unable to understand God's fiery judgment that was upon them and unfitted them for the task of the Servant. In ch. 43:22-28 he set a realistic picture of the present Israel alongside his vision in vs. 1-21 of the Israel of the future, an Israel that burdened God only with its sins and that from the beginning of its history had persisted in transgression. In ch. 45:9-11 Israel was represented as impertinently scolding God for what he was making of it and daring to tell him how he should proceed. In ch. 46:8, 12 the house of Jacob was addressed as "you transgressors," "stubborn of heart and far from righteousness." The source of the confusion is a failure to recognize Second Isaiah's homiletic method of setting the Israel of the present under the searching judgment of the Israel of God's intention. It is directly because Second Isaiah had such a profound and encouraging conception of Israel's destiny that he was so severe with the Israelites with whom he had to deal who were in serious danger of losing all sight of their future in God's plan.

There is little in ch. 48 that is new. The themes that are interwoven have all been introduced in earlier chapters. So familiar are they that it is amazing that anyone should be suspicious of its genuineness. The one change that we observe is that the prophetic severity, which has until now taken second place in relation to exuberant hope, presses into the foreground and dominates the chapter, although even here it eventually gives way to hope and confidence. The prophet held in his mind two certainties that seemed to contradict each other: the certainty of God's purpose for Israel, and for mankind through Israel, that alone made sense of history, and the certainty of the blindness, deafness, and general unfaithfulness of the Israelites that prevented them from being a ready instrument for God's purpose. The tension between these two is constant in his thought. One way to resolve the dilemma would have been to abandon Israel as a whole and to set his hopes upon the remnant of faithful believers within the nation. Later we shall have to consider the evidence to determine whether or not he eventually made such a separation in the nation, but in these earlier chapters there is no sign of it. He simply faces the contradiction and asserts that in spite of Israel's sin God will carry through his purpose to its triumph and transform Israel into a fit instrument. The blind will be given eyes and the deaf ears (ch. 43:8).

Against this background, ch. 48 ceases to be a series of widely differing oracles loosely strung together and becomes a powerful unified sermon pleading with a rebellious people to open their eyes to the destiny that God has planned for them, to recognize the hand of God in their history in past and present, and to believe that the future as well will come from his hand. In *vs. 1-2* the prophet addresses his people directly, accusing them of hypocrisy in their religious professions and calling them to open their ears to the word of God. The fourfold repetition of the command to hear (vs. 1, 12, 14, 16) and the references to the nation's unwillingness to hear make us aware of the solid wall of resistance that the prophet was meeting. The ears of his people were closed to his message. This obduracy and opposition has about it a concreteness and definiteness, particularly in ch. 48, that suggests, not communities of exiles at a distance which were known to the prophet only by letters and report, but rather, the community in which he himself was living where he could observe the practices of his countrymen and where day by day he was in personal confrontation with his opponents. The community is a worshiping community. Its members count themselves true Israelites, confess and stay themselves upon the God of Israel, swear by the name of Yahweh, and consider Jerusalem their city. But their unfaithfulness to God is so great that they have actually forfeited their right to claim the unique relation with him of a covenant people. The covenant has been broken by their refusal to fulfill its conditions, and they cannot in truth call themselves Israel, the chosen people of God, the Servant of his purpose.

In *v. 3*, God himself begins to speak. The theme of the speech is the now familiar argument from history. Can Israel be blind to the way in which in its own past God's word has ever heralded the event and the event confirmed the word? This could have been illustrated by the word of promise to Abraham, which seemed impossible of fulfillment and yet was fulfilled at least in part in his descendants, or by the revelation to Moses, which was validated by the exodus and the settlement of the nation in Palestine, or by the preexilic prophets' warnings of ruin, which were still in process of fulfillment. But in ch. 48 the argument is given a new turn. God says that he revealed the event beforehand in his word because he knew that the obstinate rebelliousness of the Israelites would lead them to attribute the events of their history to the power of idols. He forestalled this perversion by revealing his intention in the words of his prophets before he acted in history. For the same reason he is now revealing the new events that are about to take place so that, when they come to pass, they will be recognized as his doings. The prestige of a god in the ancient world depended to a large extent upon his reputation for influencing events in daily life. The power of medicine men and priests in primitive religion lay in their claim to be in communication with the spirits or gods who controlled the things that happened. Therefore the devotees of each cult were eager to attribute both the fortunate and the unfortunate happenings to the activity of their god. The more powerful a god seemed to be, the more numerous were his worshipers. The triumphs of Babylon were taken to be evidence of the power of the Babylonian gods. Was Second Isaiah then merely entering Yahweh in competition with the other gods, claiming for him what their adherents claimed for them? They too used a "proof from prediction," furnishing evidence that their diviners had predicted events in advance.

The only adequate answer to this question would be to assemble all the passages in which the prophet points to the past, "the former things," and thereby encourages his people to lay hold upon the great tradition of which they are the heirs. He points to the creation, to the call of Abraham, to the exodus, to David, to the princes of the sanctuary. It is the whole of Israel's past that is one gigantic witness to the reality of God. Where among the nations is there anything like this—a god who enters into covenant fellowship with his people and by means of his word of revelation lights up the road they have to travel, guiding them safely through fire and deep waters and bringing them steadily toward the goal of his purpose? "Look unto the rock whence you were hewn and the hole of the pit whence you were digged, look unto Abraham your father" (ch. 51:1-2); that is, look back into the past and see where the true line of your destiny is revealed and what it meant then for there to be a genuine Servant of God. Then follow this line forward into the future until it reaches its destination. If God's hand is concealed now, then consider those times in the past when God's hand was revealed and from them learn who he is and therefore what he must do. Into such regions as this none of the gods of the nations are likely to venture. As the Lord of history, the God of Israel was and is unique through all time.

V. 6. Read with Torrey: "You have heard and seen all this," which requires only a change in the pointing of the second verb. This echoes ch. 40:21, 28, "Have you not known, have you not heard?" No Israelite should have to be reminded of his nation's past. "Will you not declare it?" They should be able themselves to tell the story. But now comes the change of focus from "former things" to "new things," from past to future, from history to eschatology. Exponents of the Cyrus theory are in a dilemma here, unsure whether Cyrus belongs among the former things or the new things. They put him among the former things when they argue that, for Second Isaiah, Yahweh's prediction of Cyrus' triumph was the proof of his power, but in a chapter such as ch. 48, where the coming of the mysterious conqueror in vs. 14-15 is so plainly the "new thing," they project Cyrus into the future (note Muilenburg's uncertainty about this on pp. 554 and 556). It is hardly fair to try to have it both ways. The new and hidden things that Israel has not known, but which are now in process of creation, are the events of redemption: the in-gathering of Israel, the overthrow of the nations, and the establishment of God's universal kingdom. So new is this vision of the future that Second Isaiah's skeptical opponents may have objected that it was a baseless innovation of the prophet himself. To this he is now replying that they know nothing of it because God has concealed it from them to prevent them giving credit for it to their idols. What God is about to bring forth is nothing less than a new creation, a new beginning for Israel and for the world. It is unbelievable, unheard of, and yet true. No man could have imagined its possibility for himself. What lies ahead is the utterly impossible for man that becomes possible only when God unveils his glory and comes to man. The coming of his rule is the transformation of all things in man's existence. The accusation in v. 8 that one would expect from

Israel's history that the nation would deal treacherously (with God) since from its birth it had the reputation of being a rebel is directly in line with ch. 43:26.

V. 9 reveals how little improvement Second Isaiah saw in his people in comparison with preexilic times. Their idolatry and unfaithfulness merited only God's all-consuming anger. God would have given them only their just deserts (in ch. 40:27 they were clamoring for justice!) if he had cut them off entirely from being his people. When their redemption comes, let them not think that anything they have done has made them deserving of it. Not any merit in them, but simply God's faithfulness to his purpose, is the source of the coming redemption. He acts for his own sake, for his own praise, that his name may not be profaned, and not for Israel's sake. This may sound like an attribution of selfishness to God, as though he were concerned only for his own glory and not for sinful man, as though the sin of man made him an object solely of God's anger and no longer of his grace. But we dare not forget for a moment that God's name is God as he has made himself known to man, God in his word of self-revelation, and therefore God in his gracious purpose for his creation and for all mankind. The revelation of God's glory is the fulfillment of his purpose. Thus, to act for his own sake is to maintain the integrity of his purpose and to do what he has promised in his word in spite of the sin of Israel. God cannot let himself be defeated by the sinfulness and unreadiness of the human instrument through which he has chosen to work. This holds true equally for the church. In the midst of God's repeated assertions that he will bring his redemption in spite of Israel's sin stands v. 10 in which he says that he has refined and tried Israel in the furnace of affliction. The phrase "but not with [emended rightly in the RSV to "like"] silver" obscures the meaning which, however, is reasonably clear from the context. God hoped that in the fires of judgment that Israel had endured for years the nation would be refined and made ready for its great calling, but what has come out is not pure silver. The impurities remain. "Not as silver" is an echo of "not in truth or right" in v. 1.

Vs. 12 and 13 prepare us for the announcement of the new creation with their references to the creation of the heavens and earth

and to the calling of Israel—twin themes, creation and covenant, a
significant combination, which although hardly the appropriate setting in which to announce the coming of Cyrus, is the perfect setting in which to announce the *new* creation and the *new* covenant
people. The assembly in *v. 14,* called to hear the announcement, is of
Israelites. "Who among them" should be emended to "Who among
you" (with the support of forty manuscripts), which ties it together
with vs. 6-8, where the Israelites could declare the former things, but
not the new ones. The mysterious conqueror who is now revealed is
the Servant of the future, the *true* descendant of Abraham and Jacob
in contrast to the false descendants (ch. 48:1). The parallel of
"Yahweh loves him, he will perform his purpose" with ch. 42:1-2 is
so perfect that it should be clear to anyone whose mind is not confused by false assumptions that both passages refer to the same
reality. Note also that in ch. 41:8 it is Abraham who is loved by God.
For a full consideration of the confusion in the sentence caused by
the references to Babylon and Chaldea see the note on ch. 43:14. It is
unlikely that "Babylon" and "Chaldea" are original to the verse,[1]
but even if they were, it would not make necessary the introduction
of Cyrus as the agent of God's purpose, since the Servant has already
appeared as the instrument of God's judgment as well as of his
salvation in his dealings with the nations. In ch. 48:15, as in chs.
45:19 and 46:11, God's speaking and acting, his word and deed,
are held in close unity. His word to Israel (cf. chs. 51:16; 59:21;
49:2) was his call to Israel in which was hidden the whole of its
destiny.

V. 16 is difficult as it now stands because of the sudden introduction of God in the third person and the presence of the pronoun
"me" in the last line that would require the whole verse to be read
as the speech of the one who has been sent by God. Volz so interprets it, as a speech of the Servant. Torrey omits the whole of the
last line. Certainly the opening line of the verse, which is directly
parallel with vs. 1, 12, and 14, identifies it as a continuation of God's
address to Israel, and the second line is a repetition of God's words
in ch. 45:19. The third line, parallel with the second, affirms in a
familiar manner that nothing has happened without God's presence

[1] See p. 102 for the consideration of this problem.

and activity (cf. ch. 41:4). How then does the last line suddenly shift into a totally different key and have the Servant speaking of God's sending of him? Kittel suggests an emendation, "I Yahweh have sent him and his spirit," but this is pure conjecture. "His spirit" we would expect to be subject rather than object and to participate in the sending (cf. chs. 42:1; 61:1). But what the original reading was is so uncertain that it is best not to base an important conclusion on the present text as Volz does or on a reconstruction.

V. 17 continues God's address to Israel in a tone so similar to that of vs. 1-11 that the continuity is unquestionable. With a God who was willing to be their redeemer and to buy them back out of slavery, who would have taught them how to profit from all their experiences, and who would have shown them the way into a brighter future, they might by now have already reached the day of peace and salvation when their numbers would have been as many as the sands of the sea—if only they had listened to the commandments of God. Because they have not listened, the day of redemption has been delayed (cf. chs. 58-59, where it is said even more clearly that Israel's disobedience prevents the coming of the great day). But not even Israel's disobedience can hold it back forever. *Vs. 20-21* follow directly upon v. 19 and repeat the theme of vs. 9-11: in spite of Israel's sin God's redemption is at hand. The message must be heralded to the ends of the earth that all may hear: God has redeemed his servant Jacob. The past tense is used, as usual, to express the certainty of the future event.[2] In v. 21 the ingathering of Israel's sons and daughters from afar is described as a new exodus, God making water flow for them out of the rock even as he had for their forefathers as they traveled through the desert from Egypt. *V. 22,* regarded by most interpreters as a later addition both here and in ch. 57:21, largely because they could not conceive of the "prophet of comfort" ending an oracle on such a somber note, is not an inappropriate conclusion. Chapter 48 furnishes abundant evidence that Second Isaiah had no peace or comfort to offer to the wicked or the faithless even though they were Israelites. He could not detach the holiness of God from his grace any more than Amos or Jeremiah could. That the day of salvation would come in spite of

[2] See p. 102 for full consideration of the Babylon-Chaldea problem.

Israel's sins did not mean that the faithless would participate in the salvation. For them, as for the proud and ruthless tyrants among the nations, the day of salvation would be the Day of Judgment. It is in keeping with the whole of ch. 48 that, having announced the certainty of salvation, the prophet should end with the warning, already given in v. 18, that there is no peace, now or ever, for the wicked.

CHAPTER 49 / In ch. 49 the prophet gathers together in

a new way all the features of his vision of Israel's destiny. In its exuberant faith the chapter might be compared with chs. 40, 42, and 45, contrasting strongly in tone with the preceding chapter, ch. 48, and yet linked with it by carrying forward and developing more broadly the confidence expressed in ch. 48:11, 14, 20-21. The two elements in the prophet's hope for the future, the national and the universal, are woven together as in chs. 42 and 45. But as ch. 49 proceeds, the emphasis tends to be on the national, in contrast to ch. 45, where he moves from the narrower national hope to the broader universal one. Volz loses sight of this when, like Duhm, he detaches vs. 1-6 from the remainder of the chapter, assuming that the Servant with the missionary destiny must be someone quite other than the Servant of the following verses. Muilenburg recognizes rightly the unity of the chapter.

Chapter 49 makes a substantial contribution to our understanding of the Servant. In chs. 42 and 45 the focus was chiefly upon the achievements of the Servant in the future. Israel transformed would fulfill a mission of national restoration, rebuilding Jerusalem and gathering the exiles home, and then would establish God's just and merciful rule to the ends of the earth, breaking the power of the world's tyrants and setting free their imprisoned people. The temptation was to contrast only the glorious Israel *of the future* with the insignificant and sinful Israel of the past and present, although in chs. 43:27 and 44:1-5 we were reminded that there were two sides to Israel's history from the beginning, one dark and disobedient, but the other bright with faithfulness, and that there was, indeed, in the past an Israel that was sustained through every trial by its hearing of the word. Now in ch. 49 the true Israel of the past and the true Israel of the future are brought together so that there can no longer be any misunderstanding. A line runs from the beginning to the end of Israel's history, binding all of it together, and that line is the word to Israel in which God's purpose for man is revealed. Sometimes it is hidden, sometimes disclosed for all to see, but always it is unbroken. Wherever this word has been heard and cherished, has had its power in the shaping of life, has had witness borne to it in word and deed, there the Servant of God has been alive, and there has been an Israel that knew and possessed its destiny. All the true servants of God in the past have formed the body of the Servant. They are remembered in the traditions of Israel for this reason alone, that they heard the word out of the unseen in which Israel was called into its unique covenant relation with God and bore their faithful witness to it. When Israel in the present wants to know what it means to be truly Israel, then it has to look to the past, to the great tradition of men and women who were taken captive by God for the service of his word among men. But, having looked to the past, they have to turn round and peer into the future to see where the line runs as it comes out of the past, through the present, and into the future. It is not enough that the word has had its servants in the past; the greatest task of all lies yet ahead. God has a redemption to accomplish, not just for Israel—that is difficult enough—but for all mankind, and what he has been doing in Israel from the beginning has been the shaping of a human instrument to use in the achievement of the world's redemption.

The likeness of the potter shaping a vessel on his wheel, used in ch. 45:9, is significant for Second Isaiah's understanding of Israel's history and his conception of the Servant. From beginning to end Israel has had to live its life on the potter's wheel. The Servant is in process of creation, a long and painful process. Looking back, one can see the contours of the vessel taking shape, but in the present, amid the confusing and contradictory experiences of the moment, it is more difficult to see what God is doing. Sometimes it seems as though he has abandoned the vessel as worthless and hopeless and will make nothing more of it, as though all the labor and the suffering of the past were to be wasted (ch. 49:4). But the faith-fulness of the potter has to be trusted. What he has begun he will finish. The painful experiences of the immediate past were intended by him to be, to change the metaphor, like the refining fire of the metallurgist who purges away the dross of the metal to secure pure silver (ch. 48:10). The stubbornness of the nation in its impurities and the resistance of the clay to the potter delay the work of the Creator, but they only delay it; they cannot defeat it. He will have his way in the end. Then the Servant will stand forth transformed and complete, the finished handiwork of God, the instrument of his purpose for the establishment of his Kingdom of justice and truth. Kings and queens will bow down astonished and overwhelmed at the sight (ch. 49:7; cf. ch. 52:13-15, etc.).

Nothing has puzzled and confounded interpreters more than the way in which the image of the Servant seems at one time to be that of an individual, whereas at other times it is clearly the nation as a whole, and more than this, that the Servant is identified not only with the true Israel of the past and of the future but also with the blind, deaf, unfaithful Israel of the present. Nowhere is the individ-ualization more complete than in ch. 49:1-6, which has impelled a host of interpreters to separate it from its context and to excise the word "Israel" in v. 3, contrary to all good procedure in the critical handling of texts.[1] Everything said of the Servant in these verses is said elsewhere of Israel—that it is called from the womb (ch. 44:24), entrusted with God's word (chs. 51:16; 59:21), discouraged by what seems to be failure (chs. 40:27; 42:4), and given the tasks of restor-ing the nation (chs. 44:26; 45:4, 13) and of being a light to all man-kind (chs. 42:6; 44:4-5; 45:6, 14, 23). Moreover, when the word "Israel" remains in v. 3, the chapter becomes a splendid, unified, and comprehensive oracle. Therefore, ch. 49 should be convincing evi-dence that even when the portrayal is most intensely individual, there is no reason to assume that the prophet's conception of the Servant as Israel has been abandoned.

Torrey is so impressed with the individual character of the Serv-ant in chs. 42:1-9; 45:1-7; 46:11; 48:14; 49:1-6, and other similar passages that, although he holds them within the framework of the

[1] Bewer, *loc. cit.*

people of Israel, he concludes that in his vision of the future the prophet narrowed his conception of the Servant at some points to make of him the one anointed leader of Israel, the future Messiah. Many other scholars have identified the "individual" Servant with the Messiah or with personages of Israel's past, present, and future, the favorite identification being the prophet himself, with Jeremiah a close second. H. Wheeler Robinson has proposed a shifting image of the Servant that can range from the nation as a whole through a remnant of the nation to an individual, which comes very close to the truth.

The analogy of the church to the Servant Israel enables us, perhaps better than anything else, to enter into the mind of Second Isaiah, because the reality that he describes as the Servant stands in the same relation to God and man in the Old Testament as the church does in the New Testament.[2] The people of God is composed of sinful men who constantly resist the Spirit of God so that it is ever in danger of becoming as salt that has lost its savor and is fit for nothing but to be cast out, and thus has ever to be called to repentance. Even the apostles who stand at its beginning are pictured in its traditions as blind and blundering men who would have betrayed their Lord if left to themselves (cf. chs. 43:26-28; 48:8). Yet, in spite of man's sin, God preserves for himself a church. It was born, not of any human ingenuity, but at the call of God's word in Jesus Christ, and has its life only in complete dependence upon and faithfulness to the word by which it was created. It lives from and for the word, the word of God that is alive within it only when God himself in his Spirit is alive within it. It is both individual and collective. It is present in the fullness of its life where one true Christian disciple bears his witness to God and yet it reaches out to compass the whole earth as a community of faith. Christians can look back and see in the apostles and the faithful witnesses of the past the rock from which they have been hewn (ch. 51:1), but they have also to look forward in hope and courage toward the church that God intends to make of *them* that he may carry his purpose to its fulfillment. The true church is not an ideal that men conceive and that then hovers somewhere above the actual church, haunt-

[2] Calvin, *Commentary on Isaiah,* sees this very clearly.

ing it but never being realized. Rather, it exists within the church of sinful, disobedient men as a reality in human flesh that is sustained, and has ever been sustained, by the grace and mercy of God, and because the pure grain and the weeds cannot be separated from each other in this life, the whole community has to be addressed as the church of God and called to fulfill its destiny. Individual and community; past, present, and future; true Servant and unfaithful Servant of God; all are one, whether it be the church of Jesus Christ or the Israel of Second Isaiah.

The difference between Second Isaiah's Servant and the New Testament church is that for Second Isaiah the fulfillment is future, whereas the church looks both backward to the day of fulfillment and decisive redemption, i.e., the day of the revelation of God's glory in Jesus Christ, *and* forward to the consummation of what was then revealed. The prophet looks backward on a double history in which the Servant of the word mingles obedience with disobedience and is friend and enemy of God and he lives in hope of the day when there will be a Servant who in the perfection of his obedience will rule for God on earth, reflecting in his rule the qualities of God's own rule. As Christians we recognize the object of Second Isaiah's hope as nothing other than the coming of God and of the Kingdom of God in Jesus Christ, but at the same time we go too far if we say that the Servant of the future *for Second Isaiah* was the Messiah. It is truer to say that the Servant of the future for him was Israel, transformed, redeemed, no longer merely in covenant with God, but itself the instrument whereby the covenant relation would be extended to take in all mankind. We dare not forget, however, that Jesus of Nazareth *was* Israel historically, gathering up into himself and his words all the witness of Israel that had gone before and bringing to fulfillment the destiny for which Israel had lived from the beginning. We do no violence to Second Isaiah when we claim that his hopes were realized in Jesus Christ and his church. Because we share with Israel a double history and a double life in which faithfulness is ever mingled with unfaithfulness and the service of the word with rebellion against the word, and because we too live, not in the confidence of what we have achieved, but in hope of what God is yet to make of us, we are able to read the writings of Second

Isaiah as *Christian* Scripture, written for us, and the medium whereby God calls us to repentance for our failure to be the church and to faith in the destiny for which he has chosen us.

The chapter receives a universal setting in *v. 1* that signals its theme. The most distant peoples of the earth are called to attention to hear, this time not God, but the Servant of God address them. There has been enough of judgment upon the nations; now the good news of salvation is to be proclaimed. But what is Israel's authority for taking such a position in relation to the nations? Like Jeremiah (and most likely in direct dependence on Jer. 1:4) and like Paul (Gal. 1:15), the Servant bases his right to speak upon God's choice of him and God's call, which have compassed his life from the moment of his conception in the womb. Israel has not chosen this exalted position for itself, but has been chosen (cf. John 15:16). The prophet might have added: what nation, knowing the claims and the responsibilities that God would lay upon the Servant of his purpose, would be likely to choose that office? (cf. Amos 3:2). Name and destiny are closely associated, so that to receive the name "Israel" was to receive the destiny of Israel.

V. 2. Duhm finds it impossible to conceive of the people of Israel being given a mouth like a sharp sword. It could be true of a prophet. Jeremiah could liken his own word to fire and to a hammer that breaks the rocks in pieces (Jer. 23:29), but not Israel. Duhm forgets that the prophet elsewhere (ch. 54:13) describes the future Israel as having "all its sons taught of the Lord," and, had he recognized ch. 61 as belonging to Second Isaiah, he would have found in it a verse (ch. 61:6) in which all Israelites are priests and ministers of God. To Second Isaiah the only true Israel is the one that knows itself called, as each of the prophets was called, to be a witness (ch. 43:10, 12, etc.) to the word. A silent Israel, with nothing distinctive to say in word or deed on behalf of its faith, is one that has lost the purpose of its existence, but an Israel with God's word in its mouth is an entity to be feared by the nations no matter how insignificant it may seem to be outwardly. There is power in this word that can overthrow kingdoms. "Out of the mouth of babes and sucklings" (i.e., man in his weakness and insignificance) proceeds a word that "stills the enemy and the avenger" (Ps. 8:2). Or as Luther knew:

"A little word shall slay him." How could it be otherwise if this word on Israel's lips is the very word of God himself in which God goes forth to accomplish his purpose in the world? Israel's power over the nations depends upon its cherishing this word in its heart, not leaving it in books and oral traditions as something to be read and remembered with respect as a holy word, not leaving it in the past as a word that was once on the lips of men but cannot any longer be upon their lips in the same way and with the same power, but letting it have the mastery over life itself and letting it so permeate a people's existence that it comes forth in living speech and action as the occasion requires.

The likening of Israel's mouth to a sharp sword and Israel itself to a polished arrow in God's quiver is more than vivid poetic language. It has profound theological significance. The former image was felt by New Testament writers to be so apt in describing the nature of revelation that they use it more than once. In Eph. 6:17 in Paul's description of the Christian warrior it is the weapon with which he must win his battle, the instrument of attack. In Heb. 4:12 a two-edged sword discloses the inmost thoughts and intentions of the heart. In Rev. 1:16 it is the all-powerful word of God himself. In Luke 2:35 the child who is born is to be a sword of revelation that will pierce even the heart of his own mother. To be the servant of this aggressive word, then, is to be the instrument with which God attacks his enemies in the world, that is, with which he lays siege to the strongholds behind which men resist his will. This word cannot be enjoyed in quietness apart from the life of the world. It is not the medium of a spiritual relationship with God that men may have in isolation from their relationship with their fellowmen. It does not give them a place of safety, a retreat from which they can look out in somewhat pitying indifference upon the evils of the world. Rather, it plunges them into conflict with the world, not that they seek conflict, but that their faithfulness to this word of God brings to light the conflict between the will of God and the will of the world. They have no choice but to face the conflict or to be unfaithful to their God. God has a battle that he intends to win against all the forces that stand against him, and to be his people is to be in the midst of the battle. Surely these images warn the interpreter not to absolutize the gentleness of the Servant on the basis of ch. 42:2-3, as though there could be nothing warlike in his character. Sword and arrow are instruments of war! Both God and his Servant have their own unique way of waging war on their enemies. God's word is more powerful than all the armies of the nations. There is no contradiction, then, in saying, on the one hand, that the Servant will destroy the enemy with the breath of his lips and, on the other, that he will not trample upon or crush the poor and weak of the nations.

Hellmuth Frey[3] has drawn attention to the fact that the Servant *is* the arrow of God, just as in chs. 42:6 and 49:6 he *is* the covenant of mankind and the light of the nations. "Not just his mouth but his person is the word of God." This needs to be said guardedly, for the fundamental distinction between Old Testament and New is that only in Jesus Christ does the word become flesh, that is, a person. Nevertheless, the presence of God's word in Israel is analogous to the incarnation. It is not just an idea or a set of words in men's minds or in a tradition or in writings; it is God in personal communion with man through his word so that the man whose ear is opened comes under the sovereignty of God in his word, is bound by the word as a slave is bound, and from the word receives a freedom in his dealings with the world such as no other man possesses. The unique freedom that existed in Israel was the fruit of the unique covenant that bound Israel to God. Thus, Israel was the representative of God in relation to the world, in whom the very nature of God was reflected, and witness was borne before men to the reality of God (cf. Gen. 12:3, where the response of men to the descendants of Abraham is to reveal the nature of their response to God himself).

The hiddenness of the Servant corresponds to the hiddenness of God (ch. 45:15). The glory of God's universal sovereignty is hidden in the perverted order of the world where, for the time, power seems to belong to the unrighteous, and weakness to be the lot of the righteous, but, in this dark time when God's power is hidden, man must live in anticipation of the hour when it will be revealed. So also the true nature of the Servant is hidden from the eyes of men.

[3] Frey, *op. cit.*, p. 196.

He appears weak, insignificant, with no hope for the future according to the world's way of reckoning. But this ought not to trouble or discourage him. Because he knows wherein lies the power that will determine the future of men and nations, he can walk boldly and even joyfully through the present darkness, certain that the ultimate victory, the only one that counts, is with God. God hides the Servant in his quiver or in the hollow of his hand until the decisive hour arrives when the battle is to be fought and won. In that hour Israel will share in the glory of God—"Israel, in whom I will be glorified." Chapter 40:3-5 portrayed God's coming in glory. Here his coming is *in and through his word* in Israel. He wins his victory, not in any external manner, not with an army of angels battering down the fortresses of men, but through a human Servant who yields himself unconditionally to be mastered by God's word. Already we are on the threshold of the mystery of ch. 53, and of yet greater mysteries beyond.

The discouragement of the Servant expressed in *v. 4* corresponds in part with the mood that seems to lie behind ch. 40:6-7, in which we saw reflected the despair of the prophet himself before he found a solid basis for hope. Well might even the most faithful believer among the Israelites have become weary by the middle of the sixth century! It must have seemed as though the centuries of Israel's life and all that had been achieved by the faith and perseverance of the faithful were to be wasted and end in nothingness. But this despair in v. 4 is quickly succeeded by a chastened confidence, the confidence that the God of all the earth will be just, and that if he is just, then a future will be made where there seems to be no future.

V. 5. See the section on ch. 45:5 concerning the mission of Israel to restore Israel, which has consistently been a stumbling block to interpreters. They would have no difficulty in conceiving a mission of Second Isaiah to restore Israel (Volz), or a mission of the Messiah to restore Israel to its destiny (Torrey), or a mission of Jesus Christ and his Jewish followers to recover the lost sheep of the house of Israel, and yet all of these are in essence a mission of Israel to Israel, the mission of an Israel that has eyes to an Israel that is blind.

V. 6. Perhaps many of Second Isaiah's fellow countrymen would have been happy if he had announced only the restoration of Israel.

In that program they could have joined hands with him. But a narrow nationalistic outlook would have been to him the end of Israel. A God whose goal was nothing more than the restoration of Israel was a little national god, not the Creator of heaven and earth and the Lord of all mankind. Second Isaiah simply drew out the full consequences of his monotheistic faith; one God of all the earth implied one universal people of one God, if he were to be the same God of mercy and justice to non-Israelites as to Israelites. See the section on ch. 42:6 for comment on "light of the nations."

V. 7. Almost all interpreters have followed Duhm in separating v. 7 from vs. 1-6, failing to see that the hidden Servant is the one who is at present despised and abhorred, but who in the day of redemption will be revealed in power and honor so that kings and princes will bow before him. The passage from humiliation to triumph is the very crux of the eschatology and the essential clue to understanding the descriptions of the Servant, particularly in ch. 53. Note how the theme is carried directly forward, although the form changes from a speech of the Servant to a speech of God concerning the Servant. Whereas in v. 7 God makes an announcement about the Servant to the world in general, in vs. 8 ff. he addresses the Servant directly. The time also has changed: in vs. 1-7 the day of salvation lay ahead; in vs. 8 ff. God speaks of it as though it had already come, but the content of the speech shows that it is still future. In reference to the "covenant of mankind," see the section on ch. 42:6. As in ch. 42:7, the task of the Servant is universal: to establish "the earth" (RSV, "the land," suggests only Palestine) and to reapportion the "desolate heritages," i.e., the regions that have been left desolate by God's judgment on his enemies. The prisoners and those who are in darkness are the poor and oppressed of the nations on whom God has mercy. The description of them in the following lines as participating in the new exodus has led to their being identified as Israelite exiles, but the context here and the parallels in ch. 42:6-7 make clear that they are non-Israelites who join in the great ingathering (cf. ch. 44:1-5). *V. 12* should have prevented any identification of this return with the return from Babylon reported by the Chronicler, since these pilgrims come from the four corners of the earth. Their coming is described as usual with imagery drawn from the exodus: God sustains them in the desert, providing them with food and water and making a road for them across the mountains. As in ch. 40:11, they are like a flock of sheep with God as their shepherd. *V. 13* also is reminiscent of ch. 40:1-11 as the prophet breaks into a psalm of joy at the prospect that he sees opening before his people. God's love for man has triumphed. The time of darkness is past, and the light has come. Therefore, let the heavens and the earth, and even the great mountains, sing for joy. Nothing is more characteristic of Second Isaiah than this jubilation, and let us remember that it is the jubilation of a man who still walks in darkness so far as the outward situation is concerned. He has only the hope of what God is about to do. He walks not by sight, but by faith in the unseen (Heb. 11:1), believing so firmly that God will do what he has promised in his word that it is almost as though God had already done it.

Vs. 14 ff. As in chs. 40:12 and 45:9, the prophet turns from ecstatic proclamation to argument with the unbelieving community. The complaint is the same as in ch. 40:27: God has not dealt fairly with his own people; they have been forgotten by him; he has cast them off completely (cf. ch. 50:1). In answer Second Isaiah discloses the boundless love of God for Israel. A mother will forget her newborn babe before God will forget Israel. The walls of Jerusalem, future walls, since the old ones are now in ruins, are graven on God's hands like an architect's plan so that they are before him continually, and at any moment the actual rebuilding will begin. The day of destruction is past and the day of restoration at hand. In *v. 18,* as the prophet again sees in a vision the multitudes streaming into Jerusalem from all the earth, it is apparent that, whether in imagination or in reality, the position from which he looks out across the world is Jerusalem. This is by no means proof that he lived in Jerusalem, but at least it makes us hold the possibility open that he did. The picturing of Jerusalem, when it has been repopulated and rebuilt, as a bride arrayed in her beautiful garments and ornaments, stands in sharp contrast to the daughter of Babylon in ch. 47 who was to be stripped naked of all that showed her to have been a queen.

The first half of *v. 19* does not make sense as it stands. Torrey's suggestion of a change in the vowel pointing, however, makes it read: "True, I laid thee waste, made thee desolate, razed thee even to the ground, but now thou shalt be too strait for thy people." *Vs. 20-21* picture imaginatively a future in which the new inhabitants of Jerusalem are so many that they are uncomfortably crowded and Mother Jerusalem in amazement asks where they have all come from. How is it possible that a bereaved and barren mother should have borne so many children and not even known that it was happening? The absurdity of the mother's question is meant to emphasize the miracle of the transformation. That which has happened is nothing less than the impossible! Here again, the future that God gives his people is the impossible possibility, humanly impossible but divinely not only possible but certain. In *vs. 22-23* the kings and queens of the earth not only bow down to the Servant in acknowledgment of their subjection (as in v. 7) but make themselves the bearers and the nourishers of the returning exiles. The exaggerated expression of humility, "lick the dust of your feet," is objectionable to the modern mind (Duhm is certain Second Isaiah could not have written it), but to the Oriental it means only complete subjection. The radical reversal of fortunes in the day of God's appearing is a theme that permeates the whole of the Bible (cf. I Sam. 2:4 ff.; Luke 1:52-53; 6:25). A further echo of ch. 40 is the promise of vindication to those who "wait for me" (or "hope in me").

The similarity in form of the questions in *v. 24* to those in v. 15 indicates the continuation of the argument with unbelievers and is evidence of the unity of the chapter. As in ch. 40:12 ff., these Israelites are so impressed by the power of the tyrannical rulers (emending "righteous" to read "tyrant" in v. 24) under whom they live that they have no hope of liberation. But they do not reckon with the power of God, which makes the strength of tyrants seem as nothing. The fate of the tyrants who oppress Israel in v. 26, that they shall eat their own flesh and drink their own blood, has been even more offensive to the modern mind than the expressions in v. 23. The prophet, or his interpolator, has been accused of lusting after bloody vengeance on Israel's enemies and of giving divine sanction to such wicked lust. But the prophet is merely using terms that were common among the prophets to describe civil war (cf. Isa. 9:20; Zech. 11:9). God destroys tyrants by letting them destroy themselves, which is another way of saying that the unlimited egotism of the power state brings it into conflict with its own people and with its neighbors until eventually it secures its own downfall. Judgment upon the nations is the first stage in the establishment of God's universal rule. The chapter ends, not with the ingathering of Israel, but with the acknowledgment by all mankind that the Redeemer of Israel, the Mighty One of Jacob, is the one and only Lord over all.

CHAPTER 50/ Though one of the briefest chapters in the entire book, ch. 50 fairly bristles with problems and has an importance far greater than its size suggests for the total understanding of Second Isaiah. We sense an increasing tension as we read it, an ominous note foreshadowing rejection, bitter conflict, and deep suffering. It is a kind of forecourt to ch. 53, and we are not likely to see far into the later chapter unless we interpret the earlier one rightly, just as the story of the cross in the Gospels discloses its profound significance only to the reader who has grasped something of the nature of the conflict in which Jesus' mission involved him with the religious and political forces of his time.

As the chapter opens, we hear a lament from the mouth of God (which lets us see also into the heart of the prophet who spoke for God) that when he came no man paid any heed, and when he called no man answered (v. 2). As the chapter advances, we see someone (one of the problems is to know who) giving his ear and his whole self to the service of the word that, because God is in it, has power to transform weakness into strength and weariness into joy, but having to face public humiliation and persecution for his faithfulness to that word. There can be no doubt that whoever this is, it is the same figure that meets us again in ch. 53: despised, rejected, a man of sorrows, wounded, condemned, going silently to his death. The mind leaps forward so instinctively to recognize the very features of Jesus Christ in his suffering and death that although we need not suppress the conviction that there is a very intimate relation between the figure who confronts us here and the figure of our Lord, the two belonging together in the same mystery of redemptive suffering, we have to make a decided effort to hold ourselves in the sixth century B.C. and to let these texts speak in the context of the witness of Second Isaiah before we begin interpreting them in the larger context of the New Testament—which is the ultimate historical and theological context not only of these passages but of the whole of the Old Testament.

The problem that meets us first is the unity of the chapter. Like almost all the other chapters, the usual interpretations chop it into bits. Because God argues with an unbelieving Israel in vs. 1-3, as he does in ch. 49:14-26, Duhm, Frey, and others have attached these verses to ch. 49, in spite of the fact that ch. 49:24-26 forms a most suitable and impressive conclusion to the chapter, whereas ch. 50:3 does not. The change of speaker from God to the Servant between vs. 3 and 4 encouraged this move, although it has been made abundantly clear in earlier chapters that a change of speaker does not necessarily mean a break in the development of a theme. There is no difficulty in stating the theme that runs through the whole chapter. It is the rejection of the good news of God's redemption by an Israel that should have responded to it with joy. The fact that in vs. 1-3 it is God who complains of the rejection, whereas in vs. 4-11 it is the Servant who describes vividly the brutality of his rejection, creates no difficulty, since the rejection of the Servant is the rejection of God. The second point of attack for the dissectionists has been upon the last two verses. Duhm's chief reason for denying them to Second Isaiah is the same for these verses as for vs. 1-3: their tone is too sharply critical for a prophet of comfort! Volz agrees with him. Both disregard the appropriateness of the verses as the conclusion of a chapter in which the gulf between Israel as the Servant and Israel in its unbelief has become distressingly wide. If the prophet's message of hope was met with a solid wall of scorn and rejection, as the chapter seems to suggest, it is not surprising that an actual division should have begun to be apparent between those "who fear the Lord and obey the voice of his Servant" and those who heap upon the Servant only ridicule and humiliation. For the first time, here in vs. 10 and 11, a split appears in the nation. Until now the prophet has fastened his hopes upon the whole nation in spite of its general persistence in what he could only call rebellion against God and blindness to God, but now this solidarity begins to crack, a development of the greatest significance for the understanding of the figure of the "Servant" (and the "servants") in later chapters. But when either or both of vs. 10 and 11 are chopped away, this immensely significant fact begins to be lost from sight.

The second major problem is the identity of the Servant in vs. 4-11. Is he still the nation, highly personified as in ch. 49, or is he an individual? And if he is an individual, is he a prophet out of the past such as Jeremiah, or Second Isaiah himself, or a Messianic figure who is yet to come? All of these interpretations have found vigorous support among scholars,[1] which means that the phenomena seem to point in various directions according to the way one approaches them. The literature on the subject is immense and the weight of opinion has fluctuated radically in the past century. Before Duhm wrote in 1875 and 1892, the collective interpretation predominated, but Duhm's separation of a selection of Servant passages from the remainder of the book was so widely accepted, and personification of the Servant is so intense in some of these passages, that the individual interpretation swept the field for a time, and widely diverse identifications of the Servant with historical personages were proposed. More recently the pendulum has swung back toward a collective interpretation, largely because of the increasing recognition of the arbitrariness of separating a few Servant passages from their contexts and of the overwhelming weight of evidence in the book as a whole that for the prophet the Servant was in some sense Israel, although in what sense has not always been too clear.

Chapter 50:4-11 helps us to understand why it has been so hard for the answers to this question to come to rest in any one position. Each feature of the dialogue in ch. 49:1-7, we have seen, can be understood as an element in the personification of an Israel that is true to its destiny as the Servant of the word. This can be said of some features in ch. 50:4-11, but not of all. The "tongue of a disciple" that the Servant received from God in ch. 50:4 is parallel directly with the lips of the Servant in ch. 49:2 that God made as a

[1] See H. H. Rowley, *The Servant of the Lord and Other Essays on the Old Testament* (London: Lutterworth Press, 1952), and C. R. North, *The Suffering Servant in Deutero-Isaiah* (London: Oxford University Press, 1956).

sharp sword. Calling the Servant a disciple rather than a prophet in ch. 50:4 corresponds with the fact that in ch. 54:13 all Israel's sons are to be disciples in the day of redemption. The word to the weary is the same good news that Jerusalem was to take to the cities of Judah in ch. 40:9. The true Israel across the centuries is one who has been wakened each morning to the word of God. Also the willingness to face suffering and opposition for the sake of the word can be set down as a mark of the true Israel. But from v. 6 on it becomes difficult to maintain that the whole dramatic representation of the Servant in conflict is no more than personification.

Of course it is possible that Second Isaiah was so successful in his imaginative dramatization that we are made to see vividly before us an individual in the throes of conflict with his opponents, and yet are intended to understand this as a representation of what happens when men accept the calling and destiny of the Servant of God. But the impression is conveyed strongly that there was some one man who actually felt the blows of the smiters on his back and had people pull his beard and spit in his face for scorn of him. At once the suggestion leaps into the mind: Who could it be except the prophet himself? He was the bearer of the word to the weary, and as we have seen, the hope he offered to his fellow countrymen came at a high price. They had to give up all their idolatrous practices, all their trust in the effectiveness of religious ceremonial, and yield themselves in simple obedience to the will of God if they were to receive his cleansing forgiveness and know the beginning of the new day. The word of comfort was a sharp sword that cut across the whole existing order in the community. Like the word of God in the earlier prophets, and also later in Jesus Christ and his apostles, it was an offense to the natural man, shaking him to the depths in all his superficial securities because it claimed him totally for God. No man could receive it as the source of comfort, strength, and joy who did not first hear in it God's refining judgment. But men ever resist coming under God's judgment because it means the end of all their attempts to justify themselves and to be their own gods, in short, the death of self. The evidences of tension between Second Isaiah and the immediate community to which he ministered have been gathering from ch. 40 on. The caustic ridicule with which he treated the unbelief and idolatry of men would not earn him the gratitude of many. And the hope he set before them may well have seemed to them so fantastic that they thought him a crazy prophet, worthy only to be teased and mocked. That Second Isaiah should have been persecuted for his faithfulness to his prophetic task is thoroughly credible from what we have observed thus far in chs. 40 to 49, and we shall find even more convincing evidence of conflict in the remaining chapters. But since we have not yet considered the relation of chs. 56 to 66 to chs. 40 to 55, we shall leave that evidence to appear later.

We can understand, then, the strong appeal of an individual interpretation of the Servant. The strongest argument, however, against the Servant in ch. 50 being an individual and no other than the prophet himself arises when this theory is applied to ch. 53. The figure in ch. 50 and that in ch. 53 are one. In both he is specifically called the Servant and has many of the same features. But ch. 53 describes the death of the Servant, and although some scholars have even gone so far as to have Second Isaiah portray his own death in anticipation, this goes beyond the credible. Some have suggested that a disciple of the prophet wrote ch. 53 about his master. But ch. 53 has the same dramatic structure as we find elsewhere in the book and is recognizable also in its language as a writing of Second Isaiah. Nowhere else in the book does the prophet set himself in the center of the stage and focus men's eyes upon himself. In fact, his writings have sometimes wrongly been called impersonal because of the way in which he hides himself behind the dramatic speeches of God and behind the figure of the Servant and rarely speaks directly as a prophet of God to his people. It would be strange and contradictory if at the very climax of his book in chs. 50 and 53 he deliberately made himself and his own experiences the focus of attention and made the whole future redemption of Israel dependent upon his own patience in suffering!

How, then, shall we resolve this dilemma? The phenomena point in two directions, in each of which there are serious difficulties. Perhaps we must in some measure leave the question open because of the uncertainty, recognizing that there is at best a very thin line of demarcation between the prophet, or any true prophet, and the

Servant. We have already seen in ch. 49 that the Servant Israel has a history that reaches from its birth in the exodus, or even earlier in Abraham, through the centuries, through the present and into the future until the goal of God's purpose is reached. The Servant takes up into himself all who have heard and responded to the word of God with a faithful witness. He is alive in Abraham or Moses, and therefore also in an Amos or a Jeremiah. But this line that begins in the distant past and comes gloriously to its destination in the future runs also through the present. Second Isaiah's call to the whole of scattered Israel was to take up its destiny as the Servant in the present, but his eyes were open to the fact that not all that called itself Israel was truly Israel (ch. 48:1-2). Nevertheless, there was an Israel in the present, a remnant of the nation that still had ears to hear. In this context we appreciate the fact that in ch. 50:10 the prophet addresses a special group within Israel, distinct from the remainder of the nation, as "you who fear the Lord and obey the voice of his Servant." In ch. 51:1 and 7 the same persons are addressed as "you who pursue deliverance, you who seek the Lord, you who know righteousness," and "the people in whose heart is my law." Who can these be except the community within the community, the faithful in the midst of the unfaithful, those who responded to Second Isaiah's message in distinction from those who rejected it? If they stood with the prophet sharing his hope, they would be involved in the same tensions and conflict in which he was involved. In ch. 51:7 they are told not to fear the reproach of men or to be dismayed at their revilings.

It is possible, then, to retain the unity of the concept of the Servant even in ch. 50. All Israel is called to be the Servant, but all Israel does not respond to the call, and the Servant exists only where there is faithful witness to the word of God. But what may have given to ch. 50 its special intensity and its high degree of individualization is that Second Isaiah and those who with him constituted the community of the Servant in the present may actually have been persecuted for their faith so that this *immediate* experience would be taken up into the portrait and would lend to it a remarkable vividness. We have yet to consider the evidence for such persecution. The chapter, were it written in the midst of such conflicts and addressed to friend and foe alike, might well at some points break through the dramatic form that the prophet was accustomed to use and become direct speech to the two sections of the community in which he lived. It is as though an actor in a drama on the stage were suddenly to step out of the action of the play and address himself directly to his audience without interrupting the sequence of his part, thus drawing the audience into the play itself. The Servant mask falls for the moment and the prophet speaks. There is nothing similar in ch. 53. There the Servant mask remains firmly in its place. It is not to be assumed that with ch. 50 Second Isaiah has narrowed the conception of the Servant to include only the faithful and has abandoned all hope for the community as a whole. The opening verses make clear that this is not so. In spite of the lack of response in Israel, he insists that God has not cast the nation off but, on the contrary, is far more ready to save than the nation is to let itself be saved. Neither God nor the prophet has rejected Israel, but Israel is rejecting both God and the prophet. It is not inconsistent, then, that in the following chapters Second Isaiah continues to herald the day of salvation for Israel.

The opening scene in *vs. 1-3* links ch. 50 with the preceding chapter, continuing as it does the argument of God with Israel. As in ch. 49:15 and ch. 49:24, God asks a double question, or the same question in a double form. The Israelites who claim that the sorry plight of the nation is proof that God has abandoned the covenant relation are asked to produce the bill of divorce or to name the nation to which God was so in debt that he had to give his own children into slavery to pay the account. The question is an emphatic expression of the same love of God for Israel that in ch. 49:15 was declared to be greater than the love of a mother for her own child. God then offers the true interpretation of Israel's troubles, the interpretation of earlier prophets that in ch. 42:25 was uncomprehended by Israel: the nation's distress is a manifestation of the judgment of God upon the iniquities of his people, not with the intention of destroying Israel, but that it may be refined (ch. 48:10). *V. 2* asks why the deafness of Israel to God in the past continues in the present. Most striking and significant is the parallel between "I came" and "I called." Thus far God's coming has seemed to be entirely a prospect of the future—but his calling has been both past and present. (The various forms of the verb "to call" are used with great frequency.) His calling is his speaking in his word, his revealing of himself to Israel. In ch. 55:11, and elsewhere, this word of God contains the life-transforming power of God himself. But here the word in which God calls is the word in which he *comes* to his people. God himself is present in the word that the Servant speaks, so that to receive it is to know God in his coming. The rejection of the word of the Servant is the rejection of God himself. Therefore, there is in the prophet's mind both a present and a future coming of God, a present coming in his word and a future coming in glory and power; a hidden coming in the present, but a coming that will be seen by all mankind in the future. This is of decisive importance not only here but also for the understanding of prophetic eschatology in the New Testament. Now we begin to understand the prophet's joy and certainty. He has already experienced God's coming *in the hiddenness of his word* (cf. ch. 49:2), so that he lives in anticipation of the day when the truth and reality of God's sovereignty over all life will be openly revealed.

The conclusion of the scene in *vs. 2b and 3* has caused much perplexity. God has just spoken of his power to save, but what he illustrates is his power to destroy! Marti explains the passage as a reference to the myth of God's destruction of Leviathan and the original watery chaos in order to bring the world into being (cf. the reference to Rahab and the great deep in ch. 51:9-10). Skinner and Levy think that the events of the exodus are in the prophet's mind, but although this explains the dead fish, it provides no parallel to the drying up of the rivers. Volz and Torrey see only references to changes in nature that suggest God's power. Volz even explains the darkening of the heavens as being the result of a sandstorm! But turning well-watered land into desert or desert into well-watered land is familiar imagery in Second Isaiah. The latter occurs constantly as a representation of a dead world coming joyfully alive as it receives its God, and the former represents God's judgment upon man's godlessness. All life without God is turned into a barren desert. There is no reason to give the image a different interpretation in vs. 2 and 3. Israel's present experience of God's power, as suggested in v. 1, is in his overwhelming judgment. He who has power to bring death has also the power to bring life. If Israelites had eyes to recognize God's presence in judgment, they would have eyes also to peer into the future and anticipate his coming in mercy. One reason why the passage has puzzled interpreters is that they fail to grasp firmly the fact that God's deliverance has not yet come and that the prophet and his people are still in the midst of their time of judgment and darkness (chs. 40:27; 42:22-25; 43:22-28; 46:12-13; 48:18; 49:14; 50:1; 51:12-23). Interpreters' minds are so full of Cyrus and the return from Babylon in 539 B.C. that they cannot see what is so obvious from the conclusion of chapter after chapter and in the general situation of the Israelites who are addressed: that as yet they have seen *nothing whatever in their circumstances* that might give them hope. The great turning point from the darkness of judgment to the brightness of hope has already come in the hidden counsels of God that ultimately determine events and has been revealed in God's word to the prophet, but its consequences have not yet begun to be seen on earth in outward happenings.

V. 4 describes perfectly the mission of Second Isaiah himself (cf. chs. 35:3-4; 40:1-11, 27-31, etc.), but this does not mean that he has dropped the customary dramatic form here and begun to speak of himself, but only that his own mission and conflicts are reflected vividly in his portrayal of the Servant. Never does he confine the mission of the Servant to a special class of prophets; rather, he calls upon the whole of his nation to lay hold upon it as its divinely appointed task. To be the Servant is to hear continually from God the word in which God himself comes to men as the strength of the weak, the liberator of the prisoners, the light of the blind, and the giver of joy to a sorrowing humanity (cf. ch. 61:1-3). It is significant that the Servant is described as a pupil or disciple rather than as a prophet (cf. ch. 54:13), the emphasis being placed thus on his openness to being taught *new* words by God (cf. the "new things" yet to come). The history of the Servant is the history of his education, and the years of heavy judgment have been a most important stage in that education. The concept is not static but dynamic. The Servant does not spring full-blown into life. From the birth of Israel until it reaches its destination God will have been constantly at work, like the potter (ch. 45:9) shaping the vessel to make it fit for its task. Most interpreters regard the doubling of infinitives "to know to help" as due to an error of a copyist and omit the first.

One would expect an encouraging "word to the weary" to furnish a prophet with a comparatively easy task, in contrast to the grim assignments of an Isaiah (ch. 6:11-12) or a Jeremiah (ch. 1:10). But *v. 5* indicates that this impression rests on a misunderstanding. The word to the weary is not a series of humanly encouraging words, optimistic comments upon the outlook for the future, but is the absolutely unique word that alone can conquer human despair, the word in which God himself is able to be present with man. The God of mercy and help, however, remains the God of holiness and justice. His coming brings the dead to life, but only if the dead are willing to have their life wholly from him and to give up all their vain attempts to find it elsewhere. The forgiveness of God is not to be received without the surrender of the sinful habits and the yielding of the human will to God's will. Therefore, as every prophet knew, when God comes bearing gifts men flee in self-protection. They cannot receive God in his word and remain the men that they are. The whole order of life, the whole structure of religious ceremonies in which men put their trust, the whole of human existence, is shaken and set in question when God's word of comfort and forgiveness is spoken. This was to be revealed fully when men crucified Jesus Christ in order to silence the word of forgiveness that denied them the right to go on being what they were. Thus the Servant, hearing God's word of comfort afresh each morning, recognized how offensive it would be when spoken in its fullness to men and knew that the bearer of the word of comfort would be made to suffer for taking such a word to men. But it should be clear that the suffering of the Servant is the consequence of the offensiveness of the word he bears and is not to be identified with the suffering that has come upon Israel as a punishment for its sins. This distinction cannot be made absolute because there is a sense in which the severity of God's judgment upon Israel's sins proceeds, in prophetic thought (cf. Amos 3:2), from the special relation of responsibility in which Israel stands as the covenant people of God. But at least it warns us against any interpretation of ch. 53 that suggests that for Second Isaiah all of Israel's sufferings were lumped together as a vicarious atonement for the sins of mankind.

V. 6. Frey[2] has pointed out that the indignities suffered by the Servant are those heaped upon the prisoner in a Jewish judicial process. Spitting in the face is for us an act of the most vulgar brutality, but in Israel it was the customary way of humiliating the prisoner (cf. Num. 12:14; Deut. 25:9; Matt. 26:67). We are so accustomed to an order that preserves a studious respect for the prisoner's person until he is condemned that we find it hard to realize that such things happened in a court of law. When men were accused before Nehemiah, the governor, of having married foreign wives, he beat them and pulled their hair (Neh. 13:25). The apostles were beaten when they came before Jewish courts (Acts 5:40; 16:22; II Cor. 11:23-25). Also the language of *v. 8* is that of a lawcourt. The "adversary" is the prosecutor who makes out the case against the prisoner, and the verb for "declare guilty" is that used of the court's condemnation. What this says is that the action against the Servant of the word is not that of irresponsible individuals, but that of the official community, utilizing what are supposed to be the means of preserving justice and restraining wickedness. We know Second Isaiah's fondness for representing God's controversy with the nations and their gods, or with Israel, in the dramatic form of a legal trial in which each side presents its case, but this is something different. The Servant has been called into court by the community and is being treated as though he were an enemy of society. Volz thinks the prophet himself to have been the offender and his offense to have been his declaration of an intention to undertake a mission among non-Israelites. This narrows the concept of the Servant more than can be justified and takes no account of the diverse occasions of offense of which there has already been evidence. We have noted from the beginning the sharpness of the prophet's tongue when he strikes out at his opponents. Ridicule is a dangerous weapon. Attacks on the customary practices of religion such as sacrifice (chs. 43:22-24; 66:3), vows and prayers (ch. 48:1-2), and fasting (ch. 58:1-4) would stir the resentment not only of the priests but of all who trusted in such observances to secure the welfare of the com-

[2] Frey, *op. cit.*

munity. But if important people were mingling idolatrous practices with their worship of Yahweh (as will appear in later chapters with definiteness), the prophet was laying bare an evil whose representatives would be likely to stop at nothing to silence him and protect themselves. And, if they were afraid to lay hand upon him, they might begin by attacking some who stood with him and were less able to defend themselves.

We do not need to speculate, however, about the events that may lie behind vs. 4-11. It is sufficient that we have evidence from ch. 40 to ch. 66 of tension between the prophet and all who shared his faith with him, on the one hand, and the official religious community, on the other. Moreover, we are dealing with a prophet who was familiar with the stories of God's servants in the past. He would know the sorrows of Moses and Elijah, the condemnation of Amos by the royal priest of Bethel, and closer at hand, the bitter and almost fatal experiences of Jeremiah at the hands of his countrymen, especially at the hands of their semipagan priests and prophets who claimed to be the true patriots. How much of his dramatic portrayal of the Servant is drawn from the past and how much from immediate experiences we do not know, nor shall we ever know, nor do we need to know. What matters is that it speaks to the "called of God," the chosen people, the ecclesia through all time, concerning what is involved in their calling and destiny, laying bare both the cost of such a destiny and the basis of its confidence. The court scene has no predecessors in the history of Israel (only a single great successor) so that we may be inclined to conclude at once that it was based upon some immediate experience, but the dramatic powers of the prophet are so great that we dare not deny the possibility of it being an imaginative creation. The one interpretation that is impossible is that which makes the foreign nations responsible for the Servant's suffering and sees in the latter nothing more than a picturesque representation of Israel's experiences in the servitude of exile.

The strength of the Servant in the face of false accusation and maltreatment is his confidence that the day of God's coming is at hand and that in that day all men will receive justice. (Would anyone suggest that his hope in ch. 50 was set only on the dawning of

the new Persian era!) From it the Servant draws patience to endure
and courage to maintain his witness without faltering. He challenges his opponents to debate, but warns them that they have no
hope of victory, since God is with him. "If God is for me, who can
be against me?" If God justifies him, what need he care about how
men may condemn him? Ultimately only God's decision has any
weight. The latter half of *v. 9* is important because of the way in
which it links the Servant's adversaries with those who revile the
faithful believers in ch. 51:1 and 8. The same fate is predicted for
them in chs. 50:9 and 51:8. Clearly it is not the prophet alone who
is under attack but all who cherish God's Torah in their hearts.

There are two ways in which *v. 10* may be read, both legitimate.
The one followed by Torrey and the RSV takes the subordinate
clause, "who walks in darkness and has no light," as descriptive of
the Servant and understands the question as a rhetorical one addressed to the rebellious nation and expecting the answer, "No one."
The other takes the question as addressed to the faithful who fear
the Lord and obey the voice of God's Servant, but walk in darkness
because God's light has not yet appeared. The sentence then continues, "let him trust in the name of the Lord and rely upon his
God." The first is more strained and the description of the Servant
too elaborate if nothing more is to be said than that no one obeys his
word. The second gives a balanced conclusion to the chapter, the
faithful and the unfaithful each being addressed separately, but what
is most important and convincing is that it sets it in a sequence with
ch. 51:1 and 9 where the faithful are addressed directly. One of the
reasons why v. 10 has been regarded as an addition by some interpreters is that whereas in vs. 4-9 the Servant is speaking, in v. 10 he
is spoken about. But this would only signify that in vs. 10-11 the
prophet speaks in his own voice, and would be evidence that in vs.
4-9 he intends us to hear a dramatic speech not of himself but of
the Servant. He does not make any simple identification of himself
with the Servant, even though the Servant speaks through him. The
Servant is to him an entity far too majestic and comprehensive for
that. *V. 11.* The kindling of the fire is an occupation of the prophet's
enemies that is somehow associated with their corrupt doings, most
likely a characteristic of some pagan worship in which they engage.

Perhaps the prophet seizes upon it because he can so swiftly turn the fire in which they delight into the fires of God's judgment (cf. ch. 42:25). They have no light except these glimmering torches and they have no prospect before them except fiery torment.

CHAPTERS 51 AND 52/ Chapters 51 and 52 do

not seem at first sight to have clearly defined themes as most of the earlier chapters do, but rather, to consist of scenes or speeches, each of which is a unit in itself, some being similar to others, but a sequence of thought being difficult to discern. Duhm and Torrey agree for once in beginning a new unit at v. 17 of ch. 51 and in taking ch. 52:13-15 with ch. 53. Both decisions must be set in question. Volz indulges in an orgy of reconstruction, dividing the two chapters into five units, transferring ch. 51:4-5 to a position after ch. 51:8, ch. 51:12-14 to a position after ch. 52:12, omitting ch. 51:15-16, and setting ch. 52:3-6 at the end of the whole series. He reconstructs on the assumption that he knows what the prophet intended to say, the transference of ch. 51:4-5 being based on the fact that it offers comfort to the heathen, whereas the prophet's intention in ch. 51:1-3 and 6-8 is to offer comfort only to Israel! What we need first is a survey of the ten scenes or speeches that make up the two chapters in order to discover whether they are bound together in any way and whether there is a natural chapter division at any point.

The most striking characteristic of both chapters is the number of scenes in which the prophet speaks with his own voice, these outnumbering the ones in which God speaks. In the first scene, ch. 51:1-3, there is an unusual shifting back and forth so that it is never clear whether it is the prophet or God who is addressing the faithful. God is spoken of in the third person in vs. 1 and 3, but speaks in the first person in v. 2, and yet the continuity of thought in the three verses is unbroken. The faithful in Israel, far outnumbered by the unfaithful, are told to find encouragement by looking back in their history to their own beginnings in Abraham and Sarah, to see how, in the face of the seemingly impossible, God brought forth a nation from these two people. The God of Abraham can transform the waste places of Zion into an Eden. As though to guard against any narrow hope, the second scene in vs. 4-6, in which God speaks, pictures a salvation that not only comprehends all mankind but compasses the heavens as well as the earth so that all things are made new, and this new order is declared to be eternal. In vs. 7-8 God again addresses the faithful, this time warning them that they have nothing to fear from their attackers, whose strength is only for the moment, whereas God's victory will be forever. It is quite characteristic of Second Isaiah to break in at this point with a prayer (vs. 9-11) that begins by calling upon God to act with the power that long ago he revealed in the creation of the world and in the exodus from Egypt and that ends with a jubilant prediction of the restoration of the exiles to Zion. In vs. 12-16 God speaks again in a more argumentative fashion, dealing with the fears of those who think the nations that hold Israel captive are too strong for him to effect a rescue. These oppressors of whom we hear in the remainder of ch. 51 and in ch. 52 are not to be confused with the revilers of ch. 51:7, who are clearly the same as the persecutors of ch. 50:6-9. There are two sets of enemies for the faithful: their own unbelieving countrymen and the foreign oppressors. The failure to hold these apart results in unlimited confusion here and later. Chapter 51:16, which echoes ch. 49:1-2, shows that it is Israel, the faithful Servant, who is still being encouraged as in vs. 1-3. In vs. 17-23 the prophet addresses Jerusalem, seeking to rouse her from the stupor into which her hard experiences have thrown her and proclaiming to her that the day of God's wrath is past and a new era at hand. In ch. 52:1-6 he again calls on Jerusalem to awaken from her sleep and rejoice in a new freedom. There is no price to be paid for it, since it is God himself who bestows it as a free gift. In ch. 52:7-10 the prophet breaks into ecstatic song at the prospect of Zion's restoration. The whole earth will see the glorious vindication. In ch. 52:11-12 he suddenly turns to address the exiles themselves who are about to return, likening them to a holy procession with God guarding them both before and behind, a reminiscence of the exodus. Finally, in ch. 52:13-15 God speaks again, calling upon the whole world to see the astonishing transformation in his Servant—from a humiliation so deep that it seemed almost to efface the marks of his humanity to a glory and power so high that kings of the earth are silent in wonder before him.

Several features are observable from this survey. There is no clear line of demarcation between the chapters; the last scene of ch. 51 and the first of ch. 52 have a common theme. But it is equally difficult to make a division after ch. 51:16 or ch. 52:6. Also, the two chapters are marked in common by the doubling of verbs and pronouns at the opening of scenes—"Awake, awake" (in both chs. 51:9 and 52:1); "I, I am he"; "Rouse yourself, rouse yourself"; "Depart, depart." The repetition, which is also found in other chapters, but not with this frequency, indicates a mood of great urgency and conveys a feeling of intense excitement. It is as though the prophet were shouting, first to God to act with his mighty power, and then to Jerusalem and its exiles to meet God's action with an answering faith and joy. All Second Isaiah's characteristic themes are present: the transformation of Israel, the continuity of the history of the Servant from Abraham to the last day of time, the universality and cosmic nature of God's salvation, the inability of God's enemies to restrain his purpose, the joy of the redeemed as they return to Zion, the approaching end of the time of judgment and destruction, the free gift of salvation from God, the wonder of kings at the rise of the Servant Israel from weakness and humiliation to power and glory. *Not one of these themes is new* and yet each is presented with such freshness that it seems new. They form a unity here just as they do in the earlier chapters because they belong together as the constituent elements in the prophet's thought.

The first four scenes in ch. 51 seem to move smoothly, each building on those that came before. If there is the suggestion of a break anywhere, it comes between vs. 11 and 12, and yet vs. 12-16 can be read as God's answer to the prophet's prayer in vs. 9-10. The plea to Jerusalem to rouse herself in chs. 51:17-23 and 52:1-6 follows naturally upon the preceding announcements of the coming of salvation. Chapter 52:7-10 is an outburst of praise similar to ch. 42:10-12, and the incitement to the exiles to depart in vs. 11-12 continues its theme. Chapter 52:13-15 repeats in a new form the opening transformation theme of ch. 51:1-3 and so brings the cycle to a close on the same note with which it began.

This last point is important because it has for years been taken for granted by almost all interpreters that ch. 52:13-15 belongs with ch. 53. Its removal from ch. 52 helps to conceal both the rounded unity of chs. 51 and 52 and the fact that the impending transformation of the Servant is the theme of the two chapters, making them an appropriate bridge of transition from ch. 50 to ch. 53. In ch. 50 the Servant is in the midst of his humiliation not just in a dramatic presentation but most likely in actual fact. In chs. 51 and 52 the faithful who in the present bear the destiny of the Servant are encouraged to expect their vindication at any moment. In ch. 53 the prophet represents, dramatically, those who once were antagonists of the Servant looking back on his time of humiliation, suffering, and death and confessing that in him God had actually laid bare his arm for the salvation of his people, had made atonement for their sins, and had created a new future for Israel. But what must not be missed is that they also look forward and see, as in chs. 51 and 52, the certainty of the Servant's triumph and exaltation. The four chapters belong together and the points of similarity between chs. 52:13-15 and 53 that have caused the former to be read as part of ch. 53 are not confined to ch. 52:13-15, but are an integral part of the prophet's thought, already expressed in earlier chapters but missed by interpreters because of their insistence upon cutting apart things that belong together. The transformation of the Servant from a condition of insignificance, oppression, poverty, weakness, and blindness to become the marvel of the nations, the one who beats the mountains to dust and yet is the gentle liberator of the prisoners and the light of all who sit in darkness, was established early in the prophet's writings and is one of the essential keys to the understanding of them, although only too often a lost key. The uniqueness of ch. 53 is not in its portrayal of the transformation, but in its interpretation of the meaning of the Servant's sufferings.

In ch. 46:12 the prophet addressed his people as "the stubborn of heart who are far from righteousness," thus setting them in direct contrast to those in ch. 51:1 who "follow closely after righteousness and seek the Lord." The former we have already identified with those who "confess the God of Israel, but not in truth or right" (ch. 48:1). Torrey would have us believe that the same people are addressed in both instances, that Second Isaiah, according to his mood, sees the nation at one time as an incorrigible band of sinners and at another time as earnest seekers after righteousness. Certainly the prophet recognizes the double and contradictory character of Israel, as Servant of God and yet rebellious sinner, as having been integral to its existence from the very beginning (chs. 43:27-28; 44:1; 48:8; 49:1). It is the blind and sinful Israel that is to be cleansed and enlightened by God's forgiveness. But much more is involved here than merely a shift in the prophet's mood. In chs. 65 and 66 we find a decisive separation of the faithful from the unfaithful, the true servants (plural rather than singular) going forward to fulfill the destiny of God's chosen people, whereas those who have corrupted themselves with pagan practices are consigned to destruction. Here, we may be less inclined to think those who are far from righteousness and those who follow closely after righteousness to be merely the same people under two aspects. What we have before us here, as in ch. 50:10-11, is the beginning of the prophet's realization, under the hard blows of experience, that an unfaithful Israel that rejects God's word of forgiveness can never inherit or fulfill the promises of God. Here, at least for the moment, he turns from the nation as a whole to speak his word directly to those who are humbly open to it and who are willing even to suffer for their obedience. Even if Israel as a nation proves unfaithful, these from within Israel, and perhaps also from beyond Israel, will go forward into the glorious future that God has prepared.

The background of the encouraging words of *vs. 1-3* would seem to be the smallness of the persecuted community of the faithful. Rejected by the larger community (see chs. 65 and 66), a mere handful of believers, what could they hope for from the future? Look back and see where you came from, the prophet tells them. At one time there were only Abraham and Sarah, far advanced in years and with no children. Yet God's promise to them of a great future in their descendants was realized. The God of Abraham is still the same God with the same power. Out of a tiny group of true believers he can again fashion a great people (cf. ch. 49:19-21). The mention of Sarah in v. 2 is the only Old Testament reference to her outside the book of Genesis. This and the mention of Eden in v. 3 show the familiarity of Second Isaiah with the Genesis traditions and illustrate what he has in mind when he refers to "the former things": God's mighty acts in the past, which should open the eyes of Israelites to what he will yet do with them in time to come. The day of redemption will see Zion so transformed that it will be like Eden before sin entered it to create desolation.

But the restoration of Eden cannot be for Israel alone, just as the original inhabitants of Eden were not Israelites, but simply man and woman, the parents of the whole of mankind. There is no need to emend "my people" and "my nation" in v. 4 to read the plural, "peoples" and "nations," and to have God addressing the nations rather than Israel in vs. 4-6. The unemended text links vs. 4-6 to v. 3 as an extension of the vision of the new day. The parallel of v. 4b with ch. 42:1-4 is obvious, which suggests the possibility that it is the Servant who speaks in vs. 4-6, although it makes no difference to Second Isaiah whether it is God or the Servant who establishes justice and brings deliverance. The two are so closely identified in the redemption that God's law and the Servant's law are one. The recognition of the presence of the Servant here would strengthen the case for the retaining of ch. 52:13-15 as the conclusion of ch. 52. The three parallel terms for salvation in v. 5 make it clear that the prophet envisages the final establishment of God's rule over the whole world. His Kingdom is the answer to the hopes of all mankind. Volz indulges in speculation when he reads into these hopes of the nations an appreciation by Second Isaiah of the Zoroastrian religion of the Persians as a genuine anticipation of the one true God! The nations, creatures of God created not for death but for life, not for chaos but for order, wait for their salvation and liberation but in blindness to the one from whom it must come. In the day of salvation they open their eyes to see with amazement that the God of Israel is the one who alone can save them. Those who are redeemed from among the nations are specifically called the "blind" and the "prisoners" (ch. 42:7).

V. 6 is an exact parallel to ch. 40:6-8, saying the same thing in completely different words. Not only all flesh but the heavens and the earth themselves are creaturely and therefore perishable. The things that are seen and that are taken to be the substantial realities of life are actually as transitory as smoke or as clothes that so swiftly wear out, but the things that are not seen—God, the word of God, and the salvation that God has promised in his word—endure forever. The tendency of our minds is to jump at once to the thought of a new heavens and a new earth (cf. chs. 65:17; 66:22), but actually in v. 6 Second Isaiah does not go beyond the negative statement that the present heaven and earth will not endure. Because his people were so overawed by the present structures of power in the world and could not see how even God could create a new future for Israel in the face of such obstacles, he was concerned to show all things human and mortal in their true dimensions in the light of the one eternal God. Note how this theme is picked up and repeated at greater length in vs. 12-16. The oppressor is doomed, so why fear him?

The RSV conceals the closeness of the parallel between vs. 7 and 1 by translating *sedeq* as "deliverance" in v. 1 and as "righteousness" in v. 7. It must be the same in both verses. "Righteousness," whether followed by "of God" or not, is the righteous rule of God upon which Second Isaiah sets all his hopes. It is not a quality of life that may be possessed apart from God, but is known only as God is known. To seek or follow after righteousness (cf. "seek the kingdom of God" in the New Testament) is to await eagerly the coming of God to reveal the righteousness of his rule. Thus, to be far from righteousness is not just to be ethically deficient, but to be far from God. But, since God's righteous rule is revealed in Israel in his word, those whose ears are open to his word *know* his righteous rule already. "Law" in v. 7 is not used in the legal sense of "laws," but as "Torah," God's word, in which he reveals himself and so instructs his people in the way of life. The "law" in Israel's heart and the word on Israel's lips in v. 16 are one and the same. The translation "law" suggests only a remembering of the commandments and conceals what is central for Second Isaiah, that God himself is present in his life-transforming power in his word (ch. 55:10-11), that he *comes* in a hidden fashion when he *speaks* (ch. 50:2), and therefore, a people that knows him already in his word can live in the joyful certainty of the ultimate revealing of his righteous rule. The repetition of ch. 50:9b in ch. 51:8a and of the conclusion of v. 6 in v. 8b links vs. 7-8 closely not only with vs. 4-6 but also with ch. 50. The conflict in ch. 50 between the faithful and unfaithful in Israel reappears in ch. 51:7 and will continue to appear in later chapters (chs. 54:15; 57:1, 4; 58:4; 59:7, 15; 65:8 ff.; 66:1-6).

V. 9. The invocation of God to act speedily for the redemption of his people occurs here for the first time. The prophet is not only the herald of God's salvation and the spokesman for God to his people but also the intercessor for the people with God. We have more extensive examples of his intercession in chs. 62 to 64, where he identifies himself with his people not only in their desolation but also in their sins (ch. 64:6) and pleads passionately with God to have done with his anger and to begin the time of mercy. The intercession in chs. 51 and 62 to 64, so plainly the voice of the same prophet, is one of the many features that link together the two sections of the book, chs. 40 to 55 and 56 to 66, which have so frequently been assigned to different prophets. "Arm of the Lord" is not something or someone apart from God himself but is God himself in his might. He rules with his arm (ch. 40:10). He lays bare his arm before the eyes of all the nations when he establishes his sovereignty (ch. 52:10). The revealing of his arm is the revealing of his power in action (ch. 53:1). The two instances of God's action in the past to which the prophet's mind turns at once are the creation of an ordered world out of a watery chaos and the deliverance from Egypt. The creation, however, takes on a more mythological form for him than in Gen., ch. 1, the making of dry land in the midst of the waters being set parallel with the ancient myth, so widespread in the East, of a primeval battle of God with the dragon Rahab or Tiamat. As the parallel shows, the use of the myth is poetic and sophisticated and not naïve. The decisive moment in the deliverance from Egypt is seen as the making of a way in the depth of the sea. The day of redemption that lies in the future is both a new act of creation and a new deliverance out of slavery. That it is future is very clear in chs. 51-52, but these chapters are by no means unique in this. Rather, they are characteristic of the book as a whole and merely emphasize what is everywhere true, that the action of God is proclaimed as imminent and absolutely certain, that it is prayed for, that it is seen as delayed by the sins of the nation, but *never* does the prophet stand beyond the event except in the imagination and confidence of faith. This fact, which unifies the book from end to end and constitutes the all-encompassing expectation in which every part of it was written, is lost from sight when the assumption is made that the prophet was stimulated into activity by the events reported in Ezra, ch. 1, or at least by his observation of the movements of Cyrus. It then becomes necessary to relate some of the descriptions of the day of redemption to the achievements of the Persian king and so to regard them as past. Thereupon, the thought of the prophet falls into hopeless contradictions and confusion, and his book disintegrates into bits and pieces. Only when the consistency of his eschatological hope is grasped does it become possible to see the impressive unity of his writings.

In response to the prophet's intercession in *vs. 9-11,* God announces his readiness to redeem in *vs. 12 ff.* The repetition of God's mighty "I" corresponds to the repetition of the prophet's plea "awake." "Comfort," here as in ch. 40:1, is too weak a word in English to carry the prophet's meaning. What is needed is a word that denotes deliverance from despair into confidence and hope. That which prevents the rebirth of confidence is the fear of man. As in ch. 40, and in v. 6 of this chapter, the prophet dwells upon the mortality of these men before whom the Israelites tremble. They may seem great and powerful for the moment, but they perish like the grass when God breathes upon them. Fear of them is possible only for Israelites who have forgotten that their God is the Creator of the world and the Lord of history. The fury of the oppressor lasts only for a moment. When God acts, where then is the fury of man? In *v. 14* the fearful who are "bowed down" by their fears are assured not only of their release and of their deliverance from death but also of their daily bread. In the context of the earlier part of the chapter and of ch. 50, where there was evidence of the persecution of the faithful because of their witness, this verse may point to the severity of their situation, that they were in danger both of the loss of their daily bread and of death at the hands of their brethren. This becomes thoroughly credible when these same faithful believers in ch. 66:5 are seen to have been "cast out" from the community by their scornful "brethren." In *vs. 15-16* the two themes of creation and election are set closely together twice, the first time God's choice of Israel being described as his putting of his word in Israel's mouth, the second time as his claiming Israel uniquely as his people. "You are my people" implies "I am your God" and so points to the covenant relation. But the heart of the covenant, the means whereby God sustains the covenant relation, is the word that he speaks to Israel and which Israel has then to declare to mankind. This close association of creation and covenant suggests that the word that God spoke in the creation to bring order out of chaos is the same word that he speaks not only to Israel but through Israel to the world that he may bring a new order out of the fearful chaos of the present. The creative power lies in God's word, so that a people with this word hidden in its heart has within it the power to transform the world. How ridiculous that a nation whose destiny it has been to carry this power of God concealed within it should be frightened by the puny powers of men!

The striking feature of *vs. 19-23* is the vividness with which Jerusalem is depicted as though she were still in the throes of war and devastation. She and her sons have drunk to the dregs the cup of God's wrath. Sword and famine have desolated the country. Foreigners have trampled upon it. The inhabitants lie exhausted in the streets. Chapter 64:10-11 has the same vividness, as though the destruction of Jerusalem and the burning of the Temple had taken place very recently. The fact that Second Isaiah can describe the future as though he were looking back upon it is a warning to us that he may also be able to describe the past as though what happened many years before had happened only yesterday. His dramatic powers are sufficiently in evidence that we must take account of them at every point. But two things seem inescapable. First, as Second Isaiah viewed the years between 587 b.c. and his own time, they were an unbroken period of darkness and desolation that he interpreted as the judgment of God upon the sins of Israel; secondly, he himself had lived with his people through this time of God's wrath and tasted with them the bitterness and deadliness of despair. Perhaps he had experienced as a youth the events of 587 b.c., so that the vividness of his description is that of a prophet-poet's memory. If the time of his activity, which is so hard to place definitely, was somewhere between 550 and 538 b.c., he may well have been old enough to observe and remember what happened in 587 B.C. There is no contradiction between the harshness of his indictment of Israelites whose profession of faith was to him a superficial fraud and his great compassion for a Jerusalem that had suffered so brutally at the hands of its enemies. Interpreting the suffering as God's judgment and as evidence of God's wrath at sin does not keep him from feeling the suffering as his own and crying out for God's mercy upon himself and his people. Here there is no coldly distant discerning of divine wrath in other men's sins, as with Job's comforters, but rather, a love for Jerusalem in spite of her sins and a passionate longing for her redemption.

Against the placing of a chapter break between vs. 16 and 17 (Duhm, Torrey) it may reasonably be argued that a continuity may be discerned even here, the invocation of God's strength in vs. 9 ff. being answered by God's declaration in vs. 12 ff., and the two issuing in the plea of the prophet to Jerusalem to rouse herself from despair and grasp the new future that God's pardon is preparing for her. But if a break must be made somewhere, it is more defensible between vs. 16 and 17 than where it now stands, partly because chs. 51:17-23 and 52:1-6 have a common theme and partly because the enemies of the faithful in vs. 1-16 seem to be Israelite brethren, whereas the enemies of Jerusalem in chs. 51:17 to 52:6 are clearly foreign oppressors. But it is perhaps best to consider chs. 51 and 52 as a unit.

The lack of anyone among Jerusalem's sons who is able to guide her, that is, provide her with responsible leadership, should be placed alongside the lack of any who would answer when God called (chs. 50:2; 65:12; 66:4), the description of all as turning every one to his own way (ch. 53:6), the wonder of God that there was no one to intervene for him (ch. 59:16), and the complaint of God that when he came, there was no one to help (ch. 63:3,5). The expectations of God were that Israel would be the instrument of his purpose and that within Israel would be responsible and enlightened guides— prophets, priests, and rulers. Amos and Hosea, Jeremiah and Ezekiel, had all pointed out the fatal consequences for the nation as a whole when those who were supposed to be shepherds of Israel ceased to have any genuine knowledge of God and merely made their living from their office instead of giving responsible leadership. Verse 18 seems thus to indicate the failure of Israelites to take up these offices responsibly. Jerusalem is without true prophets or priests, perhaps also without men of integrity in its government. The life of the community is in chaos (cf. ch. 45:18).

The construction, "Hearken to me, you who . . . ," which, as we saw, is new in ch. 51, seems to draw v. 21 into association with vs. 1 and 7 and to form another of those threads with which Second Isaiah binds a number of scenes together. In vs. 1 and 7 he addressed himself specially to the faithful, but the faithful were burdened more than anyone else with the distress of being still under God's wrath. In ch. 50:10 they were described as walking in darkness and having no light. They were the afflicted, drunk not with wine but with despair (ch. 51:21), the Israelites with weak hands and feeble knees because of the hopeless outlook (ch. 35:3-4), who by their plight drew forth not only the compassion of the prophet, but, he was sure, the compassion of God himself. To these he declared the end of the time of wrath and the beginning of the time of mercy. It is impossible to think of him speaking such words to those who stubbornly persisted in mingling pagan practices with their worship of the God of Israel and who responded to his appeals with mockery and scorn.

CHAPTERS 51 AND 52 (Continued) /

It has been necessary to introduce ch. 52 together with ch. 51 and to deal with some of its problems in the larger context. From beginning to end the theme of ch. 52 is the stupendous transformation of Israel that is about to take place. It is important to see this clearly because it makes vs. 13-15 the perfect and logical conclusion. The opening verses, like ch. 51:17 f., seek to rouse Jerusalem from her sunken condition that she may exchange the rags of her humiliation for beautiful bridal garments in preparation for the return of her divine husband to her. She has been a slave, but now she shall be free and a holy city, since the God of holiness will dwell once more with her. The God who destroyed her and sent her into captivity will restore her. In vs. 7-10 the prophet sees the redemption already in process of accomplishment: a messenger crossing the mountains to carry the news that God's joyous rule has begun, watchmen on the walls of Jerusalem singing for joy as God's glory is revealed before their eyes. Jerusalem is redeemed, but this is only the beginning of a universal salvation. God's kingdom and power and glory are to be known to the ends of the earth. The return of the exiles is then described under the dramatic likeness of a holy procession in vs. 11-12, and the chapter comes to a conclusion with a speech of God in which he announces that his Servant Israel who has been so humiliated, crushed, and scorned by men, will be so highly exalted in the day of his kingdom that the rulers of the earth will be struck dumb with wonder at the sight. The nation on which they trampled will be the instrument through which God exercises his firm but gracious rule over all mankind.

The rise of Zion out of the dust and out of slavery to become strong and beautiful is the reverse of what was described concerning Babylon in ch. 47. One feature of ch. 52 that is not familiar from preceding chapters is what has been taken to be a cultic interest. Jerusalem is the *holy* city. In the day of her transformation she will not be defiled by the presence of uncircumcised and unclean foreigners. The exiles as they go out from their foreign homes to return to Zion are told to touch no unclean thing and they carry with them "the vessels of the Lord," which must be kept from all defilement. This concern for ritual holiness and purity is surprising because the Temple and its priesthood have thus far had no place in Second Isaiah's pictures of the restored Jerusalem. The mention of the Temple in ch. 44:28, as we have seen, is from another hand than his. His own attitude to the Temple and its sacrifices comes out most clearly in ch. 66:1-3 which, when taken together with ch. 43:22-24, sets him emphatically in line with Jeremiah and earlier prophets in the repudiation of sacrifices as having any place in the divine order for Israel. Chapter 56:1-7 can be left aside in this consideration because, not only in this but in other respects, it stands out of line with the solid body of Second Isaiah's writings and shows the marks of a later hand. But in themes, language, and style ch. 52 is a characteristic writing of Second Isaiah except for this one point. How then shall we explain these unusual features?

The rejection of sacrifices, or any other religious practices, such as fasting (ch. 58), by which the community expected to be able to exert pressure on God, does not carry with it the implication that

Second Isaiah would abandon all imagery drawn from the cultic practices of Israel. The death of the Servant is called a "sin-offering" in ch. 53:10, and although the word "sacrifice" is not used in ch. 66:2, the meaning is the same as in Ps. 51:15-17 where material sacrifices are rejected and the humble and contrite heart is called "the sacrifice acceptable to God."

There is also an emphasis upon holiness in Second Isaiah. God is frequently named "the Holy One of Israel," and no prophet is more insistent than he that an unholy people cannot receive the Holy God. The key to the cultic language of ch. 52, therefore, is in the naming of Jerusalem in *v. 1* "the *holy* city." Its holiness is not a quality that belongs to it of itself, but is entirely the consequence of the presence in it of the Holy One of Israel. Also we should remember that Zion or Jerusalem symbolizes, not a place, but a people, the Zion of v. 1 being identical with the Servant of v. 13. In ch. 51 the prophet's mind moved from people to city; here he moves in the opposite direction from city to people, the transition being made by the reference to the returning exiles in vs. 11-12. A holy God must have a holy people. "The uncircumcised and unclean" have usually been identified simply as non-Israelites, which then sets the verse in contradiction to Second Isaiah's universal vision of foreigners being incorporated into the new people of God. But there is no reason why the words should not include all who are unholy and unfit for the presence of a holy God, whether Israelite or not. In v. 11 those who come from the four corners of the earth are warned to leave behind them all that is unholy and unclean. There are not only Israelites but also many from among the nations who come to acknowledge themselves members of the people of God (ch. 44:1-5). The "vessels of God" that they bear with them are usually identified as the holy utensils with which the Temple was equipped and which Cyrus was reported by the Chronicler to have sent back to Jerusalem (Ezra 1:7; 6:5), but here they have a symbolic significance. The utensils for God's service in the restored Jerusalem are his sons and daughters, and this is exactly what we read in parallel passages where the nations at God's signal come to Jerusalem, carrying in their arms the precious burden of God's children (chs. 49:22; 60:4, 9). To take "vessels of God" in the literal cultic sense rather than in this figurative sense attributes to Second Isaiah a concern for the reestablishment of priestly sacrifices in the Temple at Jerusalem that not only is absent from the remainder of his writings but goes directly contrary to what he consistently asserts.

The speech of God in *vs. 3-6*, declaring his intention to liberate Jerusalem, has been the subject of much debate and has been variously reconstructed. The RSV prints it as a prose interlude, but Torrey by a few judicious changes restores to it a poetic form in keeping with its context. The fourfold repetition of "saith the Lord" is certainly clumsy and unlike the style of Second Isaiah. But the declaration that Israel's redemption will be free (cf. chs. 45:13; 55:1), the setting of the present liberation against the historical background of past enslavements, the concern of God lest the despising of Israel should issue in a despising of Israel's God, and the announcement by God of his presence, "Behold me," as the revelation of his saving power (cf. ch. 40:9)—all are characteristic themes and expressions. God did not sell his people to a foreign nation (cf. ch. 50:1) and he does not have to buy them back. There is no price to pay for the coming liberation. It does not have to be purchased with sacrifices and fastings (ch. 58:1 ff.). Neither Israel nor any other nation can control or limit the action of God. In his sovereign freedom he let foreign powers trample upon Israel as a judgment upon her sins, but now in the same freedom he is terminating the time of judgment and beginning a new era of mercy. *V. 4* may be a gloss to explain the reference, "You were sold for nothing." The descent into Egypt is a poor illustration since it was in no way a judgment of God upon Israel, and it is strange that the Assyrian oppression should be mentioned, rather than the more immediate Babylonian one. *V. 5* follows more smoothly upon v. 3 than upon v. 4. Having announced his intention to redeem, God looks down upon his scattered, humiliated, and suffering people and asks, "What have I here?", as though he were surprised that the transformation had not already taken place. It is intolerable that in the continuing misery of Israel God's own name is dragged in the dust. But all this is now at an end. God's revealing of his name afresh to his people is the revealing of himself in his righteousness and power. There may be a reminiscence here of Ex. 3:13 ff. where the revealing of God's name to Moses was the prelude to the exodus. An Israel that knows God's name and responds to him when he says, "Behold me," is an Israel in covenant with God and assured of deliverance.

The lyrical and dramatic interlude in *vs. 7-9* reveals the full dimensions of God's salvation. The opening of the chapter tended to focus attention on Jerusalem, but earlier chapters have already taught us that the restoration of Jerusalem (Israel) is only the prelude to the redemption of the whole world. Since the God of Israel alone is God, the establishment of his sovereignity cannot be limited to Israel in its claims or its benefits. The liberation of Israel leads to the liberation of a captive humanity. The herald of peace and blessing who skips across the mountains comes first to Zion with the message that the God of Israel has established his kingdom over all the earth. The time of conflict, suffering, and darkness is past. Behind the herald on the road across the mountains (cf. ch. 40:3-5) the prophet with the eye of faith sees God himself returning to Jerusalem. Volz interprets this to mean that God has been with the exiles in Babylon and now is coming back with them to Palestine. Torrey asserts that a return of Yahweh to Zion is altogether foreign to the prophet's thought. Both miss the central point of Second Isaiah's theology, that all the desolation and darkness of Israel, the barrenness of its life like that of a desert, is the consequence of God's absence, or hiddenness, or wrath. However it may be described, it is the rupture between Israel and God made by Israel's sin that is the source of the nation's misery. Zion without God is a wilderness. But God's forgiveness of Israel is his restoration of the covenant relation and is described as his return to Zion that calls for a corresponding return of Zion to him. God comes! And his coming is like the breaking forth of rivers in the desert that transform it into an Eden (ch. 51:3). The watchmen on the walls of Jerusalem are said to see "face-to-face" the return of God to his people. The customary translation "eye to eye" leaves the meaning obscure. The use of the same phrase in Num. 14:14 makes the translation "face-to-face" more likely. Its boldness is like Second Isaiah: in the day of redemption God is to be actually with his people face-to-face. There is no longer any separation between him and them. He is seen in his glory, but not only by the inhabitants of Jerusalem. The eyes of all the nations see the salvation of God.

The call to the exiles to start on their way to Zion fo_
ally upon the preceding vision. *V. 12* shows that the i_
drawn from the story of the exodus from Egypt. Like the pr_
of God in the pillar of cloud and fire that guarded Israel before and
behind on the way through the desert, so will God be to his people
in the new exodus. But this time there will be a difference: the Israelites left Egypt in haste (Ex. 12:10; Deut. 16:3), and this atmosphere of haste was preserved in the celebration of the Passover, but
in the new and final exodus there will be no need for haste, for there
will no longer be any enemies from whom to flee. God's Kingdom
will rule over all.

If this interpretation of ch. 52:1-12 is valid, then what would we
expect to be the status of the Servant if the prophet should change
his name for Israel and instead of speaking of Jerusalem should
speak of the Servant? Jerusalem enslaved and buried in the dust has
been transformed and exalted into a new creation in beauty and
power. God's universal kingdom has been established and a people
of God restored at its center. But who can this people of the restoration be other than the Servant? In the time of darkness he was trodden into the ground, scattered, impoverished, despised by his neighbors, yet all the time there was hidden in him a word and a destiny
that no one could have suspected from his outward appearance. He
was the Servant of God, unrecognized. But in the day of God's
glory and power all such concealment would fall away, and the
Servant would be revealed in his closeness to God, as the instrument of God's purpose, through whom light would shine forth to
the nations and God's covenant love would reach out to encircle all
mankind. In short, what is said of the Servant in *vs. 13-15* is exactly
what we would expect the prophet to say on the basis of vs. 1-12.
That there are phrases in vs. 13-15 that seem to bind the passage
together with ch. 53 is not unusual. It is like Second Isaiah to bind
his chapters together even where he is introducing a wholly new
theme. But there is nothing new in the theme of the Servant Israel's
future transformation. Interpreters have failed to recognize it in the
earlier chapters only because they have torn passages apart that belong together and have been blind to the fact that the exalted and
triumphant Servant is related to the humiliated, sinful, and blind
Servant as the butterfly is related to the caterpillar worm (cf. ch.

worm, Israel, is transformed into a conqueror and lib-
ell may the kings of the nations look on in astonishment!
e verb translated "shall prosper" in v. 13 has been a source of
difficulty to interpreters. It can also mean "shall deal wisely." Torrey
makes it a proper name for the Servant, *Yaskil,* on the pattern of
Meshullam in ch. 42:19, feeling that it does not fit with the other
verbs indicating exaltation. But it is hard to see why the prophet
should not say of the Servant through whom God rules in the day
of redemption that he deals wisely or that he prospers. The former
is preferable. Almost all interpreters are agreed in making slight
emendations in v. 14—reading "him" for "thee" after the preposition
"at" (as in the RSV), and *"because* his appearance was marred" in
place of *"so* marred was his appearance," thus making a perfect correspondence between vs. 14 and 15. Many were appalled at the
Servant's humiliation, but many kings and nations will be *startled*
(the RSV follows the widely accepted emendation of "sprinkle")
at his astounding exaltation. To the nations the exaltation of Israel
will be wholly unexpected, but not to Israel, since God is revealing
it beforehand in his word. The nations, like many people within
Israel, are blind and deaf to God and therefore blind and deaf to
the meaning and goal of history. They do not know what God has
in store for them, nor do they know that hidden within the Israel
whom they have despised has been the secret of their own destiny,
hidden in the all-powerful word of God in which from the beginning God has been revealing himself and his purpose to men. But
in the day of redemption the blind will have eyes with which to
see and the deaf ears with which to hear (ch. 43:8).

CHAPTER 53 / Essential to the understanding of ch. 53
is its relationship to the remainder of the book and its position in the
very context in which it stands. Many interpreters detach it and set
it either by itself or at the summit of a series of special "Servant"
passages. The Servant in ch. 53 seems to them to be sharply contrasted in character with the Servant elsewhere in the book, innocent where the other is guilty, enlightened where the other is blind,

an individual where the other is clearly collective. But we have already discovered the source of this splitting of the Servant image in the failure to maintain the unity of the prophet's thought about Israel, the unity of the sinful rebellious Israel, past and present, with Israel as God's witness before the world, past and present, and the unity of Israel, weak, blind, guilty, scattered, and oppressed now, and Israel restored, reborn, ruling the nations for God, liberating the prisoners, and establishing justice everywhere in the great day ahead. In short, the contradiction in the Servant image is the contradiction in the actual life of Israel, between Israel according to God's intention and Israel according to its own intention. The prophet has to deal with this contradiction created by the nation's sin. It is the obstacle holding back the day of redemption and triumph. How is it to be overcome? It has to be forgiven by God. But what can be done when the nation stubbornly refuses to hear the good news of God's forgiveness? That is the problem which the prophet faces in ch. 53. But first we have to see clearly the evidence for the unity of this chapter with the writings of Second Isaiah as a whole in order to overcome once and for all the persistent tendency to consider it in isolation.

Chapter 53 is marked as a writing of Second Isaiah in so many different ways that it should be impossible to sustain any theory that attributes it to another author. The dramatic form in which Second Isaiah writes is so distinctive and unique with him that it is like his signature. Other prophets introduce God as speaker, but never with the dramatic variations that are found here: God debating with the nations, God addressing Israel, God speaking to the world about Israel. But what is most unusual is that the nations or Israel or the prophet himself or a kind of chorus may do the speaking while yet carrying forward the theme begun in God's speech. There is nothing like this in any other prophet, and the suggestion that a disciple of Second Isaiah could imitate it in parts of chs. 56 to 66 or in the so-called "Servant Songs" is as unlikely as that someone could have imitated Shakespeare so perfectly that his plays would be indistinguishable from the master's. The suggestion that ch. 53 was written by an imitator could be made only by someone who had no understanding of how such miracles of literary creation come to pass. Who except Second Isaiah could compose this magnificent and over-powering confession of blindness, sin, and forgiveness and put it convincingly in the mouth of the nameless persons who by their words are shown to have let the Servant go to his death, lonely and defenseless, and then afterward to have realized that in him God had brought them their salvation? Chapter 53 is the composition of an author who possessed amazing dramatic power. Do we need to ask who he was when we have so many specimens of his work in the remainder of the book? The recognition of Second Isaiah's ability to create intensely dramatic scenes should also put us on our guard against assuming that because the chapter leaves upon our minds the impression of an eyewitness account of the judicial murder of an individual, this is exactly what we have before us. The possibility still remains that this individual figure represents an imaginative concentration of centuries of the Servant's experience into a single portrait, so that Abraham, Moses, Elijah, Amos, Hosea, Isaiah, Jeremiah, Second Isaiah himself, and all the faithful of the ages, past, present, and future are embodied in this one figure.

We recognize also the basic theme of the chapter as one that has become familiar in earlier chapters: the transformation of the Servant from a state of humiliation to one of triumph and vindication in which it is openly revealed that in him God was bringing his salvation to men. The attention is so focused on the humiliation and its significance that the chapter is usually given the title "The Suffering Servant," but the suffering is presented in a framework of ultimate triumph, so that the title should be "The Suffering and Triumphant Servant." The confessors acknowledge that while the Servant was suffering and dying they were indifferent to him, not knowing the hidden meaning of what was happening before their eyes. But after his death their blindness was struck from them, and the incredible truth dawned upon them that in this pitiful figure, despised and ignored by them, God's mighty arm was all along being laid bare for the salvation of men. But what was it in the Servant that was the secret of his power? Verse 11 says that the Servant has knowledge of salvation and makes many righteous. And this knowledge is none other than the knowledge of God, hidden in the Servant from his birth in the word of God of which we heard in chs. 49:1-2; 50:2, 4; 51:16; 55:11; 59:21.

From another perspective, however, the central theme of ch. 53 is forgiveness, God's forgiveness of the sins of men whereby he cleanses them and transforms them, delivering them from the death to which they were doomed by their sins and creating for them a new life and a new future. We have already seen that from the first verse of ch. 40 the good news of Second Isaiah is that God has forgiven his people and that his forgiveness opens the door for them to a wholly new future. But we have also seen the prophet wrestling in grim earnestness with the problem that sin creates for God, sin in which men persist and will not let it be forgiven. A holy God could not compromise with sin. A blind and sinful Israel could not be the instrument of God's salvation for the world. We have seen him cut through this dilemma by asserting that God would not let even the sin of Israel stand in his way, but would bring his purpose in Israel and in the world to its fulfillment in spite of Israel's sin. But how the sin of the unrepentant sinner was to be forgiven and overcome he made no suggestion. That was the revelation that was left to be embodied in ch. 53: the bearing of the penalty of unrepented sin by the Servant and the breaking of the resistance of the unrepentant sinner by the Servant's offering of himself to God as a sacrifice for sin. Who except Second Isaiah as we have come to know him in chs. 40 to 52 could be expected to penetrate to this depth into the mystery of God's forgiveness of human sin?

A third feature that binds ch. 53 together with the preceding chapters is the representation of the Servant as ignored, misunderstood, scorned, beaten, and condemned by the community. When chs. 56 to 66 are included with chs. 40 to 55, there is an impressive mass of evidence that Second Isaiah's message fell largely on deaf ears in the community and that he and those who stood with him had to endure severe persecution from those who resented the attacks of the prophet upon the existing order. But even in chs. 40 to 55 the evidence has been considerable. As early as ch. 40:14, 27 we are made aware of a sharp difference between Second Isaiah and some of his contemporaries. In ch. 42:18-25 the Israel that is described is blind and deaf to God and has no understanding of the sobering message of the earlier prophets. In ch. 43:22-24 the prophet not only accuses his people of failing to respond to God's call but also repudiates their sacrifices as completely unavailing with God. In ch. 45:9-11 we are made acquainted with Israelites who not only contend with their Maker but also set in question the wisdom of his purpose for them as declared by the prophet. An idolatrous Israel is attacked in ch. 46 as "stubborn of heart and far from deliverance," and even more sharply in ch. 48 for being so treacherous and rebellious against God as to be unworthy of the name Israel. In ch. 50 God asks why no one has responded to his call, and the Servant reveals what he has had to suffer in obedience to the word that God gives him each day afresh to declare. In ch. 51 the people who have God's Torah in their heart are exposed to the reproaches and revilings of men and are in fear that their enemies may deprive them not only of their daily bread but of life itself. In ch. 52:14 the Servant is so disfigured in appearance that it is difficult to recognize that he is a human being, which suggests someone so beaten and abused that one has to look closely to discern that he is a man.

The evidence of conflict continues in chs. 56 to 66, and we must anticipate the exegesis of these chapters in order to build out a full context for ch. 53. In ch. 57 the righteous, who are no doubt identical with the faithful of ch. 51:1 and 7, perish without anyone paying any heed, but their death at least brings them peace, for they no longer have to face the bitter scorn and mockery of their semipagan neighbors! Those who make sport of the righteous, opening their mouths wide in laughter and sticking out their tongues at them, belong together with those who spit in the Servant's face and pull his beard in ch. 50:6. In ch. 58:1-5 the prophet stands in opposition to a religious community that professes to be following God's commands scrupulously and expects by its religious observances such as fasting to earn his favor, and he makes the peculiar statement about the fasting, "You fast only to quarrel and to fight and to hit with wicked fist." But whom do they hit and with whom do they quarrel and fight? Apparently those who fast have been using physical violence to compel the nonconformist prophet and his nonconformist followers to conform to the community's religious regulations. In ch. 59 the same people are accused of having their hands defiled with blood and in ch. 59:6-7 they commit deeds of violence and shed innocent blood. There could not be clearer evidence of religious conflict in the community, so severe that some of those who maintained their faithfulness to God had already gone to their deaths at the hands of their brothers. It was a costly thing to be the faithful Servant of God's word in a community that preferred a more relaxed and indulgent mixture of pagan and traditional Israelite practices.

The next passage in which a divided community is evident is in the prayer of the prophet in ch. 63:15 ff. He and those who are included with him in the prayer claim God as their Father and Redeemer "though Abraham does not know us and Israel does not acknowledge us." This needs to be interpreted in the light of ch. 65 where the *servants* of God are sharply distinguished from Israel as a whole, the name "Israel" being left to these servants as a curse and God calling them by a new and different name (ch. 65:15), also the name of God being no longer "God of Israel" but instead "the God of truth" (ch. 65:16). The "servants" (plural) are the "chosen of God" henceforward, and the rebellious sinners are consigned to destruction. Thus in ch. 63:16 "Abraham" is used parallel with "Israel" to signify the nation as a whole, and the failure of Abraham and Israel to recognize the true servants of God in the prophet and the faithful who stood with him is identical with the failure of the speaker in ch. 53:2-3 to recognize the saving presence and power of God in the humiliated Servant. In ch. 64:7 the prophet, identifying himself with the nation in its sin, confesses that no one responds rightly to God, and in ch. 65:1-7 he pictures the nation not only refusing to respond to God's call but reviling God (v. 7) in its pagan forms of worship. In ch. 65:8 ff. it becomes evident that the prophet has surrendered his hopes for the nation as a whole and has fastened them upon the faithful within the nation. It is noticeable that after ch. 53 he ceases to speak of "Israel, my Servant." Already in ch. 54:17 he uses the plural form "servants," and in ch. 65 all the promises of God that earlier were held out to Israel are focused upon the servants. The fulfillment of God's purpose is as certain as ever, but the instrument that he is to use has been more narrowly defined.

But it is ch. 66 that brings the conflict and the opposing forces most clearly into the open. The prophet's opponents apparently are proposing to rebuild the Temple, as though by providing God with a "resting-place" in Jerusalem they might be sure of his presence and his blessing. He scorns their theology. They ignore the Creator of heaven and earth who holds all men in his hands and substitute for him a little god who will live quietly in the house they build for him. Not thus can they placate the wrath of God that leaves the land in desolation. That alone which is acceptable to God is the humble and contrite heart of the believer who sets all his trust upon God's word. What would infuriate religious officials more than to have a prophet publicly and in the name of God denounce their project to build God a Temple? But a Temple would also mean sacrifices. And Second Isaiah had still sharper words with which to condemn all such sacrifices by which men thought they could lay God under obligation. The ritual killing of an ox is an offense comparable to murder, and the killing of a lamb for sacrifice is no better than the breaking of a dog's neck. Sacrifice is idolatry. These are fighting words in a community that sets its main confidence upon the operations of a sacrificial cult. Then in v. 5 those "who tremble at God's word" and who in ch. 65 were distinguished from Israel as a whole are addressed as those who have been hated by their brethren and cast out for the sake of God's name, that is, because of their faithful witness to God. Their enemies are represented as *mocking* at their faith and hope, saying that they would like to see this glory of God's coming which is to be such a joy to believers. Hated, mocked, expelled from the community, the faithful can only wait for their vindication from God (cf. ch. 50:8). The record of suffering and death in these chapters provides the context for understanding ch. 53.

There are yet other lesser marks of Second Isaiah's hand in ch. 53. The central figure in the chapter is introduced merely with the personal pronoun "he." Much later, in v. 11, he is identified as the Servant, but through ten verses he remains nameless, the mysterious stranger. But this is exactly what Second Isaiah has done in a whole series of passages in which he brings God's Servant upon the scene: chs. 41:2, 25; 45:13; 46:11; 48:14-15. He describes the Servant fulfilling his destiny without naming him at first, partly as in ch. 41, that it may come with a shock of surprise when he identifies God's conqueror and agent of redemption as the Israel of the future, partly because it was an act of faith for his hearers to recognize themselves in the Servant, but perhaps also because God's servant, hidden now in the past in Israel and only in the day of redemption to be clearly revealed, was in a very real sense a mysterious figure. The mystery of God's revelation of himself to man in a word that can be heard and remembered and the mystery of the Servant in whose heart that word is hidden, which will be revealed eventually as the secret of all that has ever happened in history, are two parts of the same mystery, which was only to be deepened in its mysteriousness when the love and holiness of God were revealed in their fullness in Jesus Christ. Second Isaiah's modest "he" with which he introduces the one in whom God's redemption comes nearest to man shows his awareness of the mystery that must always surround the person of the Servant.

Another slight touch which, however, is significant of the author, is the way in which the speaker changes in v. 8 and in the middle of v. 11 without any interruption of the discourse concerning the Servant. Through vs. 1-6 the confession of sin is made by unidentified persons who appear only as "we." The description of the Servant's condemnation and death proceeds in vs. 7 ff. with no indication that the speaker has changed until suddenly at the end of v. 8 it is said that the Servant was stricken for the transgression of *my* people, where the *my* would refer undoubtedly to God. Attempts have been made to emend the word, changing it to the less personal and more colorless "for the transgression of people," and this would perhaps be convincing if the same sudden shift in speaker did not take place also in v. 11. The earlier part of the sentence in v. 10 and in the first half of v. 11 is certainly not spoken by God, yet suddenly at the mention of "the righteous one," the voice of God breaks in identifying him as "*my* Servant" and continues in v. 12 with a prediction of the Servant's triumph. The first shift in speaker appears to be the kind of error that one usually attributes to a copyist and emends without hesitation, but the second shift is too plainly intentional to be meddled with. But when we discover the same shift of speaker in ch. 51:1-3, we recognize the two occurrences of it in ch. 53 as subtle marks of the author. In his dramatic form of writing in which the theme could be carried either by God or by a human speaker and a theme placed at one time in God's mouth could be heard at another time from the mouth of the Servant (cf. chs. 42:1-7; 49:1-7), it was only human that the author should nod occasionally and leave it not entirely clear which of his speakers had the floor, or perhaps he shifted intentionally to a different speaker to enforce his point.

One final mark of Second Isaiah's hand is the double question with which the chapter begins. Rhetorical questions abound in his writings and because of poetic parallelism they are usually double (cf. chs. 40:12-14, 18, 21, 25, 27, 28; 41:1, 26; 42:19, 22, 24; 43:9; 44:7; 45:11, 21; 46:5; 48:14; 50:1-2; etc.).

With this quantity of evidence that ch. 53 is by the same author as the remainder of the book, it is hardly necessary to controvert the attempts that have been made by an analysis of the language to establish a difference in vocabulary between ch. 53 and the remaining chapters. Where the theme of ch. 53 is parallel with what we find in other chapters, the language is similar, but where it launches out daringly into new reaches of understanding and says what is nowhere else to be found in the book, it is not surprising that it uses words and phrases that are different. But the language is nowhere so strange and different that we feel we have closed the book of one author and opened the book of another.

The parallels that we have established between ch. 53 and other passages lead us to the conclusion that the Servant who meets us here is the Servant with whom we have already become familiar elsewhere in chs. 40 to 52. The restraint of the prophet in never identifying himself directly with the Servant makes us dismiss the widely favored interpretation that he was describing himself in ch. 53. Having kept himself studiously out of his oracles by a carefully constructed dramatic form, he would hardly place himself and his sufferings and an imaginative account of his own death in the very center of his profoundest oracle. But this does not prevent us from recognizing that the pain and humiliation and martyrdom that were being endured in faithfulness to God's word in the circle to which he belonged provided him with the very lines and colors that went into his portrait of the Servant. It is no ideal concept or purely imaginative creation. He knew the faithful Servant at first hand and described him from within, not from a distance, even the shortest distance.

We have now to ask whether, with the knowledge we have gathered from all parts of the book concerning the prophet, the believers associated with him, and the community that would gladly have been rid of all who "trembled at God's word," we can reconstruct a credible situation in which ch. 53 might have originated. The prophet's love for his people and for Jerusalem was such that he persisted in his hopes for the nation as a whole in spite of every discouragement. He did not easily and quickly draw back into a conventicle of disciples where he would be assured of sympathy and response. He claimed not only the Israel immediately about him but also the Israel scattered among the nations for his God and heralded a future in which this people of God would be indefinitely extended by the accession of hosts of Gentiles. Even the most persistent and flagrant pagan practices among his people did not make him abandon his vision of the future. But his attacks upon the syncretistic religion of the community, upon the whole sacrificial and ceremonial system of the official cult, and upon the project for rebuilding the Temple brought brutal persecution with bloodshed upon him and his followers, and they were driven out of the community. He then had no choice but to redefine the chosen people of God as the faithful remnant within the nation. We have to think of him then as living in the midst of this bruised and battered community of the faithful, still speaking the word that strengthened the weak hands and confirmed the feeble knees.

We can imagine what a problem their suffering would be for these faithful believers. The book of Job lets us know how customary it was to assume that suffering should be interpreted as punishment for sin. The prophetic teaching that sin inevitably brought misfortune, suffering, and death was easily turned around to mean that wherever misfortune, suffering, or violent death occurred, there must have been some grievous sin. Verse 4 tells us that the Servant's misfortunes were interpreted by the community as God's smiting or punishing of him. We know then that the suffering of the faithful must have been a painful problem for them. They knew that they

were suffering for their faithfulness to God, but their brothers who
hated them interpreted it as a just punishment meted out to them
by God for thinking and acting contrary to the accepted ways of
the community, which they identified with the ways of God. Can
we imagine the prophet of God having nothing to say to his people
in that dilemma? And if he spoke to that situation, can we imagine
him saying anything that would more perfectly meet the problem
than what is written in ch. 53? The faithful would already be
familiar with the dramatic form in which he was accustomed to
cast his thoughts, and also with many features of the Servant: the
humble and hidden form of his present appearance and the power
and glory that would be his when God triumphed in the future; the
unbroken history of the Servant in Israel's past and the way in
which that destiny had come to be focused upon themselves; the
demand upon the Servant for absolute faithfulness to God's word
and the costliness of such faithfulness in a world that was blind
and deaf to God. They would have learned from the prophet how
far beyond them the Servant towered—as far as the church of the
ages, past, present, and future, towers beyond any little group of
Christians—but also to see in the destiny of the Servant the destiny
to which they themselves were called. But what they needed to
know was why the Servant of God should seem to be abandoned by
God into the hands of sinful men and should have to suffer, not for
his sin, but for his integrity.

There is an irony in the prophet's decision to put the answer to
this problem in the mouth of one of those who had stood among
the enemy, uncomprehending, seeing only the outward insignificance, repulsiveness, and offensiveness of the Servant, totally un-
touched by the Servant's witness to God, coldly deducing from his
misfortunes some hidden sin. Here is the stiff-necked, coldhearted,
unrepentant, and hypocritical Israelite at his worst. Here is the
Israelite who is blind and deaf to God and to his own destiny.
Should we say "Israelite"? He may be simply man in his blindness,
for the prophet's vision always reached beyond Israel to the world.
But something has broken through the resistance of this man. He
is no longer proud, indifferent, and rebellious against God. He has
been humbled. He has had his sins forgiven. The sinner has been

made righteous. He has been transformed out of his unfaithfulness into a true believer. How has it happened? What power has been at work to accomplish such redemption? The repentant sinner confesses that God's power was revealed to him (God laid bare his arm, v. 1) in the most utterly unexpected place, where neither he nor anyone else would have thought to look for it: in the suffering and dying Servant. Hidden within the deceptive outward form of that Servant was the knowledge that alone is able to make men truly righteous, the word and spirit of God in which God himself comes to man to establish his sovereignty and to claim him wholly for himself. But that word would never have been revealed to the sinner if there had not been a Servant who was willing to suffer and die for it.

The repentant sinner, looking back, sees the true meaning of suffering endured in faithfulness to God's word. It was the suffering deserved by the sinner that was borne by the righteous Servant. "He bore our griefs and carried our sorrows, was wounded for our transgressions and bruised for our iniquities." And the wonder of it was that, through what the Servant endured, the sinner was made whole. The blows that beat him to the ground brought healing to the hard-hearted transgressor. Strange, almost terrifyingly strange, but true! There seemed to be no other way in which God could conquer the obtuse sinner than through the willingness of his own beloved Servant to bear the pain and burden of the consequences of sin in his own body. Therefore, God asked of his Servant that he offer himself as a sacrifice for sin. Because it was the will of God that sin should be conquered and all men brought into obedience to him, the prophet had to go all the way through and say that God willed the Servant's wounds and grief (v. 10), willed them, not in anger at the Servant, but in love for the sinner.

One thing more had to be said, but it needed to be said by God rather than by the repentant sinner, so the prophet shifted in mid-verse to God as speaker. Suffering and death would not be the end for the Servant. His death would be more fruitful by far than other men's lives. In fact, it belonged to the nature of the Servant that he gained for himself a more glorious and abundant future by dying. In his death it was as though the word of God hidden in him were

released to find its dwelling place in other men, building them into
the body of the Servant of the future. Because he humbled himself,
God will exalt him, and in the day of redemption he will share with
God the riches and blessings of his kingdom.

The miracle of ch. 53 is that within so few words so much is said
on the profoundest problems of human existence. We can imagine
the power with which it sounded into the little community of suffering servants who surrounded the prophet. We know something
of what it meant among the early Christians in their understanding
of the death of Jesus and of the costliness of their own faithfulness.
But it has its fullest meaning for us when we no longer detach it
from the context in which it had its origin, but rather, hear it in its
place as the climax of the message of Second Isaiah both to his own
time and to us.

The first problem that confronts us in *v. 1* is the identification of
the speaker. We have called him the repentant sinner because of
what he tells us of himself. He does not seem to have been one of
those who beat and abused the Servant, but rather, to have been an
observer of all that happened, yet one who let it be done. He saw
him despised and found no reason to think him unworthy of the
scorn. He acknowledges himself a sinner who strayed from God like
a lost sheep and followed his own way stubbornly rather than God's
way. The parallel between the last half of ch. 52:15 and ch. 53:1,
the two verses saying much the same thing in different words, has
led to the identification of the "we" of v. 1 with the kings and
nations of ch. 52:15. The kings and nations saw finally what they
had never expected to see, the exaltation of the Servant, and seemingly parallel with this, the speaker in ch. 53:1 announces that what
has now been revealed to him would be unbelievable to most men:
"Who would have believed what we have heard?" This identification would be convincing, in fact it would be inescapable, if we
were to follow the customary practice and attach ch. 52:13-15 at the
opening of ch. 53. But that continuity being broken, we have to let
ch. 53 stand on its own feet, and the internal evidence points primarily to Israelites who constituted the blind and hostile persecuting
community, the "stubborn of heart" of ch. 46:12 and the "blind" of
ch. 42:18. There is a possibility, however, as we have already sug-

gested, that Second Isaiah draws no hard and fast line between Israelite sinners and sinners of the Gentiles, so that all alike might be included. After all, the Gentile sinners had done their part through the centuries in providing misfortunes for the Servant and in treating him with scorn. Whether the sinner be Israelite or Gentile or both, it makes no essential difference in the meaning of the chapter. What must *not* be done is to identify the speaker in ch. 53:1 ff. solely with the Gentiles or the kings of the Gentiles. It would be not only strange but highly unlikely for Second Isaiah to represent the kings of the nations as observing the sufferings of the Servant Israel and interpreting them in typical Israelite fashion (cf. Job's comforters) as God's just punishment of the sufferer's sins. Also, "my people" in v. 8 is an obstacle in the way of this interpretation.

The revelation of "the arm of the Lord" is everywhere in Second Isaiah the decisive action of God either in destroying his enemies or in bringing salvation. It is parallel with God's "coming" because it is God himself who rules "with his arm." In ch. 51:9 the prophet prays for God's arm to waken as in the creation and exodus. Always this action or coming of God has been future except in ch. 50:2 where God's coming was equated with his calling. But in ch. 53:1 the speaker reports the event as past. The arm of the Lord has been revealed! God has acted for man's salvation! And what he expects men to find incredible is that the revelation or action of God has taken place in the person and history of the Servant and specifically in his sufferings and death! There are frequent other passages in which the future redemption of Israel and the world is described as though it were past, but ch. 53 does not belong with them unless the suffering and death of the Servant are interpreted as yet to come, which is hard to accept in the light of so many references in the book to past and present actual suffering. Also, the focus in ch. 53 is upon what God has done in the self-offering of the Servant, and in the brief reference to the Servant's future triumph the motif of vindication and reward is predominant, rather than the motif of God's saving action. The triumph is future, and the suffering past. God has conquered man's sin and made the sinners righteous through the Servant's vicarious bearing of the punishment that was due the sinners and his communication to them of the righteousness that belonged to him in his relation with God.

At this point Second Isaiah breaks through to a new level of understanding of how God deals with sin in order to conquer it and of how God comes to man for his redemption. The transformation and triumph on which he had set his hopes, the future intervention of God that he expected at any moment, was already present at the point in history where the Servant in faithfulness to God's word gave himself freely and accepted whatever cost was required of him in suffering in order to break men's resistance to God. God acted for man's salvation, not in solitary grandeur apart from any human instrument, but in the action and passion of his Servant. The word that was the Servant's life and for which he suffered and died was not a word apart from God, but was the word of God in such a way that God's own power and presence were in it. The death of the Servant was his decisive *witness* to the word that was his life, and in this witness God's forgiveness broke through every barrier to achieve man's redemption. Though the immediate purpose of Second Isaiah was to interpret the present suffering of the Servant, he could have found instances in the past (e.g., Abraham's readiness to sacrifice his own future in Isaac; Jeremiah's acceptance of the cruelest misunderstanding and persecution rather than waver for a moment in his service of God) where the readiness of the Servant to die opened the way for God's triumph, and as a thoughtful pastor of a flock he may have had an eye on the future as well, warning the faithful that the Servant of God must ever go to his victory through suffering and death. He did not know how perfectly his words would one day describe the crucial event of all history when another and greater Servant would make himself an offering for sin and by his obedience break the power of evil over mankind, establishing God's rule on earth and bringing God's forgiveness, peace, and healing to the door of every man.

Whereas v. 1 has the character of an exclamation, *v. 2* begins a narrative in which the speaker seems to be describing a person who has long been present to his observation. Scholars differ in their impressions of this narrative. Some are so certain that it is the description of a historical person that they insist the Servant was an individual, search the records for the person to whom the description is most appropriate (with a wide range of identifications, from Moses to Jehoiakim), and even debate whether or not the sickness in v. 3 ("grief" in the RSV) was leprosy. Others (Gressmann[1]) remark the vagueness of the description, are certain that a historical person would not have been pictured in such general terms, and make of the Servant a dying and rising redeemer figure of the future. Volz points out that almost all possible misfortunes are attributed to the Servant—sickness, persecution, ugliness, loneliness, misunderstanding, public condemnation, blows of men, blows of God—and suggests that, like Jesus Christ in the New Testament church, he was conceived as the bearer of the sufferings and sorrows of all mankind. This mingling of vividness and vagueness, of the specific and the general, may be explained by the fact that the Servant has his existence both in individuals in the present and in a history that reaches from the dim origins of Israel through the present into the future.

The figure suggested by v. 2 is like a spindly, unhealthy-looking plant, struggling for its life in dry, hard-baked earth, seemingly in danger of withering and dying at any moment, not an inappropriate description of God's cause in Israel through the centuries. The lusty vigorous growths were usually pagan. The Servant of the word was consistently a minority development, with his existence threatened on every side. It seemed impossible that he should long survive—Elijah and the handful of the faithful in the ninth century, Amos and Hosea and the few who stood with them in the middle of the eighth century, Jeremiah fighting his lonely battle in the years of Judah's tragic end. The description fits, not the history of Israel as a whole, but only the history of the faithful Servant. Whenever the collective interpretation tries to make the details of ch. 53 fit the entire nation of Israel in its history, it becomes quickly involved in absurdities not only in the impossibility of attributing innocence and integrity to Israel in v. 9 but in almost every detail of the description. What does it mean to say that Israel had no comeliness or beauty that would attract anyone's interest or attention? Applied to the nation it is almost inane, but as a description of how a vigorous,

[1] Hugo Gressmann, *Der Messias* (Göttingen: Vandenhoeck & Ruprecht, 1929).

pleasure-loving unbeliever felt about people whose most earnest concern was their witness to God in word and action, it is full of meaning. Such people seem to him to lack all the qualities that are most graceful and delightful. They are like death's-heads at his feast. They are people with whom he does not care to associate. A slight emendation should be made in v. 2, changing "before him" to "before us."

V. 3 describes the repudiation of the Servant by the community as a whole. The best commentary on it is in ch. 66:5 where the "servants" of God who "tremble at his word" are hated and cast out by their brethren, hated because their brethren do not want to have the word of God setting in question their established way of life both in their religious practices and in their treatment of their fellow citizens (ch. 59). "A man of pains" is a better translation than "a man of sorrows" because the context is the violent expulsion of the Servant from the community. This context also demands that "sickness" be understood in the more general sense of bodily brokenness as a consequence of maltreatment. The Servant is pictured as a lonely, broken, helpless creature, so encompassed by misfortunes that he is a horror to his neighbors. They cannot even bear to look at him. This was perhaps in part due to the cruel interpretation of his misfortune, common not only in Israel but in all Oriental nations in the ancient world, as a sign of God's anger and rejection (cf. Job 19:14-19), but also to the general inclination of men to avoid any unpleasant sight. The passive verb "he was despised" alongside the active verb "we esteemed him not" seems to indicate that the speaker, although he took no active part in the persecution of the Servant, accepted the common judgment of society, had no understanding of his true nature, and so shared in the guilt of rejecting him.

With *v. 4* begins the reinterpretation of the Servant's sufferings in the light of God's revelation, or better perhaps, in the light of the redemption effected by the Servant's death. We have looked at them through the eyes of the unrepentant sinner; now we look at them through the eyes of the repentant and forgiven sinner. The misfortunes are still seen as a sign of the wrath of God, not God's wrath at the Servant, but God's wrath at the sinner. So begins the strange and mysterious exchange. The Servant who deserves blessing is cursed, and the sinner who deserves God's curse receives the Servant's blessing. To the minds of men it is unfair, unjust, unreasonable, a contradiction of what they conceive to be God's way of dealing with men in order to encourage virtue and discourage vice. It is the sinner who is destined to die and the righteous man to live, but here the righteous man has died the death of the sinner, and the sinner has been made righteous by the beholding of it. Unreasonable, wholly unexpected by any man, and yet the only way in which the bottomless gulf between the sinner and God can ever be bridged! Another logic than human logic is at work here, the divine logic, which confounds human logic (cf. the divine thoughts that are infinitely higher than human thoughts in ch. 55:9). And the Servant has to learn at least the ABC's of this divine logic that he may think God's thoughts after him and be guided by God's mind rather than his own. This is what makes the Servant's way so difficult in the world. The kind of logic at work in his words and actions differs from that of men who are blind and deaf to God, and the conflict between God's mind and man's mind comes to a focus where he has his life among his fellowmen. God has no other way of invading a world of men who are in rebellion against him that he may bring them to the free acceptance of his rule. Volz is right in asserting the centrality of the idea of substitution to the chapter, pointing out how often it is repeated in vs. 4-6, 8, 10-12. The same thing is said in no less than thirteen different ways: he suffered and died in our place, giving himself as a sacrifice for us that we might know the peace and blessing of God's forgiveness.

What creates perplexity for many in ch. 53, and not only here, is the assertion in vs. 6 and 10 that the Servant's suffering was God's will. "God laid on him the iniquity of us all." "It pleased the Lord to bruise him; he has put him to grief." They can accept an interpretation of the suffering in which it is freely borne by the Servant for his brethren and has profound redemptive consequences, but to say that it *pleased* God to make the Servant suffer seems to them to make God responsible directly for the brutal abuse. The statements in the text are open to serious misunderstanding if God's action is conceived as a kind of mechanical control of everything that happens in the world. But the Biblical understanding of God's relation to the world is personal rather than mechanical, intensely personal so far as men are concerned. God's willing and acting is always a willing and acting in the context of personal relationships. He does not establish his rule over men by an external compulsion, but waits with infinite patience for the response of a true obedience. What, then, if man withholds the response? Has man in his freedom the power not only to resist but even to defeat God's will in the world? God wills that sin should bring in its train destruction and death, but this, as Second Isaiah well knew, only restrains sin and does not overcome it. How, then, was God to reach man in his blindness and rebellion, penetrating past his defenses to his heart and shocking him awake to the horror that sin is not only for God but also for man? The answer lay in God's *sending* the man who was open to him, who trembled at his word both with fear and with joy, who already had his life in the truth of God, to speak his word and to be a witness to his righteousness in the midst of the sinners. But in the act of sending, whether it were Moses, Elijah, Amos, or Jeremiah, or any one of the nameless faithful, God already knew the cost to a man of going at his bidding and more than once he warned the prophets of it. The witness could not be given without the willingness to suffer. Therefore, God willed the suffering of his Servant because he willed his going no matter what it cost. There was no other way in which to overcome the resistance of man.

V. 7. The silence of the Servant through all his sufferings is a more powerful protest against the injustice of his captors than anything he could say. He does not need to defend himself, because no valid accusation has been made against him. It was not usual in Israel for a prisoner, guilty or innocent, to bear his punishment in silence. Therefore, the Servant's grim and unbroken silence, setting his face like flint and looking not to men but to God for his vindication (ch. 50:7), had in it an ominous and warning quality, a sign to some at least that something of great moment was happening here. It was the silence in which the Servant waited for God. The likeness of the lamb led to the slaughter is most likely a touch of Jeremiah in the portrait ("I was like a gentle lamb led to the slaughter," Jer. 11:19), but the silence of the lamb under the knives both of the shearers and of its slaughterers comes more likely from the conduct of Second Isaiah's own people under persecution. They were deprived first of their wool and then of their lives (cf. section on ch. 51:14).

V. 8 narrates the Servant's death. As in ch. 50 the language suggests a judicial process that implies that the official community with its constituted authorities was guilty of the death of the Servant. From the combined references to the shedding of innocent blood in ch. 59 and to the expulsion of the "servants" by their brethren in ch. 66, we might conclude that some were killed in the general violence attending the expulsion. But the two suggestions of judicial process are not to be ignored. The community apparently desired to make at least a pretense of justice in order to clear its conscience. This gives us some idea of the dimensions of the opposition. "Restraint" may be understood as imprisonment and "judgment" as the court of justice. "Taken away" may indicate the haste with which the proceedings were conducted. The question, "Who considered his generation?" ("generation" being used as in ch. 41:4 to signify history, the life history of the Servant) points to an unconcern of those who participated in the condemnation of the Servant to know anything about him. His judges were not interested in the truth about their prisoner, but only in being rid of him. The interpretation of the Servant's death as being "for the transgression of my people" identifies the "we" of vs. 1-6 as basically Israelites, although for Second Isaiah there could be Gentiles included in "God's people." Interpreters who identify the "we" with Gentiles alone have therefore to do something to evade the expression "my people." Torrey says that the kings of ch. 52:15 are still speaking in v. 8, and each confesses that the Servant died for *his* people, a strained interpretation. Others simply emend it to remove the first person suffix. But, as we have seen, the sudden shift in speaker is not unlike Second Isaiah (ch. 51:1-3) and occurs again unmistakably in v. 11. Following the rule that the text most difficult to explain is likely to be original (if it makes sense), we must retain the text as it is. The consequence is that the suffering of the Servant is seen to be at the hands of his Israelite brethren and not to be the more generalized suffering of Israel at the hands of its enemies.

V. 9. The fact that the grave of the Servant was among criminals shows once more that his death was an official execution. "With a rich man" is impossible, but with the addition of a single letter it becomes "with doers of evil," a perfect parallel to "wicked." The latter part of the verse may perhaps be taken as an echo of the false accusations against the Servant, that he had been guilty of violence and deceit. The court condemned an innocent man. But in doing so it condemned itself in the eyes of men and made them begin to ask questions about the conduct of the authorities. When selfish evil tries to masquerade as justice it prepares its own unmasking. Thus understood, the declaration of the Servant's innocence does not mean that he was sinless, but only that he was not guilty of any violence or deceit that warranted a death sentence. Second Isaiah would never have said this of Israel, but on the contrary, he continually accuses his people of violence and deceit of the grossest kind.

V. 10. The note on v. 7 has dealt with the recognition of the suffering as God's will, but it is significant that in v. 10 the freedom of the Servant in offering himself as a sacrifice for sin is set alongside God's willing of the sacrifice. As in Gethsemane, the will of God becomes the Servant's will, not by compulsion, but by the unconditional surrender of obedience. The Servant goes forward to the sacrifice confident that in some strange way this is the only road to God's victory. Without emendation the Hebrew can be read "when his life makes atonement for sin," the Hebrew *'asam* carrying the idea of substitution that is dominant in the chapter. It is not a sacrifice to God but a trespass-offering by which one makes good an offense that has been committed. There is no basis anywhere in the chapter for the later church doctrine of a payment made to God in order to assuage his wrath at man's sin. The second half of v. 10 says very simply that by his surrender to death the Servant prolongs and multiplies his life. He lives by dying. If he were unwilling to die in the service of God's word, he would soon perish from the earth. Applied to the Servant as we have understood the concept, as the faithful Servant of God in all generations, this truth is most impressive. Moreover, the seeing of a numerous offspring in the future is the promise made frequently to a lonely and humiliated Israel (chs. 44:1-5; 48:19; 49:5, 12, 18 ff.). Those who see an individual in the Servant have on their hands in this verse the resurrection of an individual from the dead, a somewhat embarrassing phenomenon if the chapter is to be retained as written by the prophet in the sixth century B.C. Volz solves the difficulty by detaching the chapter from the book and assigning it to an author in the fourth or third century. But this ignores all the marks of Second Isaiah's authorship. It would surely be surprising for a prophet to introduce for the first time a doctrine such as the resurrection of the dead in the incidental fashion in which it occurs here.

V. 11. The text furnishes serious difficulties, but its intention is reasonably clear. The Servant is assured by God that he will see the fruits of his toil and suffering. He will not spend himself in vain, a fear that apparently troubled some, according to ch. 49:4. The first line is one word short and the second one word too long. In ch. 51:7 the faithful are called "those who know righteousness." Perhaps "the righteous one" should be changed to "righteousness" and transferred to the end of the first line "he shall be satisfied when he knows righteousness," i.e., he shall be satisfied with God's salvation. The second line would then read, "my servant shall make many righteous." "Many" is one of those indefinite words that Second Isaiah loves to use. It is perhaps deliberately indefinite as it is when it is repeated in the New Testament, pointing not only to Israelites but also to the many beyond Israel who await their liberation and transformation. The words "to be accounted" in the RSV introduce a judicial idea that is alien to Second Isaiah and is nowhere present in the text. It may be translated "he made many righteous" or "he turned many to righteousness" or simply "he saved many" but not "he made many to be accounted righteous."

V. 12. The future exaltation of the Servant, promised him by God, has been described in earlier chapters and is only slightly touched on here. In ch. 41:2-3, 15, 25 he is to triumph over the nations. In ch. 42:1-7 he is to establish God's justice and mercy to the ends of the earth and to set all the prisoners free. In chs. 43 and 44 his sons and daughters are to be gathered from the ends of the earth and restored to their homeland, together with new believers from among the nations. In ch. 45 the wealth of the nations is to be poured out at the feet of the Servant. In ch. 51:3-6 Zion is to be transformed into a new Eden, and the old heavens and earth are to vanish with the coming of God's eternal kingdom. Against this background ch. 53:12 is very restrained when it says only that God will give the Servant an inheritance with the many and that he will "divide the spoil with the strong." "Spoil" carries with it here no connotation of plunder, but must be read in the light of ch. 45 as signifying the reversal in the fortunes of the Servant. He goes from humiliation to exaltation, from weakness to power, and from poverty to wealth. There is no idea present of a vengeance of Israel upon its enemies or of an enrichment of Israel at the expense of the Gentiles. All that Second Isaiah is concerned to say in v. 12 is that God will eventually vindicate his Servant. He who let himself be counted a criminal and went to his death for the sake of sinners will receive his justification from God.

The mention of the Servant's intercession for transgressors is significant because of the fact that we have such an unusual number of prayers of intercession for Israel in various parts of the book. Few examples of intercession are preserved in the writings of the earlier prophets. We know of Jeremiah's intercessions for his people from his hearing God's command to intercede no longer for Israel. Habakkuk lays the complaint of his people before God and mounts his watchtower to await God's reply. But it is Second Isaiah's voice that we hear most plainly in passionate intercession (chs. 51:9-11; 62; 63:15-19; 64), identifying himself with his people in their sin (ch. 64:5-6) and pleading with God to have mercy. The community of faith that gathered about him would have the same spirit, not separating itself self-righteously from its disapproving brethren and thinking only of its own salvation, but continually making intercession and taking upon itself a responsibility for the community as a whole. It is not inappropriate that the chapter ends on this note of intercession. The Servant who intercedes for his brothers begins thereby to take their sins upon his own shoulders and finds no point of return until the task of sin-bearing has been finished.

CHAPTER 54/ The first impression that ch. 54 makes on the reader is likely to be that it contrasts with ch. 53, like coming out of a shadowed place into the light. The note of triumph was not absent from ch. 53, but the emphasis was upon the costliness of the triumph. In ch. 54 there is jubilation from beginning to end. The sorrows of the past are remembered only as the dark background against which the joys of redemption are all the brighter. It is as though the prophet had had a vision of the New Jerusalem so real to him that its day seemed to have already come. The time of barrenness, desolation, and conflict is past. God's perfect rule has begun. The restored Jerusalem is more glorious by far than it has ever been before. Can this be the same prophet who a moment ago saw the Servant of God taking the dark road down into death in order to win his victory for his fellowmen? Not only is it the same prophet, recognizable by his language and style and also by his familiar themes, but one of the central themes of ch. 53 is repeated in ch. 54 in a different form. In chs. 49, 51, and 52 we have seen that Second Isaiah uses the figure of the Servant and the figure of Mother Jerusalem interchangeably to represent Israel. In ch. 53 the lonely, desolate, and seemingly hopeless Servant passed through death into a new and more fruitful life, exalted by God above the nations. In ch. 54, Mother Jerusalem, barren, humiliated, forsaken by her husband, afflicted, storm-tossed, comfortless, experiences an unbelievable transformation into a great and almost blindingly beautiful city, densely inhabited by her children and happy in her reunion with the husband of her youth. One thing that is not entirely clear is whether, as in many of the earlier chapters, this hope was for Israel as a whole in spite of its sin or whether it was focused upon the faithful alone. The final words of the chapter, "This is the heritage of the *servants* of the Lord and their vindication from me, says the Lord," suggest the latter. This is the first instance in which the prophet speaks of "servants" instead of "the Servant," which is significant in the light of ch. 65, where this change in terminology denotes an abandonment of hope for the nation as a whole and a fixing of all hope for the future upon the faithful. But the love of the prophet for his people and for his city was so great, like the love of God himself for them, that even when he was forced to narrow God's promises to the "servants," his heart reached out to compass all. It should not be forgotten that the "vision" of ch. 53 was of an ingathering of the *sinners* through the faithful Servant's witness.

It is hard to grasp that anyone could walk the hard, dark road that was Second Isaiah's lot and sing with joy as he does. One of the absurdities of the "Servant Songs" theory is the impression it creates that some four or more passages (usually denied to Second Isaiah) alone are songs and that there is nothing elsewhere in the book worthy to be called a song. Actually, from beginning to end the book is full of singing. More than one of the psalmists who enriched the praises of Israel may have learned to sing from this prophet. From time to time, when his thought of what God has in store for his people has lifted his spirit higher and higher, he soars out into a song of praise and calls on the whole creation to join him in his singing. But we must not be deceived by the joyfulness. It was a man of sorrows, acquainted with grief, despised and rejected of men, who sang like this and taught other men to sing. He sang, not because all things were going well with him, but because, even when all was darkest and death was staring him in the face, he was absolutely sure that God was reigning, so that at any moment the darkness would be at an end and the light would shine. The world around him might seem to be a chaos, but he knew that God did not intend a chaos and that he had only to wait to see God's new order. He lived as seeing the invisible. The reality of the new Jerusalem that he sets before our eyes in ch. 54 was the primary reality for him, and the wretched, paganized Jerusalem on which he looked out each morning was like a bad dream from which they would all one day awaken. Like Abraham in Heb., ch. 11, he was in search of a city that has foundations, whose maker and builder is God, and it was this vision of God's intention for man that made him such a troublesome disturber in the community where he lived. People who think that an eschatological hope makes a man sit down with folded hands to await the coming of the day of the Lord should study Second Isaiah with care. It was the intensity of his hope for Israel and for man that made him a revolutionist among men, a devastating critic of his society, who could not leave things as they were, even though his shaking of the existing order should cost him his life.

The contrast is built up between the barren mother who has not even once been in travail with a child and the great brood of children that suddenly surround her in the day of restoration. The identical theme is developed in ch. 49:19-23. Some interpreters have identified the desolate woman with the Israel of the exile and the married woman with postexilic Israel, deducing then that the prophet was referring to a higher birthrate among the exiles that had produced a more numerous Israel! But the multiplication of sons and daughters is part of the miraculous transformation, like the turning of Zion into Eden and the desert into a garden. In *v. 2* Jerusalem is likened to a tent that will no longer hold the family. A new and bigger tent has to be made, and with it longer ropes and stronger stakes. In fact, Jerusalem in its descendants will reach out to the ends of the earth and possess the nations for God. The rule of God and the rule of the Servant Israel were inseparable in Second Isaiah's mind, but already in chs. 42, 49, and 53, if not elsewhere, he had made it clear that Israel's rule would be the reflection on earth of God's own rule and not in any way like the rule of even the most beneficent tyrants that the world had known. One of the first effects of Israel's rule would be to restore not just Jerusalem but all the desolate cities (*v. 3*).

The prophet Hosea likened Yahweh and Israel to husband and wife. The early years in the wilderness, when the covenant was new, were a time of confidence and joy, but the later years in Palestine were darkened by the adultery of the wife and the breaking of the marriage relation. Hosea saw in God's love for Israel the hope of a restoration of the bond beyond the time of judgment and separation that were to serve as a discipline. This may well have been one of the sure words of God out of the past on which Second Isaiah based his faith. At least it can be said that he picks up Hosea's image and carries it forward, proclaiming that the time of judgment and discipline is at an end, that the covenant relation between Yahweh and Israel is about to be restored and all the promises of God embodied in the covenant fulfilled. The joy and fruitfulness of the new relation will be so great that the dark unhappy past will be forgotten. For Second Isaiah the covenant had in it no legal quality, but rather, was intensely personal, a relation not of equal partners but of the Sovereign Lord of the whole earth with little insignificant Israel, and with all mankind through Israel. How could so great a God wed himself to a people so obscure among the nations of the world? Yet this incredible fact was the secret of Israel's destiny, the source both of her humiliation and her glory. She had been chosen and called to be the bride of the Holy One, of the Creator of heaven and earth, whose holiness and love claimed from his bride the entire devotion of her heart and life. This devotion Israel had withheld in the past, refusing to let herself be bound to God alone and thinking to enrich her life from a variety of sources rather than from the one unseen God. Yet it is only in this narrow pass that a man can escape from a vague, generalized relation with a vague and generalized God into a personal relation of infinite depth in which his whole being is possessed and yet liberated, judged and yet justified, burdened with intolerable responsibilities and yet given the power to bear them with lightness and joy, called upon to die to himself and yet promised a life in which there is no death in time or eternity. God with Israel, as a husband with his wife, means God with man, and therefore man at the threshold of a life that has infinite new possibilities because henceforward it will be a life in fellowship with God. This was Second Isaiah's vision, but it was not to have its true power and to begin its invasion of the world until the vision came out of the future and became the reality of a life in human flesh and blood in Jesus Christ. In him the oneness of God with Israel, of God with man, was fulfilled, complete, and the doors were opened for man out of the old world into the new.

The return of the divine husband to his human wife is simply another form of the proclamation of forgiveness with which Second Isaiah began in ch. 40. Israel without God may be likened either to a wilderness or to a desolate, barren wife, and the return of God may be likened either to the flowing of waters in a desert or the restoration of the marriage relation with the creation of a numerous family. But everything depends first upon the love of God for Israel and his willingness to forgive, and second, upon an openness to the love of God on the part of Israel and a willingness to be forgiven.

Sometimes a chapter such as ch. 54 has been read as though God's forgiving of Israel were a divine act that occurred at a certain time and automatically brought the era of judgment to an end. But all the glowing promises of ch. 54 are dependent for their fulfillment upon God's call being answered, upon God's offer to renew the covenant being accepted, that is, upon the love of God so warmly represented being responded to with love. Where there is no such response, the time of judgment continues, and God is still experienced as wrath rather than love. The fact that the prophet speaks as though the turning point were past and the decision made must not deceive us into thinking that the day of redemption was as yet more than a hope and a vision for him.

The prophet's familiarity with the traditions of Israel that were ultimately to form the book of Genesis is evident again in his likening of his own time to the days of Noah (vs. 9 ff.). Torrey thinks that he uses the Priestly account in its final form and quotes this as evidence for a late date for the book. But the traditions were in circulation for centuries before they reached their ultimate construction, and their use is no sufficient basis for so important a conclusion. A man who had lived through the disasters of the first half of the sixth century might well feel that it had been like the days of the Flood all over again. God, in anger at the sin of man, had come close to blotting out his people. But as God saved a remnant through Noah to make a new beginning, so also in this evil time God had preserved a remnant to carry forward his purpose in a new day. The use of the Flood story, like the term "servants" in v. 17 points to an identification of the Noahite remnant with the reduced community of the faithful. It is to them and not to an unfaithful community that the promise is made that they shall never again experience such wrath and desolation. They are the people of the new covenant of peace who already know God's forgiveness and live under the promise of the rainbow.

The vision of the New Jerusalem with its walls and gates and towers resplendent with precious stones was to appear again in the book of Revelation in the New Testament, reminding us of the similarity between Second Isaiah and the Christian seer of visions. Both lived in dark times when it seemed impossible that a people of God should survive and both encouraged the faith of their people by setting before their eyes a vision of the holy city in which evil no longer has any power and God's righteousness, truth, and peace prevail over all. This was their way of saying: "God reigns and his purpose will ultimately be fulfilled. Evil, however mighty it may seem, will be overthrown." How could the city in which God's glory would actually be revealed on earth be other than paramount in beauty. The precious stones with which it is adorned are meant only to suggest the infinite beauty of a life that is wholly compassed by God. If the knowledge of God's truth and justice and love brings such joyous beauty into life now in the days of brokenness and darkness, what will it be like in the day of redemption when it is complete! Muilenburg draws our attention to the fact that there is no Temple in this new Jerusalem, a significant fact. In *v. 13,* the inhabitants of the new Jerusalem are described. They will all be *limmudim,* learners or disciples of God. This is the word used twice in ch. 50:4 by the Servant to describe himself, one who is constantly learning from God, one whose ear is open each morning to hear God's word for that day. Thus the community of those who "tremble at God's word" is an anticipation of the new Jerusalem. The city in which all are disciples is the offspring and fruition of the suffering Servant of the present. *Vs. 14-17* emphasize so strongly the freedom of the disciples in the new Jerusalem from fear of oppression, terror, or strife that they reflect vividly the perils that were being faced at the time of writing. God's servants may be exposed now to the attacks and false accusations of evil men, but the time will come when they will be invulnerable. The promise of the coming of that new day is to enable them to endure with patience their present wrongs. These last verses, understood in this way, form an additional link between chs. 54 and 53.

CHAPTER 55/ If ch. 54 is like the book of Revelation in

its vision of the New Jerusalem and the disciples of God with which it is to be populated, ch. 55 is like the Gospel of John in its passionate appeal to men to open their eyes to the richness of the gifts that God is offering so freely and to grasp them in faith and repentance while yet there is time. Also like the Gospel of John, it sees the gifts as offered through a particular channel, through the word of God in which resides the life-transforming power of God himself. The water, wine, milk, and bread that men are encouraged to "come and eat" are not gifts of God apart from God himself, just as the righteousness (or salvation) of God is not a quality of life bestowed upon men by God and then retained by them in independence of their relation with him. To know the righteousness of God (ch. 51:7) is to know God in his righteousness, that is, to live one's life in the openness and defenselessness of a personal relation with the God of righteousness so that God's righteousness is reflected in man. In the same way, to know the love of God is to respond to God's love in a personal relation, so that the responding love is like the love that is received from God. Throughout Second Isaiah water is a symbol of God's presence in the world. Waters flowing in the desert represent God's coming into the deserts of human life. So also, we may infer, the bread, wine, and milk that alone can give man life are symbols of the God for whom man hungers and thirsts because he has been so made that he is truly alive only when his whole being is responding in thankfulness and obedience to God. Man without God is an aching void for which the Easterner could find no closer likeness than the painful thirst of the body for water when it has been baked dry of its strength by the burning sun. He does not thirst for "something" from God; he thirsts for God, for the living God (cf. Ps. 42:2).

One of the weaknesses of Volz's commentary is that he makes Second Isaiah responsible for the idea that what Israel had to offer to the nations was essentially a great religion. It would be closer to the truth to say that for Second Isaiah the chief obstacle to the fulfillment of Israel's destiny was its trust in its religion and its religious institutions and its unwillingness to be the humble Servant of the word of God in which nothing less than God himself is offered to the world as its one and only possibility of life. Religion and religious institutions would be classified by Second Isaiah among those things that can be bought with money and effort. Men are always willing to spend some time and money on religion if they think that through it they can secure the things they want. But the water of life and the bread of life cannot be purchased or earned by any human effort. They have to be accepted as gifts that put one evermore in debt to God, gifts that one can never deserve, because in giving them God gives himself and in receiving them man receives God himself, the sovereign God, to be the center of his life.

That the gifts are free does not mean that man has to give nothing in return, but only that he can give nothing less than himself.

The address of the invitation in *v. 1* is purposely general; the "everyone who thirsts" is like the "whosoever" in John 3:16. It could not be more universal, for it belongs to the nature of man as *man* that just as his body thirsts continually for water, so does his whole being thirst continually for God, whether he knows it or not. The invitation goes out from God himself, for it is he who speaks through the voice of the prophet. And it is his speaking that is the channel through which the water, wine, milk, and bread flow out to men. To receive the gifts that conceal the presence and power of God himself one has only to *hear,* but hearing of this kind is not something done with the ear alone. Not without reason, in Hebrew "hear" and "obey" are expressed by the same word. Really to hear is to respond with heart and life. Deafness to God's word is what shuts man in upon himself and sends him stumbling on his way in blindness. Second Isaiah has had much to say about the blindness and deafness both of Israel and of mankind in general. His appeal now is for open ears to hear the word in which God comes and for open eyes to see the gifts that are offered in the word.

In the last chapter we dealt with the misunderstanding of Second Isaiah's jubilant announcing of God's forgiveness and redemption of Israel as though it were a divine act independent of the human response. One would almost think that in ch. 55 the prophet himself was guarding against this misconception. The thirsty man has to *come* to the waters or they flow in vain for him. He has to *take* (buy without money) what is offered and *eat.* He has to *incline his ear* and come. He has to *hear.* He has to *enter into a new covenant relation.* He has to *declare* what he knows and *be a witness* to the nations. He has to *seek, call, return.* The emphasis upon the freeness of God's gifts had perhaps an important polemic point to it in sixth-century Judah. Those who were opposed to Second Isaiah had great confidence in sacrifices as a means of securing God's favor for the nation. If only the people would make more generous sacrifices to God, God would certainly do more for them! But Second Isaiah knew that it is to the man whose hands and heart are empty that God can give himself most freely. The suggestion has been made that the invitation was to a royal feast. Water and milk are common and inexpensive articles with us, but not so in the ancient East. Water was often scarce and had to be paid for. A land flowing with milk was an Eden. But, like the bread and wine of the sacrament, they were more likely chosen for mention as the commonest articles of food and drink that were needed every day and yet indeed were symbols of the royal feast that God provides for all mankind if only they will take and eat.

V. 2 makes plain that this is no private address to the faithful few. Many of those addressed go hungry and thirsty because they seek to satisfy their need for God with that which is not God ("not bread"), perhaps with the worship of idols, or with any of those substitutes for God with which men have deceived themselves through the ages. They pay much and receive nothing, when with an open ear they might receive the greatest of blessings, life itself. "Fatness" to the Oriental denoted the choicest food. The fat was the part of the meat offered to God. In *v. 3* word and covenant are bound together. It was through God's revealing himself in his word and Israel's responding to that word in faith and obedience that the covenant relation came into being in the beginning. Israel's deafness to the word of God ruptured the relation. But now, God has spoken a new word not just for Israel but for all men through Israel, and the hearing of this new word will bring an everlasting covenant (cf. ch. 54:9-10) into being that will transform the whole earth, everlasting in contrast to the old covenant that was so tragically broken.

The closing phrase of v. 3 has been variously interpreted. Some have seen in it an introduction of the Davidic Messiah (Torrey), but Volz is right in his contention that the Messiah is strikingly absent from Second Isaiah at the very points where we would expect to hear of him. There is no room in Second Isaiah's theology for a Messiah in the sense of a royal individual who comes to rule, because the instrument of God's redemption in past, present, and future is the Servant. Chapter 45:1 may be taken as his declaration that there is no Messiah to be expected except the Servant. Thus in v. 3 what we have before us is a transfer of the hopes that centered upon the royal line of David to the people of the new covenant. By their hearing of the word, all God's promises to Israel in the past, to Abraham, to Moses, to David, become concentrated upon them. God's faithful love toward David has become his faithful love toward them. The force of this transfer is not felt unless one reads II Sam. 7:8-16; Ps. 89:20 ff.; and Jer. 33:20-22 and sees how completely the hopes that centered on David have been incorporated by Second Isaiah into his vision of the Servant's future. Volz contends that all political elements have been purged from the figure of the Servant and that Second Isaiah discarded the Messiah concept deliberately because of its nationalistic and political character. This keeps him from seeing that there is a royal aspect to the Servant that is a reflection in him of the royalty of God. But it is distinctly possible that Second Isaiah was setting the Servant in the place of the Messiah.

V. 4 speaks of David, but David has now become a symbol of the Servant so that what is said has to be applied, not to a king in the distant past, but to the Servant in the present and future. King David could hardly be called a witness to the nations of the earth or a leader and commander for them, but this is specifically the destiny to which Second Isaiah calls the Israel of his time. "You are my witnesses," God says to Israel in ch. 43:10, a light to the nations in chs. 42:6 and 49:6, from whom God's Torah goes forth to establish his rule of justice in chs. 42:1-4; 51:4-5. The Servant as conqueror and commander is seen most plainly in chs. 41 and 45, but also in other passages. Chapter 55:4 is important because of the way in which it brings the prophetic and regal aspects of the Servant's task together, witness and commander. The separation of the two has resulted not only in a fatal misconception of the Servant (e.g., Duhm's rabbinic teacher of the law) but also in a transfer to King Cyrus of many of the passages that are intended to describe the Servant in his role as commander of the peoples. It is a mistake to change the suffix "him" in v. 4 to "you" to correspond with "you" in vs. 3 and 5. This shift in person without any break in meaning is typical of Second Isaiah. *V. 5* makes clear that those addressed as "you" are to lead and command the peoples, calling nations that have been strangers to them. The position of the Servant in vs. 4 and 5 is like that in chs. 42:1-7; 44:1-5; 45:14-15; 49:1-23; 52:7-15. The nations of the earth recognize at last that there is no other God worthy of their worship and devotion except the God who has been revealed in Israel. The glory of Israel is nothing that she possesses in herself, but only the word that God speaks in and through her that holds within it the secret of life for all men.

V. 6. Again the appeal goes out to an Israel that has forgotten where its only true life is to be found that it turn from its own thoughts and its own ways before it is too late to seek and to call upon God in sincerity. *Now* is the moment of greatest opportunity. *Now* God's word is living and powerful and sounds into the midst of the community like a trumpet note. *Now* God offers food and drink to the hungry and thirsty. He is near. He is ready to be found. But there is no response, no one to answer when he calls (ch. 50:2); tomorrow he may hide himself again (ch. 45:15). Today he is waiting to forgive. But if his forgiving love is spurned, tomorrow there may be only his wrath that can be known, and this is what makes it so urgent that men should seek and call upon God and turn about in repentance at once. The appeal is made to the "wicked" and "the unrighteous man." Some commentators take these expressions as denoting only the sin of not seeking God where he is to be found (Frey). But if we have taken seriously Second Isaiah's picture of the blindness to God, the religious hypocrisy, the hatred of God's word, the readiness to persecute those who maintained their integrity, the indulgence in pagan practices, and the prevalence of violence and bloodshed that characterized the community, we shall give both words their full force. Only a radical repentance could save such a community from self-destruction.

Vs. 8 and 9 lay open the abyss between God and the community of men in which the prophet lived, the abyss that startled the first Isaiah when the holiness of God revealed to him the unholiness of the Israel in which he had his life (Isa., ch. 6). To be the people of God was to be called into a personal relation with him in which his holiness, justice, truth, and mercy would be reflected even though brokenly in the life of his people. The children of God would be fashioned in the likeness of their Father. Therefore the accusation: "Your thoughts are not my thoughts nor your ways my ways" is not an abstract statement of the infinite distance between God and man, but rather, a warning to Israel that its thoughts and ways are not those of a people in covenant with God. To let his word have its power in their heart and life would make their thoughts and ways like his thoughts and ways. To be God's people is to have his mind dwell in them in all its fullness. To make of the verses only a prophetic anticipation of the Kierkegaardian principle that the finite cannot comprehend the infinite is to miss the astounding element in Second Isaiah's concept of the Servant that sets it in line directly with the incarnation: God has chosen to create, in the midst of humanity, a people in whose heart and life he sets the word in which he himself is revealed in his holiness and love and in his life-transforming power. Heaven and earth do not remain forever in pitiless separation, but heaven comes to earth when a people on earth responds truly to the word that God speaks from heaven. But men lose not only God but all the possibilities of life that are hidden in God when they confuse their thoughts, their fallacious religious thoughts, and their ways, that is, the established practices of their community, with God's thoughts and ways and no longer recognize any need for repentance in themselves. They make God in their own image instead of letting the image of God be fashioned in them. To hear the word of God in truth would bring men ever afresh to a consciousness of the deadly abyss between themselves and God that can be bridged only by their responding with their whole being to God's offer of forgiveness.

It is evident now that the great passage about the power of God's word in *vs. 10-11* does not stand by itself in the chapter, but rather, comes as the climax of all that has been said. The "word" has been central from the beginning. And now, in conclusion, comes the promise that this word controls the future, for in it resides the power of God to transform the earth from a chaos into a kingdom of justice, truth, and peace, from a desert into a garden. It is peculiar that at this point Volz should choose to define the word of God on which Second Isaiah based all his hopes for Israel and for mankind as including a revelation in history and nature. It is impossible to find passages in Second Isaiah that give even the slightest support to such a generalized concept of revelation. Certainly the prophet points to the history of Israel, but always as the story of how God's word validated itself in events and never as though the history in itself, apart from God's word through his spokesmen, were a source of revelation. Also he sets great emphasis upon the fact that the God who chose Israel to be his people is the Creator of the heavens and the earth and the Lord of history in whose hands the most powerful nations are as nothing. All nature has been made for his praise. But there is no suggestion anywhere that the prophet looked to nature for a supplementary revelation. Nature was where the pagan prophets sought their inspiration. Both in the Old and in the New Testament the word in which God speaks to man, and speaking, comes to him, is absolutely unique as the means whereby God establishes a community in covenant with himself. To set alongside it a revelation of God in history and nature, which of necessity remains vague and ill-defined, in fact so vague and ill-defined that man in each generation can make of it what he will, introduces a confusion in which ultimately the unique word is lost from sight and hearing. Part of the uniqueness of the prophetic word is that, in distinction from all else that man through the ages has been pleased to call revelation, it confronts man as the expression of a mind that is not his mind and a will that is not his will, but rather, a mind and will that constantly demands a revolution in his human mind and will. The so-called revelations of nature and history are more comfortable and can be received without any such revolution in the present order of life. In fact, they are usually in some way or other the basis of a divine validation of the existing order.

As the rain and snow water the earth and make it fruitful, so the word of God, going forth among men, brings the life of man to its fruition and fulfillment. It is not necessary for the prophet to describe that fulfillment more fully. Chapter 54 had already done so quite adequately. God's purpose is that all mankind should be brought into willing obedience to him, and his instrument for the accomplishment of that purpose is his Servant. It is surprising that when Volz remarks that the word of God in ch. 55:11 has the same task assigned to it as Cyrus in ch. 48:14b, it does not occur to him that this equation of the Persian king with the word of God either reduces the Cyrus theory to an absurdity or makes of Second Isaiah a prophet who could see no difference between the power of Cyrus and the power of God's word. Although the power resides in the word, the word does not proceed on its way among men without a bearer. And the bearer is certainly not Cyrus but the Servant, whose mouth God makes to be a sharp sword (ch. 49:2). *Vs. 12-13* have traditionally been interpreted as a description of the return from Babylon, but the picture is thoroughly eschatological, describing the great restoration that is to take place in the day of redemption when God will gather not only Israel but all his people from the ends of the earth. That the chapter should have had a universal outlook in its earlier part, with Israel as witness, leader, and commander to all the nations of the earth, and then should end with a glowing representation of the little exodus from Babylon in 539 B.C. is most unlikely. The purpose of God of which the fulfillment is promised in v. 11 is a purpose that compasses the whole earth and has in it blessing for all men. At the prospect all nature bursts into a song of praise in vs. 12-13. The redemption of man is the redemption of God's creation. The mountains and the hills sing in thankfulness, and the trees clap their hands, keeping time with the singing. The image is that of a joyous festival in celebration of a victory. Nature as well as man is transformed. Instead of useless thorns and briers, which are the mark of desolation, the forests of cypress and myrtle are seen. Conquerors in the ancient world were accustomed to set up memorials that would preserve their names and tell of their conquests to future generations. The transformed earth would be the memorial of God's victory, and because it would last forever it would remain forever a sign to all of the power of the living God. What more convincing sign of the reality of God could there be than a transformed earth, a transformed community, and a transformed humanity? That the word of God has such power could not be questioned for Second Isaiah, for he and the faithful who stood with him had experienced it and known it for themselves. Yet what they knew was only the promise of what was yet to be.

CHAPTER 56/ Again we have to face the question of unity in the writings of Second Isaiah. It is not surprising that so many interpreters have been conscious of a sudden change in ch. 56. The first verse inverts the order that is usual in Second Isaiah. We expect to hear from him: God's salvation is near, therefore give ear to his word that creates in you a new righteousness and justice in anticipation of the glory yet to come. But in *ch. 56:1* the hearers are exhorted to keep justice and do righteousness that God's salvation may come. The difference may seem slight, but the second, inverted order is already moving in the direction of the later legalistic system of Judaism in which the coming of God's salvation was made to depend upon the nation's keeping of the law. Then in *v. 2* we find ourselves still more deeply involved in legalism when the keeping of the Sabbath is given a prominence and an efficaciousness that are utterly alien to Second Isaiah. In *vs. 3-7* attention is focused upon the status of proselytes and eunuchs in the congregation of Israel and in the worship of the Temple. Apparently the author is contending with an attempt to exclude them, or with a fear on the part of proselytes and eunuchs that they have no rightful share in Israel, most likely because of certain prohibitions they have found in the law (Deut. 23:1-8). However, the speaker assures them that as long as they keep the Sabbath and hold fast the covenant, they will be treated as true Israelites, in fact, they will have a name better than sons and daughters, and their sacrifices in the Temple will be most acceptable to God. The Temple will be called a house of prayer for all peoples.

There is nothing similar to this anywhere in chs. 40 to 55. The universalism is in line with the thought of Second Isaiah, but it is expressed in a totally different way. There is reason to think that he would feel the same about Sabbath-keeping as a way of securing God's favor as he does about sacrifices, fasting, and formal religious ceremonies in general. The problem of the status of proselytes and eunuchs in the congregation is not the kind of problem with which we have found Second Isaiah to be concerned. It would be strange if he should declare the sacrifices of proselytes and eunuchs acceptable to God when he had already denied that sacrifices had any place in the divinely established order of Israel's life (ch. 43:22-24; cf. ch. 66:3). And here not only the Sabbath but also the Temple is given a central place in his thought, although it has been wholly absent before this time. Torrey tries to rescue ch. 56:1 by joining it with vs. 7-8 and adding the three verses as a conclusion to ch. 55, an unhappy suggestion, since ch. 55 already has a much stronger and

more appropriate conclusion in vs. 12 and 13, and ch. 56:1, 7 contain
so much that is alien to Second Isaiah. Few interpreters have attempted to defend ch. 56:2-6 as coming from the pen of the same
author as chs. 40 to 55.

A fact, however, that has received too little attention is that ch.
56:1-7 is as alien in content to the author of chs. 56:8 to 66 as to the
author of chs. 40 to 55. The one passage in which the Sabbath is exalted as it is in ch. 56:1-7 is ch. 58:13-14, which is so clumsy an addition to ch. 58:1-12 that very few interpreters have had difficulty
in recognizing it as the work of a later hand. What prophet of any
stature or discernment would begin a sermon by declaring the
worthlessness of religious ceremonies and days of fasting as substitutes for the deeds of love, justice, and mercy that God requires of
his people and then would end it with a postscript in which he
agrees that if only God's people will keep the Sabbath, all will be
well! Chapters 56:1-7 and 58:13-14 are by a later writer, orthodox
and legalistic in contrast to Second Isaiah, but in sympathy with his
universal vision, who wished both to apply the prophet's principles
to a specific problem and to make his writings more acceptable in
the orthodox community. It is possible that the Cyrus and Babylon-
Chaldea insertions are by the same orthodox editor, since by means
of them Second Isaiah was brought into line with the official version of Israel's history as it is preserved by the Chronicler in the
book of Ezra. Interest in the Temple is central in the tradition of
the Chronicler.

Torrey is under the impression that once ch. 56:2-6 is removed,
the remaining text of chs. 56 to 66 follows so naturally upon chs. 40
to 55 that no break is perceptible. He even asserts that each chapter
follows so logically the one upon the other that we may conclude
that they were written in the order in which they now stand to form
a magnificent unified literary whole. In this he pushes his argument
too far, because even with the removal of chs. 56:1-7 and 58:13-14,
there remain certain differences, not so great as has been usually asserted, but nevertheless, differences, between chs. 40 to 55 and 56 to
66. Chapters 40 to 55 are like a great symphony whose themes were
announced in chs. 40 to 42, then developed and brought to their
climax in ch. 53, being constantly intertwined in the most skillful

fashion, with chs. 54 and 55 forming the triumphant conclusion. Chapters 56 to 66 are like briefer works by the same hand, containing many of the same themes but merely gathered into a collection rather than knit together into a unified work. They fall into four divisions: chs. 56:8 to 59, which are of a somber and intensely critical cast like ch. 48; chs. 60 to 62, which are jubilant with hope and promise like ch. 54; chs. 63 and 64, which are passionate intercessions like ch. 51:9-10; and chs. 65 and 66, which stand by themselves as addressed to the faithful in complete separation from the Israelite community. All four divisions have such close parallels in thought and language in chs. 40 to 55 that there would need to be very strong evidence to prevent their attribution to Second Isaiah. The differences are explicable by assuming that chs. 40 to 55 were composed by the prophet himself just as they stand, addressed by him to an Israel scattered across the face of the earth, and distributed widely among them in written form, whereas chs. 56 to 66 consist of briefer oracles delivered by him orally to the community in which he lived and later added to the original great work by himself or a disciple. This theory would explain why it has been so difficult to decide where the author of chs. 40 to 55 was located, whereas it is beyond dispute that the author of chs. 56 to 66 was in Jerusalem. Oracles written for distribution among scattered exiles would naturally be less likely to have in them clear indications of the locale of the writer. But oracles such as those in chs. 56 to 66, most or all of them spoken directly to the local community or offered as prayers for the local community, have in them much clearer indications of locale. Also, it is to be noted that wherever in chs. 40 to 55 the relation of the prophet to an immediate community in which he was meeting with opposition comes to the surface and we are able to recognize the features of that community, it is identical with the one that he addresses in chs. 56 to 66. The dramatic style in which he conceals himself, however, tends to conceal also the evidence of a specific locality.

How, then, has it come to pass that chs. 56 to 66 have been so widely denied to Second Isaiah, especially when the similarities of language, style, and thought have been so universally recognized? The primary initiator of the division was Bernhard Duhm, and we must examine the evidence that he, and others who followed him, found so convincing. First, he distinguishes rightly that in chs. 56 to 66 the prophet addresses a community that has long been established, a Jerusalem that is inhabited and no longer completely waste, that has sacrificial worship and fast days on which the people fight with each other, whose leaders are corrupt, and whose rich oppress the poor. But is this not the identical community that we have discerned behind the text of chs. 40 to 55 as the one in which the prophet was living when he wrote those chapters: people who with their leaders place a false trust in sacrifices and religious forms, who think they can teach God a thing or two about justice, who have not yet digested the message of the earlier prophets, and who, like their fathers, mingle pagan practices with their worship of Yahweh and become brutally hostile when a true prophetic word is spoken to them? What it looks like more than anything else is the direct continuation of the Jerusalem community as we see it at the beginning of the sixth century in the books of Jeremiah and Ezekiel. The features match remarkably. In chs. 40 to 55 as in chs. 56:8 to 66 we have the impression of a community that is still shattered and paralyzed by the disaster of 587 B.C., in which the Temple is still in ruins (ch. 64:11), although many are eager to rebuild it in some fashion (ch. 66:1), where many of the people are drastically impoverished, and where the old antithesis continues between a ceremonial religion indifferent to ethical issues and a prophetic faith that ruthlessly exposes the hypocrisy of any religion that offers God less than an unconditional obedience to his will in everyday life. In short, if we no longer assume that chs. 40 to 55 must have been written elsewhere than in Judah, we become free to recognize the similarity between those addressed most directly in chs. 40 to 55 and in chs. 56:8 to 66 and the absence of any essential difference in this respect.

A second argument of Duhm is that in chs. 56 to 66 God has no human helper like Cyrus but must himself overcome his enemies. But this ignores the fact that in chs. 40 to 55 God is represented both as acting alone to subdue his enemies and to effect salvation (chs. 40:10, 24; 42:13, etc.) and as acting through the Servant (chs. 41:2, 10, 15; 42:1-7; etc.). In chs. 46:12-13 and 48:11 God is described as bringing the day of redemption in spite of the sinfulness and unreadiness of the Servant. When the Cyrus passages are recognized as an orthodox intrusion, the two sections of the book become identical in this regard at least, that in neither of them has God any hope of a human helper except in his Servant Israel.

A third distinction claimed by Duhm for chs. 56 to 66 rests on a false interpretation of chs. 65 and 66. He identifies the enemies in these chapters as "heretics, bastard brothers, false brothers in the Jerusalem congregation who are about to build a rival temple and do not know where to build it," in short the schismatic Samaritans. But on what basis does he identify the author of ch. 66 with the orthodox Temple devotees in order to pronounce his enemies heretics and label the temple they propose to build a "rival" temple? He assumes that chs. 56 to 66 are being written in a later time in Judaism long after the Temple was rebuilt and that the enemies of the prophet could not possibly be the officials of the orthodox community. Many interpreters have followed him in this, accepting as fact the identification of the enemies with the rival Samaritan community of which we hear so much in Ezra and Nehemiah. But we have already become acquainted with paganizing Israelites in chs. 40 to 55 whose worship is unacceptable to their God (ch. 48:1ff.) and who fight bitterly against the prophet who attacks them (ch. 50:4-11). These are the people who are so certain that they are right, who sit in judgment upon those who refuse to conform to their ideas and practices, and condemn as fools and heretics all who agree with Second Isaiah. In chs. 65 and 66 the persecuting community whose name "Israel" is to be used henceforth by the persecuted only as a curse (ch. 65:15) and upon whom God's judgment falls, is situated within Jerusalem. In fact, the judgment comes upon the persecutors in the very Temple that they are building (ch. 66:5-6). The Jews who sympathized with the Samaritans in the time of Ezra were expelled from the Jerusalem community, but in ch. 66 the enemies of the prophet do the expelling. The prophet and his followers are the ones who are pronounced heretics.

The other arguments of Duhm fall to the ground when one refuses to make his assumptions. He declares that the author of chs. 56 to 66 had a high esteem for the Temple and sacrifices—in spite of the plain meaning of ch. 66:1-3—because he assigns the repudiated temple and sacrifices of ch. 66:1-3 to the "heretical breth-

ren" and makes the passage read as a defense of the true Temple
and sacrifices against these half-pagan upstarts; he attributes to him
a high esteem for the law, and especially the Sabbath law, because
he fails to recognize that chs. 56:1-7 and 58:13-14 are as alien to the
body of writings in chs. 56 to 66 as they are to chs. 40 to 55. He accuses the author of chs. 56 to 66 of showing his inferiority by quot-
ing constantly from Second Isaiah, an accusation that becomes ludicrous when the identity of authorship is recognized. One disciple of
Duhm who made a meticulous comparison of the language of the
two sections concluded that the author of chs. 56 to 66 was " a very
intimate disciple of Second Isaiah" who copied his master's style,
language, and thought so closely that it is almost impossible to detect
the difference! Except of course that a copyist *must* in the nature of
things be inferior!

Duhm thinks he can detect in some of Trito-Isaiah's "quotations"
of Second Isaiah a use of the same images with a slightly changed
meaning. It does not occur to him, or to Volz who follows him in
this claim, that an author such as Second Isaiah might himself vary
the significance of his images in different contexts. He does not operate with stereotyped images that must always have exactly the
same meaning. One last argument of Duhm's is simply incomprehensible: that the author of chs. 56 to 66, in distinction from
Second Isaiah, often speaks of himself, and takes as his task, first,
to show his people their sins, then to preach the gospel to the poor,
then to announce the approaching time of both salvation and vengeance. That the author in either part speaks often of himself would
be hard to prove. But the task described fits the Servant or the
prophet in chs. 40 to 55 quite as well as the author of chs. 56 to 66.
In short, to accept all of Duhm's arguments for the separation of
chs. 56 to 66 from chs. 40 to 55 one must approach chs. 40 to 55 with
the same inadequate assumptions with which Duhm himself ap-
proached them.

Volz has some additional arguments for the separation of chs. 56
to 66. He says that in chs. 56 to 66 a return of exiles is no longer
expected, which is evidence that the return is a thing of the past. But
this is true *only* on the assumption that the return anticipated in chs.
40 to 55 is that of the Babylonian exiles rather than an ingathering

of both Jews and Gentiles from the four corners of the earth. This great ingathering, so plainly heralded in chs. 40 to 55, is still anticipated in chs. 60:3-22; 61:5-6; 62:4-5, 10-12; 66:23. The isolated verse ch. 56:8 leaves upon our minds the impression that when it was written, some Jews had already returned from exile and that this was seen as a small anticipation of the much greater ingathering that was yet to come. But ch. 56:8 is a fragment whose origin is so uncertain that one dare not build heavily upon it. Again, Volz notes that whereas the nation is addressed in chs. 40 to 55, the oracles in chs. 56 to 66 seem to be directed to small groups. It is hard to think of any part of chs. 56:8 to 66 as being intended for any lesser audience than the nation as a whole. When Volz goes on to distinguish between the author of chs. 40 to 55 as "a prophet in the grand style" and the author of chs. 56 to 66 as "a preacher, pastor, leader of the exilic synagogue and pious psalmist" who busies himself mainly with the conflicts and detailed problems of the life of the synagogue and for whom the glory of Jerusalem is much more central than the glory of God, we can only confess that what he claims to see in the text is invisible to us, perhaps because we do not approach it with his assumptions. It should be remembered that he found in chs. 40 to 55 evidence that Second Isaiah, after returning to Palestine with the Babylonian exiles, heard a call to become a missionary to the Gentiles, and disregarding the angry objections of his countrymen, set out alone to turn the Gentile nations to God! In chs. 40 to 55 Second Isaiah definitely shows himself to be a preacher and pastor of the first rank and a psalmist, though hardly a pious one. We have seen reason to believe that he was leader of a group of faithful believers who knew righteousness and cherished God's Torah in their hearts (chs. 50:10; 51:1, 7), whereas their brothers turned a deaf ear to God (ch. 50:2) and were far from righteousness (ch. 46:12). Therefore, except for the identification of the faithful in chs. 65 and 66 with the members of a Babylonian synagogue, Volz's description of the prophet in chs. 56 to 66 fits quite adequately the prophet in chs. 40 to 55, and we need merely to distinguish between his massive prophetic work in chs. 40 to 55 and his occasional oracles in chs. 56 to 66.

Muilenburg's conviction that chs. 40 to 55 were written in Babylon and his recognition that chs. 56 to 66 were addressed to a community in Jerusalem make him certain that the two are by different authors. This certainly is reinforced for him by his inclusion of chs. 56:1-8 and 58:13-14 as integral to and even determinative of the character of the author of chs. 56 to 66. His statement (p. 383), "In chs. 40 to 55 the Jewish community is in exile in Babylon," takes no account of those sections of the Jewish community that were in Palestine, Egypt, and elsewhere in the sixth century, and when he continues, "in chs. 56 to 66 it is in Jerusalem," he conveys the impression that the "Jewish community" had now moved from Babylon to Jerusalem. This is the Chronicler's thesis, but it leaves too many facts out of account to be taken over in this manner. The simple truth is that if the assumption that chs. 40 to 55 were written in Babylon proves unfounded, the major ground for separating chs. 56 to 66 from chs. 40 to 55 is removed.

The background for the problem of the status of proselytes and eunuchs in the congregation is found in Deut. 23:1-8, where eunuchs and certain foreigners were excluded by law. In the Diaspora where Jews and Gentiles lived in such close proximity and Gentiles were attracted by the superiority of the Jewish religion, it was only natural that there should be greater tolerance than in Palestine where, from the time of Ezra, the zeal for a pure congregation created a narrowing of perspective and a spirit of exclusiveness. Conflict would arise when foreigners, and especially eunuchs, who had been received into the synagogue abroad came to Jerusalem for one of the religious festivals and found themselves excluded from the Temple. But this situation presupposes a date much later than the time of Second Isaiah. One can understand the supporter of the foreigner and eunuch appealing to the writings of Second Isaiah for the validation of his more liberal viewpoint, since Second Isaiah more than any other prophet had heralded the day when Gentiles would find their place within the people of God. Chapter 56:1-7 is, then, an oracle composed and inserted among the prophet's writings by this later universalist who probably felt that he was merely applying the principles of Second Isaiah to a specific situation. But he goes beyond Second Isaiah in his enthusiasm for the proselytes, promising them in the Temple a name *better* than sons and daughters. The passage has its greatest significance in showing the continuing influence of Second Isaiah in the orthodox community many years after his own time. Not all Israelites became narrow and exclusive. There remained a tradition, never completely covered over, in which it was not forgotten that since the God of Israel is the one Creator and Lord over all the earth, the door could not be closed against any man who was willing to accept the obligations of the covenant.

Whether *v. 8* is the conclusion of vs. 1-7 or stands by itself is uncertain. The formula, "Thus says the Lord God," suggests a new oracle. There has been nothing in the preceding verses about the gathering of the outcasts of Israel. This is the only passage in the whole of chs. 40 to 66 that posits a return of exiles as already having taken place. Elsewhere the ingathering is always future. The idea that in chs. 56:9 to 66 a return has taken place is based, not on any text which mentions it, but simply on the fact that the text implies the existence of a definite community of some kind in Jerusalem. We have already seen that such a community existed apart from any return. Also in v. 8 the outcasts who have been gathered and are to be gathered are Israelites and not Gentiles as in vs. 3-7. It is best, therefore, to take it as a fragmentary oracle that was included in the collection of Second Isaiah's occasional oracles but most likely comes from a later time.

Vs. 9-12 constitute an independent oracle that has nothing in common with vs. 1-7 or v. 8. It is also different from any that we have examined in chs. 40 to 55, the attack on false prophets having no parallel there. But it is quite wrong to say that it is different in tone from anything in chs. 40 to 55. It is biting and ferocious in its denunciation of prophets who fail to perform their office of watchmen over Israel, giving no warning to the nation of its dangers but instead indulging themselves with sleep, food, and drink. But it is no more biting than Second Isaiah's attacks on hypocritical religion and paganizing idolatry in earlier chapters. Also, as other passages show, degenerate prophets of this kind are a credible element in the community that Second Isaiah was facing. It would have been a strange Israelite community in the sixth century if there had been no false prophets in it. The exiles in Babylon and in Egypt had them, and undoubtedly there would be some left in Palestine. A single phrase,

"they have all turned to their own way," is an echo of the words
placed in the mouths of the repentant sinners in ch. 53:6 and is a
definite link with chs. 40 to 55. The most serious problem is that
these prophets seem to think they are living in a great day that will
continue indefinitely (v. 12), which sounds like a time of prosperity
rather than the meager and poverty-stricken days of Second Isaiah.
For this reason many have followed Ewald in dating the oracle in
preexilic times. But there is no reason to think that all were impoverished in sixth-century Jerusalem. Even in the worst situations
there are always some who manage to fare well. They are re-
proached in ch. 58 because they have no eyes to see the hunger,
nakedness, and homelessness of many of their brethren. The picture
of the false prophets becomes even more damning when we realize
that, patronized by the people of means, they were gorging themselves with food and drink in a community where many were starv-
ing. Second Isaiah's denunciation of their irresponsibility would not
make him beloved either by them or by their patrons. The tone of
ch. 56:9-13 is perfectly in keeping with the following chapter, and
it may well have been the introduction to it originally.

It is worthy of note that so many scholars have been inclined to
assign chs. 56:9 to 57:13 to preexilic times. They do so only because
they assume that "preexilic times" in Palestine came abruptly to an
end in 587 B.C. We need to be on our guard against expecting the
clear-cut lines that historians draw as the boundaries between epochs
to be present with the same sharpness in the day-to-day life of the
community. The disasters of 597 and 587 B.C. in Jerusalem were
very great. However, similar great disasters that did nothing more
than depress and dislocate the general order of the communities
have befallen nations large and small in both ancient and modern
times. The institutions of such communities remain, even though in
a damaged condition (e.g., sacrifices without a Temple), and the
habits of the people show a remarkable tenacity. Therefore, the impression of a "preexilic" community is actually evidence that the
community addressed by the prophet was the sixth-century continuation of the shattered Jerusalem and Judah that Jeremiah had
known. For those who remained in Palestine it was still "preexilic"
times.

It is noteworthy that the text begins to give much more difficulty in ch. 56:9-12 and in ch. 57. This and the incidence of words unfamiliar in chs. 40 to 55 have been taken to indicate a different author, but the directness with which these oracles are spoken to an immediate audience must be allowed its full weight. A prophet writing out his message in dramatic form for transmission to people at a distance would be likely to use somewhat different language from when he lashed semipagan fellow citizens with his tongue at close range. The former would also be better preserved than oracles that were perhaps only remembered by disciples and written down later.

V. 10. The blind watchmen remind us of the blind Servant in ch. 42:18 ff. who had no consciousness of the fires of God's judgment that were burning round him (ch. 42:25). Here the watchmen eat, drink, and sleep in great contentment while God summons the beasts of the forest to execute his judgment on them. In *v. 11* the identification of the dogs as shepherds of the people is rather clumsy and unnecessary, and the line may be a gloss to make sure that no one failed to understand who the dogs were. The last word in v. 11, translated in the RSV "one and all" is obscure, but from its use in Gen. 19:4 we may infer that here it means that each seeks his own profit to the very limit of his power. The dramatic scene in *v. 12,* where the false prophets have only to open their mouths to betray their stupidity and blindness, shows clearly the hand of Second Isaiah.

CHAPTER 57/ The caustic attacks of Second Isaiah

upon the folly of Israelites who forget their God and make for themselves idols and bow down in worship before them form the background for ch. 57. In the dramatic scenes of chs. 40 to 55 he painted word pictures of the idolaters, mocking their stupidity. But in ch. 57 the prophet stands face-to-face with the crude and paganized idolaters and addresses them directly. Because the practices at which he lashes out—child sacrifice, sexual orgies in the fertility cult, the offering of sacrifices to idols—are similar to those attacked by preexilic prophets, many interpreters have felt sure either that the

oracle must belong to the preexilic period (Volz) or that the prophet
is attributing to the postexilic congregation the sins of preexilic times
(Köhler, Orelli). But why do they assume that these deep-rooted
pagan practices suddenly ceased in Palestine with the destruction
of Jerusalem? The conduct of the Jews who fled to Egypt would
suggest that the disaster, which to many was a sign of the powerlessness of Yahweh, would lead to a wholesale increase of pagan worship and practices among Jews both in Palestine and in the exile
(Jer. 44:15). If Second Isaiah had his ministry in Palestine some-
time in the middle of the sixth century, the conditions he faced
religiously would be a continuation and perhaps an accentuation of
those pictured by Jeremiah and Ezekiel. There is no reason to think
that the people attacked in ch. 57 are any different from the treacherous Israelites of ch. 48:8 whose worship of the God of Israel was
a gigantic hypocrisy to Second Isaiah. Indulgence in pagan practices
may go on behind a facade of the most meticulous and proper observance of prescribed religious ceremonies. But such hypocrisy when
unmasked is dangerous. The prophet who spoke the words of ch. 57
into a living situation was taking his life in his hands to do it.

It is striking that interpreters without exception fail to see any
relation between the death of the "righteous" in *ch. 57:1* and the
death of the Servant in ch. 53. Volz remarks that v. 1 means no
more than that good men disappear in this evil time and insists that
the death of the righteous man was not the result of violence. But
v. 4 pictures the persecution of the righteous by their paganizing
brothers in terms parallel with those of ch. 50:6, and when the same
people are accused in ch. 59 of "shedding innocent blood," there
can hardly be any doubt that when the chapter attacking paganism
in Israel begins by reporting the death of the righteous, it is por-
traying them as the victims of pagan brutality. The connection with
ch. 53 is indicated by the emphasis upon no one giving any heed
and no one understanding what is happening when the righteous
die, an exact parallel to the heedlessness and blindness confessed by
those who speak in ch. 53:2-4. The Servant suffered and went to his
death, ignored by most of his fellow countrymen. The "righteous" is
not an individual, but a company, as is evident in the parallel term
"men of grace," and these are to be identified with the faithful of

chs. 50:10; 51:1, 7 and the servants who tremble at God's word in chs. 65:8-16; 66:2, 5. "Men of grace" is a significant title similar to "you who know righteousness" (ch. 51:7). Grace and righteousness are God's nature, and men who are open to him and cherish his word in their hearts have his grace and righteousness reflected in them. "Devout men" (RSV) is a weak translation suggesting the religiousness of the men rather than the grace of God manifest in them. That which makes them an offense to their brothers is that God himself in his grace and righteousness is revealed in their witness so that their brothers are brought under the judgment of God. The death of the righteous in such an evil time is not seen by the prophet to be entirely a misfortune. At least they are at peace and do not any longer have to face the conflict and humiliation of the faithful who must live on (cf. ch. 59:15). The beds in which they rest are their graves, perhaps a deliberate contrast to the beds in which the false prophets take their ease (ch. 56:10) and the beds of lust that figure so prominently in vs. 7-8.

The ferocity of the attack on paganizing Israelites in vs. 3 ff. should be compared with the bitter denunciation of the sacrifices offered, not to idols, but to Yahweh in ch. 66:3 and the castigation of very proper but empty ceremonies of the cult in ch. 58. Plainly the evil is not that Israelites desert the worship of Yahweh, but rather, that while they maintain all the prescribed ceremonies of the Yahwist cult, they indulge themselves also in all manner of heathenish practices. Israel was likened to a harlot by Hosea when she divided her favors in this way, and Second Isaiah uses the same image, harlot and sorceress. Unfaithfulness to God opens the door to rank superstition. The mockery of the idolaters at the righteous is true to life. They consider themselves worldly-wise, skilled in making a profit and a pleasure for themselves out of every situation, keeping one foot in each of two worlds in order to reap the advantages of both. The righteous, with their offensive one-sidedness, surrendering worldly advantages and making themselves objectionable to the society of their time, and particularly to people in places of influence, for the sake of uncompromising faithfulness to their God, seem to them to be fools who ought to be discouraged with ridicule and scorn, and if necessary with blows. *V. 5* refers to the fertility cult to which the people looked for fruitfulness for their land and prosperity in their business, and to child sacrifice, still practiced secretly, particularly in bad times when some great offering seemed necessary in order to appease the wrath of the gods. The reference in *v. 6a* is obscure. There is a play on words, the consonants of the word translated "smooth stones" being the same as those for "portion." The smooth stones may be images or the smoothness may suggest deceit or slipperiness. This is what a false Israel has chosen as its "portion" instead of the life of the covenant. Here they offer their sacrifices. The interjection at the end of v. 6, "Is it for these things that I am to have compassion?" has been suspected of being a gloss, but it is perfectly in keeping with the caustic tone of God's address. It uses the key word with which the prophet announced God's forgiveness in ch. 40, "comfort, have compassion, encourage." And now God asks, somewhat sarcastically, "Do you think that your pagan practices will draw forth my compassion?"

With child sacrifices in the valleys and the fertility cult on the top of every hill, the heights and depths of the land are polluted with idolatry. The text of *v. 8* is uncertain, but it clearly continues a description of the fertility cult. The image of the god is behind the door. Some have seen in this line a reference to ancestor worship in the home, but that would break the continuity of the passage, which portrays a public cult. Both Torrey and Volz think that *v. 9* has a political significance, presents being taken to some king and ambassadors being sent to enter into agreements with a foreign power. They justify the sudden change of theme by the fact that in preexilic times political compacts with other countries usually involved participation in the worship of their gods. The two forms of national adultery for Hosea and Jeremiah were the fertility cult and political alliances. But the political theme has no parallel elsewhere in Second Isaiah and enters with a disturbing abruptness here. Therefore, it is better to assume that the description of pagan practices continues in v. 9, gifts being offered to "Molech" or "Milkom." Messengers are even sent far off to sacrifice to distant gods, but such abasement to idols is actually a bowing of oneself down to Sheol, a descent into death. "You were wearied with the length of your journey" (*v. 10*) is sarcasm, the journey being into the depths

of Sheol and despair. But the blindness of the idolaters is such that
they do not even recognize their own despair. They imagine that
they are finding new life and strength from the gods they worship.
But this is a lie, a self-deception to which they are victims in their
idolatry. False gods produce men who no longer know the truth
about themselves. "Whom did you dread and fear that you were
so deceived?" is a rhetorical question, the preceding verses having
already given the answer, and has the force, "How could you let
yourselves be terrified into worshiping such false gods?" It was
men's fear of what harm such gods might do that led them into
superstitious practices. But no Israelite who remembered who his
God was, the one and only Lord of heaven and earth, could ever
be captured by such fear. The fear of the God of Israel cast out all
other fears of gods or men. The source of Israel's sin was a forgetting, a failing to set their minds (hearts) on God. The last line of
v. 11 is difficult: "Am I not (or have I not been) silent and hidden
(changing the vowels of this word) and you do not fear me?" This
may refer to the time of God's wrath in which he has been silent
and hidden, so that the Israelites have thought themselves deserted
by him and have turned to other gods. Or it may mean that they
do not fear him because he seems to them to be silent and hidden
now. But in this as well they are mistaken, for even in this very
hour God is revealed in his word, laying bare the truth concerning
his people and coming upon them in judgment.

The sarcastic or ironical tone, heard earlier, alone makes *v. 12*
comprehensible (so also Muilenburg). The "righteousness" of Israel
of which God will tell is the very reverse of righteousness. He will
expose their works. And in that moment nothing will be able to
save Israel. The gods in whom they have trusted will be helpless.
A breath of wind would be sufficient to carry them away. Volz ends
the oracle at this point, treating the last two lines of *v. 13* as an intrusion, because they seem to be directed to the faithful, whereas,
the oracle as a whole is addressed to the nation. But he forgets that
the nation included both the unfaithful and the faithful, and having
begun the oracle with a word not only *about* the righteous but *to*
the righteous, it is not inappropriate that there should be a word of
encouragement to them again in v. 13. Also, the promise that "he

who takes refuge in me shall possess the land" is a warning to the unrighteous Israelites that by their worship of other gods they will forfeit their destiny and their inheritance. "He who takes refuge in me" is another synonym for "He who trembles at my word." Chapter 57 is closely related to ch. 65, where the paganizing Israelites are consigned to destruction and the inheritance of Israel is promised to the faithful alone. In ch. 57 this final breach has not yet been made. There is still hope of healing for the nation in vs. 16 ff.

The transition to the very different mood of *vs. 14 ff.* is made in v. 13 with the change of focus from the idolaters to the faithful. The repetition of the opening verb, the image of "the way," the emphasis upon God's majesty and holiness, and the promise of his presence with the humble to be their strength, are all echoes of familiar passages in chs. 40 to 55. (Muilenburg notes the parallels and the very close relation.) Those who deny these chapters to Second Isaiah and assert that the author of ch. 57 was imitating Second Isaiah must explain how such a second-rate prophet could speak with incisiveness and fearlessness for God into the desperate situation of his society, and if he was not Second Isaiah, show himself quite the equal of Second Isaiah in integrity and courage? Also, Volz informs us that whereas the "way" in chs. 40 to 55 was the road for the *Babylonian* exiles through the desert, the "way" in ch. 57:14 has a purely eschatological significance, being merely the road by which God's salvation reaches his people. This he finds necessary because he dates vs. 14-20 long after the "return." But there is no reason to assign the "way" any different meaning here than it has in ch. 40:3-5 and elsewhere, the miraculous road across mountains and seas by which God comes to his people, bringing with him not only the scattered Israelites but also the redeemed of the nations. Sins such as those of the Judean community are a stumbling block in the way of God's redemption. Mention of the stumbling block helps to link v. 14 with vs. 1-13. The transcendence and eternity of God stand in contrast to the puny, perishable character of the gods that the people have been worshiping, just as the holiness of God brings into stark relief the unholiness of his people. But where the Creator and Lord of the universe comes upon a humble and contrite heart, he makes it his dwelling place and becomes the source of an unending and unconquerable strength to these humble souls that seem to be bowed so low. (Cf. chs. 40:28-31; 66:2.)

V. 16. As in earlier chapters, God promises that in spite of the sin of Israel, the days of his wrath will not last forever. This does not say that the sinners will find themselves sharing in the day of salvation regardless of their sin, but only that the sin of man will not forever obstruct the saving purpose of God. Beyond wrath, and even in the wrath itself, there is mercy, and the intention of the days of wrath is to prepare God's people for the day of mercy. The sinner has to be healed of his sin, and for that healing to take place there has to be a repentance. Verse 16b brings creation and redemption into close relation. The spirits of men proceed from God and are his creation. Even in their depravity they remain his creatures and the objects of his loving concern. He may discipline them with judgment (*v. 17*), but his purpose throughout is their redemption. The last line of v. 17, like ch. 42:25 and other passages, expresses the failure of God's heavy judgments to turn man to repentance. The Israel of Second Isaiah was no improvement upon the Israel of Jeremiah. But even though God sees the full depravity of Israel, the promise remains that he will heal his people of their sin and lead them into a new time of consolation. Torrey is right in his assertion that the consolation is "for him and his mourners," the latter signifying all those who are in mourning at the plight of the nation. "Creating the fruit of the lips," which is a strangely complicated way of saying that God gives his spokesmen the message (cf. chs. 49:2; 51:16; 59:21), introduces the universal proclamation of peace in *v. 19*. In the brief phrase, "Peace, to the far and to the near," he sums up his vision of a world and a humanity in which God's righteousness has triumphed. But as he finishes, his mind reverts to the present grim prospect of an Israel and a world in the grip of evil. This is the reality that has to be faced without faltering. The evil lives of men seem to him like a great ocean that is never at rest, the waves battling each other incessantly and tossing up all manner of dirt on the shore. As long as men remain in their wickedness there is no prospect of peace for them. The chapter closes with the same ominous warning as ch. 48.

CHAPTER 58 / Chapter 58, like ch. 57, has to be understood, not as a literary composition primarily, but as direct address to a single religious community. God speaks through the mouth of the prophet to his people. The first person pronoun in the opening verses denotes not the prophet (as Volz assumes), but God. For Torrey the chapter is an imaginary dialogue discussing the relative importance of the faithful observance of a ritual, taking the subject of fasting as typical. For Volz the chapter is a two-stage answer of a postexilic synagogue leader to the congregational problem of how to observe a fast day so as to secure the favor of God. Neither interpreter grasps the dimensions of the passage, the one making it a cool, somewhat philosophical discussion, the other reducing it to "pastoral instructions for synagogue life." They do not discern that here in a very specific situation a prophet lets God's word of judgment and mercy sound faithfully into the life of his people, and therefore into the life of all men for all time to come. His concern is not with defining the true character of fasting. Rather, he seeks to expose the hypocrisy of prayers and fastings that create the appearance of deep religious earnestness, but in their insincerity are just another expression of the community's total incomprehension of God.

The fasting is merely the surface expression of the deep sickness of which the nation is dying, its blindness to the true nature of the God whom it professes to worship. God looks upon the heart and life and is not content with anything less than the trust and obedience of his people. He cannot be deceived by ostentatious appearances of humility, a whole community clothed in sackcloth and sprinkled with ashes, all keeping their heads properly bowed as though in submission to God. They are no more humble in the sight of God than a field of bulrushes with their heads bent! (Note the typical sharpness of the sarcasm.) God knows that in their fasting they are concerned only to establish religious merit for themselves and to make a claim upon him. "We have fasted for you, so why do you not do something for us?" The fasting is to please themselves, not God. The prayers they make on the fast day never reach

God because they are no true prayers at all. Their heartlessness and cruelty toward their brothers in the very midst of their fasting reveal the true state of their hearts. Obedience to the will of God, which would mean taking decisive action about the problems of poverty and oppression in the life of the community, is the last thing they think of. Therefore, no matter how they multiply their religious ceremonies God's hand in judgment will still rest heavily upon them. There can be no deliverance, no redemption, until there is a people ready to respond to God with complete sincerity.

The inferiority of the author of ch. 58 to Second Isaiah has been claimed by some interpreters on the score that whereas Second Isaiah offers God's grace and forgiveness as his free gift to faith, the "later writer" thinks his people can merit God's salvation and actually bring it to pass by performing works of love and mercy. It would be as reasonable to say the same of Jesus because of his words to the religious lawyer, "This do and thou shalt live" (Luke 10:37). The total context has to be kept in view, and there it is made sufficiently plain, perhaps too plain for some of the hearers, that in this oracle they are confronted with a God who has great blessings in store for man, who is eager that his light should shine in all man's darkness, but who will leave him in darkness and despair until he is willing to open his life to God in that costly way that makes it open also to his brother. One of the unique features of the Biblical faith is that there is no genuine relation with God that is not at the same time a relation with the brother. No man can know God and close his heart against his brother. This was what the Israelites of Second Isaiah's day did not understand. They thought that by the performance of certain religious ceremonies they could repair their relation with God, but they were not prepared for the changes in their ways of dealing with each other, and particularly with their more needy brethren in the community, that would be demanded by a true covenant relation with their God.

The opening words, "Cry aloud, spare not," are directed by God to an undefined audience, like ch. 40:1, 9. Whoever hears is expected to obey and to become the messenger of the word from God that follows. We may be assured that the prophet himself "lifted up his voice like a trumpet." We have already heard the trumpet notes in ch. 57, sufficiently piercing to wake the dead. Now the task is to tear away the thin veneer of religious piety with which the community deceives itself and reveal the flagrant indifference to God's will that actually characterizes its life. What the prophet proceeds to describe is a people that has the appearance of earnest piety. "They seek me daily" means that daily they engage in the worship of God. Volz interprets *v. 2* as though it were the "leader of the synagogue" to whom the members went daily with their religious questions. But God is the speaker throughout. The worshipers act as though nothing gave them more joy than to be instructed in God's ways. Not only do they put on the appearance of righteousness and innocence but they profess that they want to hear God's word of righteous judgment (appropriate to a day of fasting and repentance) and to be brought into a closer relation with God. Nearness to God, they say, is their delight, but actually they are in flight from God and dread nothing more than that they should be brought face to face with him in his holiness and righteousness. There is a striking likeness between the people described here and the Pharisee pictured in Jesus' parable in Luke 18:10 ff. They expect by their performance of religious duties to lay God under obligation, and when they see no clear evidence of God's response and God's recognition of their righteousness, they begin to feel that he has been unfair to them. He asked for humility. Have they not shown it abundantly? The direct quotation by which the prophet lets them condemn themselves out of their own mouths (as in ch. 56:12) is a clear mark of Second Isaiah's style.

Verse 3b begins God's exposure of the hypocrisy of the fasting. "Behold," here and in v. 4, has the force of "look with fresh eyes at what you are really doing. See yourselves as I see you." The first criticism is that the fasting is a pleasure to them. Fasting was intended as an acute expression of man's humiliation before God, of man's acknowledgment of his sins, and of his earnestness in seeking God's favor and pardon. To enjoy fasting was an immediate evidence of its insincerity. A person who enjoys confessing his sins is not coming before God with an honest confession, but rather, is giving a performance before men (or perhaps merely before himself) that is intended to demonstrate his religiousness. The second criticism employs a debatable expression. It may be translated "and oppress all your workers" (RSV), which would be in line with vs. 6 ff., accusing them of laying heavy exactions on their workers at the very time that they themselves were fasting. But this forms a poor parallel to the first half of the line. Torrey translates it "and exact in full your own profit," which is a better parallel but leaves vague what connection their profit had with their fasting. The suggestion may be that they extort a profit for themselves even out of the fast day.

The third criticism goes farther: their motive in the fasting is not to be at peace with God and man, but is itself contentious, causing strife and conflict and leading to the striking of blows. This is plainly something more than a quarrelsome mood that causes a day of public fasting to degenerate into a public brawl. We have heard of contention in ch. 57, in which the righteous are being mocked for their righteousness, and we shall hear of strife again in ch. 59, this time leading to bloodshed, with men being attacked because they refuse to conform to the evil practices of the community (ch. 59:15). We have reason to expect that the strife, contention, and cruel blows mentioned in ch. 58 relate to the same incidents. The fast day is intended to put the people whom the prophet calls "the righteous" in the wrong and to demonstrate that the opponents are more righteous and godly then they. If the prophet and his "righteous" believers refused to conform to the fast day and to take part in the public performance, as we may be reasonably assured would be the case, then steps would be taken to compel them to conform or to punish them for their nonconformity. If men could be put in the public stocks and made objects of ridicule to the population for failing to conform to the Sabbath law in seventeenth-century New England, we can believe that refusal to participate in a public fast day might be treated as a severe offense in Judah in the sixth century B.C. A fast day could thus be a powerful weapon in the hands of pseudo-orthodox authorities with which to put their opponents in the wrong legally and to strike a blow against a movement such as that which was centering round the person of Second Isaiah. Our chapter would thus be the prophet's answer to the attack and v. 3 the unmasking of the hypocrisy of using a fast day for such a purpose. *V. 4b* can be translated: "You do not fast with the intention that it be a day on which your voice is heard by God."

There has been disagreement whether the prophet rejects the institution of fasting totally or just the perversion of it. The question is parallel with that of his attitude to sacrifice. In chs. 43:22-24 and 66:3 he seems to deny any validity to sacrifice, and when here in vs. 6 ff. he describes the "fast" that would be acceptable to God, it has in it none of the customary observances. It consists first of all in the release of all who are being enslaved or oppressed by their brothers, and then in the sharing of bread, clothing, and housing with the poverty-stricken. We see before us a community in which many have become so poor that they have been sold, or in their need have sold themselves, into slavery. The community has become sharply divided into the comfortable and the dispossessed, and as usually happens when that is the case, the comfortable consciously or unconsciously separate themselves from the dispossessed in their housing, social activities, and even their religious observances so that they may not be disturbed by unpleasant sights. They "hide themselves from their own flesh." If the prophet and many of the faithful had their locale among these impoverished brethren, it would explain some of the contempt and indifference with which they were treated by the official community and why there was no one to speak for them when they were brought before the court on some trumped-up charge. In the light of *v. 7*, where else would we expect the prophet to be? The care of the hungry, naked, and homeless poor would be his unceasing concern. This would greatly increase the fear of the authorities that his inflammatory oracles might have a serious effect in stirring revolution among the lower classes. Oppressors do not like preachers to talk publicly about freedom for the oppressed.

Vs. 8-9a, with their promise of light and healing, do not make God's response the reward of good deeds. Primarily they say that there is no hope of any response or blessing from God until Israelites show a willingness to be a people of God with a compassion for each other like the compassion that they expect from God. Their prayers cannot be heard by God until the openness of their hearts to God is evidenced by the openness of their hearts to their brothers. The promise of salvation is only to an Israel that returns with all its heart to God. The repetition of the thought of vs. 6 to 9a in *vs. 9b to 12* is not unexpected in Second Isaiah. He drives his points home by constant repetition, yet always adding something more in the repeating of it. Here in v. 9b he adds to the number of the sins to be abandoned by the community "the pointing of the finger and slander." "The pointing of the finger" is the self-righteous sitting in judgment upon others. Slander is the customary weapon of the self-righteous hypocrite to assure himself that he is superior to those who challenge his claim to righteousness. The portrait of Second Isaiah's religious opponents becomes ever more clearly etched, and its features are consistent throughout the chapters from the very beginning in ch. 40:14.

The promise to a faithful community draws together a variety of images: light in darkness, the guidance of God, good things, strong bones, a watered garden, an unfailing spring, the rebuilding of ruins on ancient foundations, the repair of broken walls, the restoration of streets of homes. We may assume that what is promised represents what is lacking in the present reality, and so we may extract from these images a picture of the city as the prophet knew it: a community in spiritual darkness without the guidance of God, living an impoverished life among the ruins of its ancient buildings, unprotected from marauders because of its broken walls, with many of its people living in rude shelters, its existence more like that of a desert than a garden. This is exactly what we would expect Jerusalem to be like in the middle of the sixth century B.C. But in spite of the ruins, the surrounding land was still being farmed, and all the necessary forms of business would be carried on with the resources available. Not all were poor and not all lived in hovels and caves. But no one could forget for a single day that this was a land that had fallen into the depths and still had no clear sign of any change in its fortunes.

Vs. 13-14 copy vs. 9b to 12 in form, but with a very different content. Their inappropriateness has already been pointed out in the section on ch. 56:1-7 where the Sabbath is exalted in a similar fashion. Volz writes a long note on the Sabbath being the glory of Old Testament religion and retains the verses as integral to the chapter, but this is possible for him only because he so completely misunderstands vs. 1-12. It makes nonsense of the prophet's sermon to have him reject a religious observance such as fasting because it has become a substitute for works of love and mercy and then add at the end a note to the effect that if only the members of the nation are scrupulous in the keeping of the Sabbath, God will reward them abundantly. The Sabbath was the enthusiasm of a later orthodox community, not of Second Isaiah.

CHAPTER 59/ Chapters 56:9 to 59 seem to belong closely together. Second Isaiah was almost overwhelmed by the evil of the community. It appeared to him like the angry waves of a great sea that is never still. The problem was forced upon his mind: how can God fulfill his agelong purpose for Israel, and for the world through Israel, in the face of such persistent evil? And yet he was as sure of God's victory as he was of the present wickedness of the nation. God's word, at work in the heart of Israel from the beginning and still at work there, must eventually accomplish that for which it was sent. Chapter 59:21, concerning the promise that resides in the word, is not an alien oracle that somehow became attached to the chapter (Muilenburg and others), but is its intended conclusion and essential to the understanding of the prophet's mind. The assertion in v. 1 that God is ready to deliver his people and that his ear is open to their cry is based upon the word that "endures forever" (ch. 40:8). God is more eager for the day of redemption than Israel is (ch. 42:13-14). It would long since have come had it not been for the blindness and sinfulness of Israel (ch. 48:18-19). God, however, cannot let his purpose be forever held back and defeated by the sin of man. If Israel continues unready to be the instrument of salvation, then God will have to bring it himself without Israel. This is the same solution to the dilemma that was offered in ch. 48. For his own name's sake and in spite of the sin of his people God will carry his purpose to victory.

There is no hint in ch. 59, or in ch. 48, of the solution that the prophet gives in ch. 53 to this same dilemma. In chs. 48 and 59 he simply cuts the Gordian knot. However great the sin of Israel, he will not surrender his confidence in the coming salvation. Yet it remains impossible for him to think that an unholy Israel should abide in the presence of a holy God or to conceive any other way of getting rid of sin except through repentance and forgiveness. Perhaps it was in the time of suffering for the faithful, which is reflected in chs. 57 to 59 and in both chs. 50 and 66, when he saw a handful of Israelites scorned by their brethren and willing to die in faithfulness to God's word, that it came to him how God so strangely wins his victory over sin. Israel may have failed God tragically, but within Israel there is a people of the word, ready to be his servants regardless of the cost. But in ch. 59 there is as yet no sign of this answer that was to be of such great significance for the future, except in v. 21 where he anchors his hope upon the word that remains in Israel through all changes.

V. 1 begins abruptly as though the prophet were answering the complaint, "Why has not our salvation come?" A man who had announced so often that the day of salvation was ready to come at any moment and had portrayed it as though it were already present, would undoubtedly be asked that question often. Here the question may be contained in ch. 58:3, where the worshipers ask why God has done nothing in answer to their prayers. "The trouble is not with God but with you," the prophet answers in ch. 59, and with this he begins an arraignment of the community for its sins. The people addressed are the same as in ch. 58, and the sins described here correspond with the sins of ch. 58. We heard of violence in connection with the fast day; here the violence results in the shedding of blood. There we saw men self-deceived in their religion; here lies and dishonest practices corrupt the life of the community and prevent justice in its courts. Whether the language of *v. 4* is as much that of the courts as the RSV translation supposes is uncertain. The expressions may have more to do with justice in general. But "no one gives truthful judgment" certainly suggests a court and is parallel with the court scenes in chs. 50 and 53. Apparently the courts were used to dealing with nonconformist followers of the prophet. Again in *v. 5* death is the lot of those who become involved with the workers of evil. Their practices are likened to the hatching of poisonous snakes, which imperil the lives of men. They weave a spider's web in order to catch men as a spider catches flies. But the web they weave furnishes them with no clothing and leaves them naked for all to see their iniquity. In *v. 7* the blood they shed is "innocent blood," in short, the blood of the faithful who refuse to go along with the evil practices of the community (v. 15).

It should be noted that whereas *God* speaks in ch. 58, it is the prophet himself who speaks from the beginning of ch. 59. Then in *v. 9* a change occurs as the prophet becomes intercessor for his sinful nation and confesses its sins as though he himself were a participant in them. To suppose that this is a different oracle because of the change is not only to break the unity of ch. 59 but to ignore the fact that such changes are not unusual for Second Isaiah. A shift from prophetic arraignment to prophetic intercession is wholly in character. Moreover, v. 9 is an exact parallel to vs. 1-2. Since "justice" and "righteousness" were used by Second Isaiah here and elsewhere as synonyms to denote God's day of redemption, the confession "Justice is far from us" is identical with the accusation in ch. 46:12, "you who are far from righteousness." Torrey misses the eschatological meaning when he translates "righteousness" as "uprightness." The parallel with "salvation" is evident in *v. 11*.

The prophet's identification of himself with his people in his intercession for them is important for our understanding of his relation with them, just as Jesus' identification of himself with sinners was of the greatest importance in his conquest of their sin. The identification is not to be conceived as having its reality only in words and in the time of the prophet's prayer, but rather, formed the substance of the prophet's daily relation to the sinners. He exposed their sin ruthlessly. He unmasked their religious pretensions. But he did not set himself apart from them and look down upon them from a position of exalted righteousness and holiness. They knew that he made continual intercession for them and that behind his intercession was a love for them like the love of God himself for his people. In the description of the Servant in ch. 53:12 there is good reason for the final stroke that he "made intercession for the transgressors." It is a serious mistake to forget that vs. 9-15 in ch. 59 are intercession and to think that the prophet himself had been guilty of "lying words, oppression, and revolt." It is an equally great mistake to assume that conditions could not have been as bad as the prophet describes, and so to regard his phrases as literary exaggerations, or like Torrey, to change the final phrase of the confession, "he who turns from evil makes himself a prey," which is so graphic, to the innocuous, "piety has fled because of evil." The "justice" and "righteousness" of v. 14 are synonyms for "salvation" and not qualities of social life. The community's scorn of God's truth obstructs the coming of God's great new day of justice and righteousness.

The background of *vs. 15b-21* is the confidence expressed continually by Second Isaiah that Israel is to be the instrument of God's redemption. For this purpose Israel was called from the beginning, and the secret of God's dealings with his people throughout their history had been his shaping and equipping of them for this task. God required a human instrument for the fulfillment of his purpose. Eventually Second Isaiah was to fasten upon the faithful remnant that clung to God's word in spite of persecution as the human agent in redemption, but at the time ch. 59 was written he had not yet reached this solution. Israel as God's Servant had abdicated its destiny, refusing to be the covenant people. The absence of justice and the presence of so much violence and evil in the nation were evidence of the completeness of the breach between Israel and God. When God looked for his human covenant partner, he found no man (*v. 16*), no one through whom he could effectively implement his purpose. But in the mind and for the faith of Second Isaiah, it was impossible that the sin of Israel should defeat the purpose of God. Therefore, he proclaims that in spite of the absence of any human helper, God will have his victory. As in ch. 42:13 he again portrays God as a warrior, but his armor is not like the armor of men. His breastplate is righteousness, his helmet salvation, his garments vengeance and fury. Again here the two sides of God's action should be noted: salvation and judgment. The intervention of God is the joy of his friends, but the terror of his foes. The scene of his intervention is the whole world. From the far west to the far east God will be seen as the God that he is: Redeemer and Avenger. So will he come to Zion, but only those who turn from transgression will know him as Redeemer (*v. 20*).

With this limitation of redemption to those who turn from transgression, the prophet is on his way to the doctrine of the Servant that appears more fully in chs. 65-66 and reaches its climax in ch. 53.

But facing the question of what hope there was for the future, he fastened, not upon the righteousness of a remnant in Israel, which would have been too much a trust in man for Second Isaiah, but rather, upon the living power of the word of God in one generation after another in Israel (*v. 21*). The basis of hope lay, not in man's faith or virtue, but rather, in God's faithfulness, that in each generation he continued and would continue to speak his word and to put it in the mouths of at least some of his people, at the same time setting his Spirit in their hearts. Though Israel shattered the covenant, God would remain faithful, and through all time he would keep his word alive somewhere within Israel. He would speak and some would hear, and where there was such hearing, there would be a covenant people in whose midst God's purpose would unfold itself as inevitably as the flowering of the earth after rain (ch. 55:11).

CHAPTER 60/ Chapters 60 to 62 are all of a piece and undoubtedly stem from the same occasion. They are a rapturous, unshadowed proclamation of the nearness of the day of salvation for Jerusalem, with no references to the nation's sin such as dominate chs. 56:9 to 59:21. The prophet sees the glory of the Lord already shining as a great light around the city. So bright is it that there is no longer need for sun or moon to give light. Darkness is banished and the nations that dwell in darkness stream toward this center of brightness from all corners of the earth. They do not come empty-handed. They bring with them the sons and daughters of Zion and gifts without number, gold and frankincense, camels and sheep. The kings of the nations come with their people and are content with humble tasks such as the rebuilding of the walls or the keeping of the flocks of Judah. Gold, silver, and bronze will beautify the city, and violence will be banished from it. All its people will be ministers of God. This is the prophet's way of saying that the Kingdom of God is at hand.

We must not be misled by the material images—kings becoming servants of God's people, the wealth of the nations being poured out at their feet, their city being rebuilt with the most costly materials.

Like the costly jewels in the walls of the New Jerusalem and the gold of its streets in the book of Revelation in the New Testament, these features are meant only to represent the gloriousness of the fulfillment that God has in store for his people. All things will be transformed. Where there has been restraint there will be liberty (ch. 61:1). Where there has been mourning there will be joy. In place of broken and ruined cities there will be beautiful new ones. A people that has long endured the hardships of poverty will no longer have to concern itself about the wherewithal of living. But none of these features has any meaning apart from the central reality of the new day, that God is with his people and that they are "clothed with the garments of salvation" (ch. 61:10). The passionate hunger of the prophet is not for wealth, or a beautiful city, or to have kings as his servants, but for God and God's redemption. The disparagement of Old Testament eschatology as materialistic in contrast to the spirituality of New Testament eschatology is unjustified and fails to grasp the true intention of the prophet. His hope, like that of the New Testament writers, is for a city of God in which righteousness dwells. In ch. 62 Second Isaiah uses bold figures of speech as he impatiently calls upon God to fulfill his purpose. He says that he has set watchmen upon the walls of Jerusalem who will give God no rest until he has made the city "a praise in the earth." Then he quotes God as having sworn by his right hand and by his mighty arm that the enemies of his people will no longer eat the produce of the land.

These chapters create the impression that they come from an early period in the prophet's ministry. In their thought and language they are typical of Second Isaiah in his most lyrical and exuberant mood. Many interpreters who have denied most of chs. 56 to 66 to Second Isaiah have made an exception in favor of chs. 60 to 62, so compelling are the parallels. God is coming to redeem his people; Israel, when it fulfills its destiny, will be a nation of priests and ministers to God; the whole earth is to share in God's salvation. The description of the prophetic task in ch. 61:1-3 fits perfectly what Second Isaiah represents as the task of God's Servant Israel in chs. 35, 40, 42, 49, 50. One point at which a question arises is in vs. 7 and 13 of ch. 60 and in v. 9 of ch. 62, where there is favorable mention of the Temple and its altar. They do not necessitate, as some have thought, that the Temple should have been already rebuilt when these passages were written, because it is the city of the future that is being described. But there is at least a contrast here with what we have seen to be a sharply critical and denunciatory attitude of Second Isaiah toward the Temple cult. However, if these chapters come from a very early period when his emphasis was upon the certainty of God's salvation as he tried to overcome the hopelessness of his people and before any conflict had arisen between him and the community that centered its religious life in the priestly sacrificial cult, the inclusion of a Temple and sacrifices in the city of the future would be quite understandable. Love for Jerusalem was very strong in this prophet and comes to expression not only in chs. 60 to 62 but also in many other passages. It may be that the Temple was part of the Jerusalem he loved and desired to see transformed—until it became the stronghold of those who stubbornly refused to hear the word of God.

V. 1. As ever with Second Isaiah the anticipation of God's coming to his people is so intense that he describes it as though it had already happened. With the eye of faith he sees the brightness of God's glory compassing Jerusalem and the nations streaming toward it, even though the actual community where he dwells is still in darkness and ruin and most of its people in utter despair about the future. His words must have seemed fantastically absurd to many of his fellow citizens and the prophet himself may well have been thought deranged. He saw what others did not see. He not only anticipated the coming of God but in the anticipation of faith it was for him as though God had already come and the transformation had already begun. His eschatological hope, like that of the early Christians, was not just a looking forward to a possible future event but was a laying hold upon the future in such a way that he lived in the present in the light and strength and joy of that future.

V. 4. The coming of kings and nations and of sons and daughters are so linked that no sharp separation can be made between the two. Already in chs. 42, 44, 45, and 49 the definition of God's people was widened to include those from among the nations who turned to the light that they saw shining from Israel. The coming of kings and nations in v. 3 is a coming to God, an acknowledgment of the one true God. The fact that in v. 10 they build the walls and in ch. 61:5 tend the flocks and plough the ground does not signify their enslavement to Israel, but rather, their willingness to perform such services now that they have become members of God's own people. They set the Israelites free to give themselves wholly to their ministry for God. The kingdoms of the world become the kingdoms of the Lord. *Vs. 6-7.* Representative places and their typical possessions are mentioned but they are meant to suggest the universality of God's sovereignty. *V. 12.* Most commentators, including both Duhm and Torrey, regard this as a prosaic gloss out of keeping with the spirit of the oracle. It interrupts the narration that began in v. 3 in which the nations come willingly from all parts of the earth, bringing with them their wealth to enrich and beautify Jerusalem. In *v. 14* even Israel's former oppressors come and submit themselves. *V. 21.* The inhabitants of the New Jerusalem will all be righteous. Sin and evil will be no more. In short, God's work of redemption will be complete.

CHAPTER 61 / Chapter 61 furnishes us with our clearest

example of the shifting of the person of the speaker that we have already detected in chs. 51:1-3 and 53:8, 11-12. The chapter begins with either the prophet himself or the prophetic Servant as the speaker, most likely the latter. How anyone can fail to recognize it as a writing of Second Isaiah is difficult to understand. The Servant describes his task as the liberation and healing of the brokenhearted prisoners of Zion (vs. 1-3). But as he goes on in vs. 4-9 to speak of this restoration, the rebuilding of the city and the mediatorial function of Israel between God and the nations that are to participate in the glorious future, the focus shifts and God becomes the speaker, without any break in the sequence of thought being perceptible. But in vs. 9-11 the first person clearly designates Israel, which suggests to us that also in vs. 1-3 we were intended to understand that the Servant Israel was the speaker. The dramatic form and the subtle shift from one speaker to another are in themselves sufficient to

identify ch. 61 as a writing of Second Isaiah, but even more convincing is the exact correspondence of the description of Israel's task
as Servant with what we find in chs. 35 and 40 to 55. He is empowered by God's Spirit (ch. 42:1) and anointed for the task (ch.
45:1) of bringing to the burdened and afflicted the good news of
God's healing forgiveness (chs. 35:3-6; 40:1-2, 9-11, 27-31; 50:4, etc.).
The coming of God is to set the prisoners free (chs. 42:7; 45:13;
49:25) and to bring joy where there has been only mourning and
sorrow. These liberated and joyful children of Zion, both Israelite
and Gentile, will rebuild the ancient ruins (chs. 44:26; 45:13; 49:17).
The passage takes us into the very heart of Second Isaiah, his understanding of the Servant's ministry being identical with his understanding of his own ministry, since for him, to be a prophet was
simply to be a true Israelite, a true son of the covenant, in whom the
destiny of the chosen people of God was being fulfilled. Therefore,
when the prophet speaks with the voice of the Servant, he also at the
same time speaks most personally and passionately for himself. The
Servant is a concept that reaches far beyond Second Isaiah, behind
him in history, beyond him in the present and the future, yet it
always includes him as an immediate embodiment of his nation's
destiny.

Vs. 1-3 describe the ministry and priesthood that belongs peculiarly to Israel (v. 6). To discharge these tasks is to be priests and
ministers to God. God requires a Servant to stand between him and
the world, to have an ear open continually to his word, and to
speak that word faithfully to men no matter how difficult it may be.
Through the word God will establish his sovereignty over the lives
of men and by bringing them under his rule make his justice prevail
to the ends of the earth (ch. 42:1-4). Therefore, the Servant as
spokesman of the word is both the one through whom God liberates
the prisoners and gives sight to the blind and the one who rules for
God. He is both prophet and king, so that both prophetic and royal
characteristics are attributed to him. Whereas the emphasis throughout is upon good news and liberation, the second clause in v. 2 reminds us that the establishment of justice entails the overthrow of
the strongholds of injustice. The day of liberation for some is a day
of vengeance for others. God's sovereignty brings with it the destruc-

tion of those who are unrepentant in their evil. "Vengeance" in English, as Torrey points out, is open to misunderstanding. He suggests "requital." That evil receives its just reward is all that is intended.

A double reference to prisoners is unlikely at the end of v. 1. The LXX reads "the blind" instead of "prisoners," which is what we would expect with the particular verb used here for "to open" (cf. ch. 42:7, which speaks of prisoners and blind in sequence). There is no reason to limit the reference here to Israelite prisoners and blind. The Servant's task, as in chs. 42 and 49, has a universal scope. God's coming is good news to *all* the poor of the earth. *All* broken hearts are to be bound up, and *all* prisoners set free. Israel is to fulfill a ministry on behalf of all mankind. Only in v. 3 does a special promise begin to be made to "those who mourn in Zion." The change from third person to second person to designate the redeemed in *vs. 5-7* furnishes a problem, particularly when the third person recurs in v. 7b. Torrey thinks v. 5 a later insertion in the second person that brought a change in vs. 6 and 7a. To him the verse has a narrow spirit unsuitable to the context. But like ch. 60:10, v. 5 contains no suggestion of the subjection of foreigners, and the sudden change from speaking *about* the Israelites to speaking directly *to* them is in keeping with the style of Second Isaiah (cf. ch. 62:1-2). The change back to "they" in v. 7b, however, is impossible. Either the second person should be read throughout, as in the RSV, or the second person should be changed to the third in vs. 5-7a. *V. 6.* That all Israelites are to be called priests does not mean that they are to be occupied with ceremonial duties. "Priests" is used here parallel with "ministers," a more general term, to signify the total engrossment of Israelites in the service of God. The primary priestly duty, according to Hosea, was to give knowledge of God. In this, priest and prophet cease to be sharply differentiated. That all Israelites should be priests meant, for Second Isaiah, that all should be "taught of God" (ch. 54:13) and should have from God a word with which to sustain the weary and fainthearted (ch. 50:4).

The text of *v. 7* is uncertain, the repetition of "double" being most likely an error through dittography, but the meaning is not difficult to discern. In place of humiliation and shame, Jerusalem is to receive a double blessing. Klostermann's emendation on the basis of ch. 50:6, "insult and spitting their portion," forms a more fitting parallel to the first clause. *V. 8.* The "everlasting covenant" stands in contrast to the former covenant whose breach brought such ruin upon Israel. The new covenant relation is not just a renewal of the old covenant, a kind of second chance for Israel, but rather, posits a new Israel that will respond to God's love and faithfulness with an unfaltering love and faithfulness, in short, a people no longer in process of redemption, but redeemed. Their life, being one of unbroken obedience, will be one of unshadowed blessing, so that all nations will recognize them as the covenant people of God. The Christian church rightly sees the fulfillment of this promise in Jesus Christ. In him alone was found the perfect obedience of the New Israel and so in him alone was the new covenant a reality, an unbroken fellowship with God in which the life of God becomes so fully the life of man that God's Kingdom can be said to have come on earth. The realization of the new covenant in Jesus Christ thus inaugurates a wholly new era in the life of man because it makes possible a life that has its source in a wholly new relation between God and man. Second Isaiah, like John the Baptist, lived in hope of such a day, seeing it from afar, and yet rejoicing in it as though it had already come. The Christian who stands with him and learns what it is to live in hope of that day is much more likely to grasp the dimensions of the good news in the New Testament that "the time has been fulfilled" and that the great day has come in Jesus Christ. *V. 9* is parallel with ch. 45:14. The recognition of Israel as a people blessed by God is at the same time an acknowledgment that the God revealed in and through Israel is the one and only God. Through Israel all nations are to come to a knowledge of the one true God.

The song of praise to God that begins in *v. 10* is typical of Second Isaiah (cf. chs. 42:10-11; 44:23, etc.). It is an expression of Israel's gratitude to God for the salvation that, although it is only promised, begins already to clothe God's people as a garment. God has already forgiven his people. The decisive moment behind the scenes is past. What is yet to come is the realization in actual events of the implications of the changed relation with God. As in the New

Testament, the salvation is described with images drawn from the joyful marriage ceremony. Behind this lies the thought of the covenant relation of Israel with God as that of a bride with her husband. The certainty of the salvation is likened to the certainty with which the earth produces fruits when seed has been sown in it (cf. ch. 55:10-11). As yet there may be nothing visible above ground, the seeds being hidden, or there may be only the slightest signs of the growing plants, but the harvest is sure.

CHAPTER 62 /

In chs. 62, 63, and 64 we meet the prophet as intercessor more vividly than anywhere else in the Old Testament. It is significant that in ch. 62 intercession for the coming of God to save is mingled with confident assertions that God is coming to save. Duhm misunderstands the relation of the two when he sees an antithesis between the two representations of God, as eager to redeem Israel in ch. 42:14 ff. (as in 62:8 f.) and as having to be urged to do it in ch. 60 (as in 62:1, 6-7) and on the basis of the supposed antithesis assigns the two passages in ch. 62 to different authors. There is actually no contradiction. As a prophet speaking *for God,* Second Isaiah proclaims the nearness of salvation, but as an intercessor speaking *for Israel* and in a time of darkness expressing the nation's eager longing for God's saving act, he pleads with God to delay his redemption no longer. Behind ch. 62 we can trace the conditions in Jerusalem at the time: the land desolate and forsaken not only by men but also seemingly by God; the fruit of its fields and vineyards seized by foreign overlords so that the people themselves go hungry. The mention of walls in v. 6 has led some interpreters to the conclusion that the chapter must come from a time after Nehemiah's rebuilding of the walls, but this ignores the dramatic and imaginative character of the writing. The watchmen or remembrancers are not actual men on actual walls but are an expression of the prophet's urgency in intercession. All who join with the prophet in praying for the peace of Jerusalem are watchmen and remembrancers. The situation as reflected in the chapter best fits the Jerusalem of the mid-sixth century, before the land had begun to recover from the heavy blows of 597 and 587 B.C. The country is inhabited. People live in the ruins of Jerusalem. Farmers and vine growers carry on their work in Judah. But it is a broken and oppressed community, burdened with rapacious rulers from beyond its borders and even more by its own consciousness of God's hand resting heavily upon it in judgment. As time passed, the latter deepened into a despairing sense of Godforsakenness. In short, the situation reflected in ch. 62 is identical with that which appears in chs. 40 ff., and the message of ch. 62 is that of ch. 40 in another form: the return of God to his people, the restoration of the covenant relation, the consequent transformation of the nation's life and its vindication before all the world.

V. 1. There is no way of determining whether the "I" here is the Servant Israel, as in chs. 49:1 and 61:1, 10, or the prophet himself. The latter seems more likely. He announces that he will keep up a continual intercession with God for the coming of the day of transformation, and that he will not do it alone, but will call into being a whole corps of remembrancers who will give God no rest as they remind him day after day what he has promised in his word (vs. 6-7). This passage raises the problem that intercession always does: why God should need to be reminded of his own promises! Is not the conception of God deficient when men think they have to urge him to do what is in accordance with his nature and will? Is it not crudely anthropomorphic for Second Isaiah to think that God will be influenced by the urgency of his intercession? Yet intercession has an important place in both Old and New Testaments in the relation between man and God. Abraham's prayer for Lot had important consequences (Gen. 18:23 ff.). Jesus' prayer for Peter was a decisive factor in his rescue from failure (Luke 22:32). Paul's intercessions for his churches were not wasted time (Phil. 1:4; Col. 1:9). We are so bound together in our humanity that when doors open between us and God we are able to reach out in prayer and draw others with us into the presence of God, whether they know it or not. Intercession is a sign of the inseparableness of our human lives in their relation with God. Because all are their true selves only in God, there are hidden bonds that link us with each other in the unseen, so that just as our prayers for ourselves open the way for God to come to us, so our intercessions for others open the way for God to come to them. Intercession is possible only as an act of love in which God's own love for us is reflected.

V. 2. The "new name" for Jerusalem is here meant to signify the completely transformed condition of the city and is so explained in v. 4. It is not to be confused with the promise of a new name in ch. 65:15-16, where the name "Israel" has been so degraded by the official community that the faithful remnant will no longer use it, but will speak of the "God of truth" instead of the "God of Israel." *V. 4.* The restoration of the covenant is likened to the restoration of a marriage relationship as in ch. 61:10. *V. 5.* Clearly something is wrong in the description of Jerusalem's sons as marrying their mother! The usual emendation, which requires only a change in pointing, "Thy builders shall marry thee," is not quite satisfactory. The singular "Thy builder" is possible. In both v. 4 and the second half of v. 5 God is the husband of Jerusalem, so that a parallel term is required.

V. 6. It is like Second Isaiah that he should address Jerusalem, telling her of the watchmen he has set on her walls, and then quickly turn in imagination to address the watchmen themselves. The image of the remembrancers is drawn from Eastern court life, where sometimes a king would have such a functionary.

V. 8. The form of intercession gives way to the most positive assertion of God's intention: God has sworn by his right hand and arm, again a vivid anthropomorphism to emphasize the certainty of God's promise.

V. 9. A happy festival in the Temple courts with feasting and drinking of wine is envisaged, something that for some time has been impossible. The fact that the Temple has a place in the prophet's vision of the future suggests a date early in his ministry for these chapters.

V. 10. The repetition of verbs occurs frequently in Second Isaiah. The preparation of the highway for the coming of God, of the exiles, and of the nations to Jerusalem, is a salient feature of his eschatology. There is no basis for the usual narrowing of its significance to make it a highway for the return only of *Babylonian* exiles to Jerusalem. The exiles come from the four corners of the earth and so also do the nations. The last line of v. 10 and the first of v. 11 emphasize the universality of the expected salvation.

CHAPTERS 63 AND 64/ These two chapters, which cannot be broken apart, are different from any other section of the book. This is perhaps because they form a sustained meditation and prayer of intercession. In ch. 62 the prophet spoke of his intention to engage in unceasing intercession for his people: here we have an example of his intercession. Naturally a prayer offered on behalf of Israel would differ in style and language from an oracle intended to be delivered or to be read. It was undoubtedly a meditation and prayer spoken in the hearing of others or written to be read by others, yet never are the Israelites addressed directly, and for the larger part, from ch. 63:15 on, God is addressed.

The dramatic opening passage, ch. 63:1-6, has troubled many interpreters because of what has seemed to them to be its savagery, a picture of God dripping with the blood of his enemies as he comes to his people. We understand it only when we grasp the fact that neither for Second Isaiah nor for any other prophet could there be a day of salvation without a day of judgment. God's mercy and God's wrath stood, not in contradiction, but in union. His faithfulness was both in love and in holiness. The final triumph of his will involved not only the establishment of an order of justice and peace in human society but also the destruction of all the forces of injustice and evil that resisted his will. Without their destruction there could be no justice or peace for the redeemed. Therefore, God's coming to redeem his people is necessarily a day of terror for his enemies. Readers are usually unprepared for the picture of the God of wrath in ch. 63:1-6 because interpreters have so emphasized the elements of gentleness and comfort in Second Isaiah's conception of God that they fail to see in the earlier chapters the uncompromising holiness of a God whose redemption of the world is delayed by the tenacity of sin. Perhaps also we are accustomed to separating from the person of God the judgment in which evil is destroyed, thinking of it as something that works itself out inevitably in the nature of the creation rather than something with which God is personally concerned, whereas the prophet sees God himself hurling his thunderbolts and trampling upon his enemies.

The relation of ch. 63:1-6 to the remainder of the passage is not immediately clear. Why does the prophet begin his meditation and intercession for Israel with this vision of judgment? Is it necessarily linked with what follows in vs. 7 ff. or does it perhaps stand by itself? Why begin with a vision of God's coming and then go on to pray so passionately for his coming? What links the two is the fact that both have as their background the seeming *inactivity* of God, that God seems to be doing nothing about the plight of his people. The nations before whom they are helpless and by whom they are oppressed are as strong as ever. There is no sign anywhere on the horizon of a change in the order of things. But the prophet sees what no one else can see. From the south through Edom he sees God approaching, coming ever nearer Jerusalem, the blood on his garments a sign to all that he has broken the power of his enemies and is about to establish his perfect rule not only over Israel but over all mankind. This vision is followed in vs. 7-14 by a historical reminiscence. God's mighty deeds on behalf of his people in the past are for Second Isaiah a revelation of what God will yet be to his people. If they want to know what he will do in the future, they have only to look back and see what he did in the creation or in the calling of Abraham or in the exodus. Then, in v. 15 begins the intercession in which the prophet pleads with God once more to show himself the Father and Redeemer of his people and to open before them a new future.

V. 1. The mention of Edom has given interpreters unnecessary trouble. Poor little Edom seems to be made the object of a wholly disproportionate judgment. Therefore some, following de Lagarde, have changed "Edom" to "reddened," which requires only a change of vowels, and Torrey has made Edom here, as in ch. 34, a representative figure symbolizing the powers of evil, like Babylon in the book of Revelation. But v. 3 says clearly that God has been trampling on "the nations," and v. 4 that it is the universal day of judgment and salvation that is envisaged, so that when God is seen coming from Edom,[1] this means only that he has finished his more distant works of judgment and is drawing near to Jerusalem by way of Edom to effect its salvation. The vision is cast in the dra-

---

[1] Prof. George Landes has pointed out to me that in Deut. 33:2 and Hab. 3:3, Yahweh is represented as approaching through Edom as he comes from Sinai.

matic form of question and answer. The prophet sees a mighty figure approaching from the south and asks who it can be. God himself answers that he is coming to the rescue of his people. In *v. 2* the prophet asks why God's garments are so stained with red, and in *v. 3* receives the report of the universal judgment that God has just completed. The emphasis in v. 3 and in *v. 5* that God had to act alone to judge and save (cf. ch. 59:16) can only mean that neither Israel nor any other nation was ready to be the instrument of his purpose.

The sudden change in *v. 7* from the fury of world judgment to the recounting of God's kindnesses to Israel throws into sharp relief the greatness of his mercy toward the people of the covenant. The speaker has changed: "I" stands no longer for God, as in *v. 6,* but for the prophet himself as spokesman for his people. Note the shifting between first and third person in the references to Israel, from "us" to "them." *V. 8* has in mind the earliest days of the covenant, the time of the exodus. God expected of Israel a faithfulness in response to his own faithfulness. The text of *v. 9* is difficult. We have perhaps to be content to know from the context that the reference was to God's responsiveness to his people's need when they were crushed in Egypt. He redeemed them from bondage and led them through the wilderness. *V. 10* summarizes the centuries-long rebellion of Israel against God and the devastating judgments that the nation brought upon itself (cf. chs. 48:8; 43:22-28).

V. 11. The remembering of the days of old is not by God but by Israel. Therefore, the subject "he" in v. 11 cannot be a continuation of the "he" in v. 10. Torrey tries to overcome this difficulty by reading "one recalled the days of old." Perhaps the verb should be plural to agree with "they rebelled" in v. 10. Various proposals to emend the latter half of the line have been made. "Moses, his people" is clearly too fragmentary. "Moses, his servant," which is found in some MSS., presupposes "God" as subject. Torrey's "the saviour of his people" is possible with only a slight change in text. But perhaps the simplest of all is the assumption (KJV and Vulgate) that "and" has fallen out between "Moses" and "his people." Remembering the exodus, the Israelites are represented as beginning to ask where the God is who acted so mightily in the days of Moses. If in those days he could rescue from the sea the shepherds of the flock, set his Spirit in the midst of them, and lead them surely into a new life in Palestine, can he not do the same now in Israel's present distress? *Vs. 13-14* are obscure. God's leading his people in the depths is "like a horse in the desert" or "like cattle that go down into the valley." In the middle of v. 14 is the phrase, "the Spirit of the Lord gave them rest" in which the verb may very simply be emended to read "led them." The reference must be to the difficulty with which horses find their way in a desert or cattle in their descent from the heights into the valleys. God's guidance of his people, step by step, is sure. Twice over, once in v. 12 and once in v. 14, God's doings are said "to make him an everlasting (or glorious) name." Through his great acts in the exodus God's name (i.e., his true nature) was revealed once and for all, and the remembrance of those acts was ever in Israel the means whereby God was known afresh in his greatness.

In *v. 15* the prophet's intercession for Israel begins. He calls on God to open his eyes to the distress of his people. He does not say what God is to see, for that is clear to all for whom he prays. The mention of God's "holy and glorious habitation" is intended to stand in contrast to the unholy and inglorious habitation of his people. Boldly the prophet asks God what has happened to the zeal and power and compassion that were revealed on behalf of his people in ancient days. No longer does Israel know anything of them. God's love and power are concealed from his people. *V. 16.* Though Israel has been untrue to the covenant relation, God cannot be untrue. Israelites may have built up a barrier between themselves and God with their sin and rebellion so that they walk in darkness seemingly forsaken by God, but beyond the barrier God remains their father. His love is withheld, not destroyed.

The phrase "though Abraham does not know us and Israel does not acknowledge us" is very puzzling. Is it not Israel for whom the prophet intercedes? Or does he perhaps make his intercession for all Israel in the presence only of the little remnant of the faithful who have been rejected by the official nation (ch. 66:5) and are no longer willing to bear the name "Israel" (ch. 65:15)? "Abraham" and "Israel" in this context would thus be names to denote, not ancient historical personages, but the present nation, and v. 16 would take its place alongside chs. 50:4-11; 65; and 66 as evidence of a division in the community between the faithful believers who stood with the prophet and the religious and civil authorities who together with the main body of the population resisted and repudiated the smaller group. In ch. 65:8 ff. Second Isaiah fastens upon the faithful remnant the destiny of the Servant and consigns his enemies to destruction, but in chs. 63 and 64 he still intercedes for Israel as a whole. He merely asserts the right of the remnant to call God Father, i.e., to claim their place within the covenant people of God and to name God as their Redeemer even as he has been the Redeemer of their forefathers in the past. *V. 17* is intercession on behalf of the nation as a whole. The prophet is perplexed that God should let the heart of Israel, his covenant people, grow hard against him and the nation that he created for his service give itself so completely into the service of evil. Here as elsewhere in the Old Testament where God is said to "harden the heart" of man so that he does evil (Ex. 7:3), or as with Saul, to let an evil spirit take possession of him (I Sam. 18:10), the implications of God's sovereignty over human life are drawn out so far that God seems to be made responsible for man's evil actions. That this is not intended by the prophet (or by other writers) is made plain in other passages where man's full responsibility for his own evil actions is asserted most emphatically. The words of v. 17 must therefore be read as the words of a prayer in which the prophet does not accuse God of making Israel err from his ways, but rather, expresses how great a mystery it is to him that a nation in covenant with God could drift so far from God. The use of the plural "servants" links ch. 63 with ch. 65 where the plural is used deliberately for the remnant in place of the collective "Servant" that pervades all the earlier writings of the prophet (except ch. 54:17). It is for the sake of God's "servants" that he prays for the "tribes of thy heritage," i.e., the whole of Israel, to be restored. *Vs. 18-19.* The LXX suggests a better reading for v. 18: "For a little we possessed thy holy hill but our enemies have trampled thy sanctuary; we have been from of old as those not ruled by thee, not called by thy name." The depth of Israel's distress is not the agony of enemy occupation but the abrogation of the covenant. The prophet seems here to be expressing the despair of Godforsakenness that tortured his people, a despair that he countered more directly in passages such as chs. 40:27-31 and 50:1-3.

Ch. 64. V. 1. The last line of ch. 63:19 belongs with ch. 64 and should be v. 1 as in the RSV. Again the passionate outcry of the prophet for God to break through from the heavens and come to the rescue of his people may seem to stand in contrast to the confidence in God's speedy coming that is expressed elsewhere. The contrast disappears only when it is remembered that the prophet speaks here as intercessor for his nation, identifying himself with his people in their distress and darkness. The coming of God for which he prays is represented as a fiery presence that dissolves the mountains as in ch. 40:4. *V. 2.* God, appearing in his fiery splendor, strikes terror into the hearts of the nations as he alone is seen to be God. The two images of fire—as burning brushwood and as making water boil—suggest, on the one hand, the destruction of the evil forces that resist God's will, parallel with ch. 63:1-6, and on the other hand, the power of God to break through the quiet surface of life and make things happen. The God who is likened to fire is a living God who acts in the midst of history. *V. 3.* The repetition of "thou camest down, the mountains dissolved before thee" is likely a gloss. The phrase "when thou doest marvellous things that we did not expect" then forms the conclusion of the preceding sentence. The nations tremble at the unexpected advent of God with its accompanying acts of judgment and redemption. *V. 4* thus continues v. 3 directly, the nations being the "they" who had not heard or seen a God such as this from of old. The nature of the God of Israel, which will be revealed decisively in his appearing, as it was in his deeds on behalf of Israel in the past, is that he acts in history to redeem those who set their hopes upon him and wait for him. They may have to wait long, weary years, but they can wait with confidence because God's vindication of them is sure. Because he is Creator of all things and Lord of history, the outcome of events is in his hands. His carrying through of his purposes may be hidden for a time, but it would be a denial of the sovereignty of God to think even for a moment that they might fall short of their fulfillment. The glory of the God of Israel is that his word has ever been and will ever be fulfilled in history, and the shame of the gods of the nations is that they have no power to do anything either for good or for ill in history, i.e., they are irrelevant to the life of man. *V. 5.* The present text is impossible, and the original hard to determine. Torrey's suggestion is as good as any: "Thou bringest rejoicing to those who do right, who walk in thy ways." It rein- forces v. 4 in its assertion of the faithfulness of God to a people that keeps covenant with him. Suddenly now, the intercession changes to confession: "Lo! Thou wast angry and we sinned," but the remainder of the sentence is hopelessly corrupt "in them forever and we shall be saved." Torrey suggests "dealing treacherously, wickedly of old," but this is merely a guess. Whatever the original text was, it continued the confession, perhaps "against thee from of old we transgressed" (cf. chs. 43:27; 48:8). *V. 6.* In the phrase "all of us," the prophet identifies himself with the nation as a whole in its sin (cf. Isa. 6:5). The intercessor not only speaks for his fel- lowmen but takes upon himself the burden of their sin as though it were his own. He bears it with them before God, and bearing it with them, is recognized by them as bearing it for them (cf. ch. 53:4 ff.). The effect of God's anger is not a sudden overwhelming judgment, but a gradual fading away of the people like the gradual disappearance of the leaves as they drop from the trees and are car- ried away. *V. 7.* The ever-repeated lament of Second Isaiah is that no one truly calls upon God. There are many who offer prayers and sacrifices to him (ch. 48:1 ff.), but it is not the true God upon whom they set their hearts. God himself is hidden from them by their sins, so that they cannot know him. This is the greatest disaster of all that sin brings upon men and nations, not that they meet with outward misfortune in consequence of God's anger, but that God is withdrawn from them and they can no longer pray in sincerity to him, since he is not there for them. The final verb in v. 7 by a slight change in the vowels becomes "thou hast delivered us" in- stead of "thou hast melted us."

V. 8. Yet in spite of Israel's sin, God remains the Father of his people. They may cast him off, but he does not cast them off. He is hidden from them by their sins, not divorced from them (cf. ch. 50:1-3). The plea, "Thou art our Father" in ch. 63:16 and ch. 64:8 links the two chapters. The likening of God to a potter and Israel to clay in his hands is reminiscent of ch. 45:9 where Israel is represented as rebellious clay reproaching the potter for what he is making of it. But in the prophet's prayer the nation in its guilt and helplessness consents to be clay in God's hands that he may shape it anew. *V. 9.* The promise that lay in God's nature as revealed of old to Israel was that he would not keep his anger forever but would show himself a God of compassion, forgiving his people when he had chastised them for their sins. The prophet is therefore reminding God of his promise. The passage of long years after 587 B.C. with no sign of restoration must have made it seem as though there were no longer any compassion in Israel's God, as though he had finally come to the end of his patience and cast off his people. "We are all thy people" belongs therefore with "Thou art our Father" as a reassertion of the covenant relation on which Israel's hopes were based.

Vs. 10-11. If these chapters are a *real* prayer of intercession offered in an actual historical situation on behalf of *real* people and not merely a poetical creation in which the author transports himself imaginatively into an earlier situation, these two verses demand a time of composition not too long after the disasters of 597 and 587 B.C. Torrey's theory that Second Isaiah lived in the latter part of the fifth century, perhaps about 400 B.C., attributes the vividness to the poetic imagination of the prophet rather than to his immediate experience of Palestinian desolation. Here, as at other points, Torrey seems to exalt the poet in Second Isaiah at the expense of the prophet. The earnestness of the prophetic intercession dare not be tampered with. We are listening to a prayer in which through the lips of the prophet a nation in its Godforsakenness cries out passionately to God for forgiveness and rescue. That Jerusalem and the towns of Judah are still largely in ruins does not mean that they are uninhabited. The prayer would be comprehensible in the middle of the sixth century when a generation had passed since the great disaster but there was as yet no sign of any change in Israel's fortunes. *V. 12.* The prayer ends with a plea to God to bring the era of judgment to a close, to break his long silence, i.e., by speaking the word of forgiveness that would open a new future before his people.

CHAPTER 65/ Chapters 65 and 66 seem to stand somewhat by themselves within chs. 56 to 66. Their closest relation is
with chs. 56:9 to 59, containing as they do such bitter denunciation
of the community. Duhm separated them completely from chs. 63
and 64, since he could not believe that the people for whom the
prophet interceded could be the same ones whom he castigated.
Torrey, however, insists on direct continuity from ch. 64 to ch. 65,
interpreting God's speech in ch. 65 as the answer to the plea voiced
by the prophet at the end of ch. 64. To the question why he remains
silent and hidden, God answers that he has long been waiting for
the return of a disobedient people. If, however, chs. 56 to 66 are
a collection of utterances of a varied nature, no such close unity need
be sought. In the one he speaks as intercessor for Israel, in the other,
God's judgment on the nation is proclaimed through him.

The most significant feature of chs. 65 and 66 is the radical split
in the community that appears in them. The identity of the two
parties is of the greatest importance. The assumption that the author
was the spokesman of the group that returned to Jerusalem from
Babylon and that these returnees were of the most exemplary purity
required that the opponents be identified with the semipaganized
"people of the land." The temple, therefore, was identified as a
rival temple in Samaria. But surely the primary context for interpreting chs. 65 and 66 should be chs. 40 to 64 rather than the book
of Ezra. We have already discovered in many of the earlier chapters evidence of a deep split in the community addressed by Second
Isaiah and have identified the opposing parties, the one as a profes-
sedly orthodox group that had great confidence in the efficacy of
sacrifices and fasting, a tendency toward syncretism in religious
practices, and little concern about justice or mercy in human relations, the other as a small prophetic group whose principles had
made it an object of scorn and persecution. The former was not
above using the courts of justice to rid itself of its critics.

Until now the hopes of Second Isaiah have remained focused
upon the community as a whole in spite of its stubborn resistance
to his message. This chapter, however, constitutes a decisive turn-

ing point in the prophet's thought, the surrender of his hopes for the nation as a whole, and the fixing of them upon the small group of those who "trembled at God's word," or perhaps it can better be described as the revelation to him that God's purpose for the world is to be fulfilled in the future, not by Israel as a whole, but only by those in Israel and from among the nations who will remain faithful to the covenant. The wrath of God will be as overwhelming for his enemies within Israel as for his enemies in the world at large. (Muilenburg recognizes the evidence of a split in the Jerusalem community in chs. 65 and 66 and the likelihood that the conflict between the two parties issued in an opposition of the pious faithful to the rebuilding of the Temple. But since he assigns the chapters and also the closely related passage, chs. 63:7 to 64:12, to a hypothetical Third Isaiah, he fails to utilize this situation of conflict for the interpretation of the remainder of the book.)

It must be kept in mind that this is not Second Isaiah's final answer to the problem of how a God of righteousness is to fulfill his purpose through an unrighteous and rebellious people. Through most of his ministry and writings he held fast to the nation as a whole as the appointed instrument of God's purpose, even though he was fully aware of the continuing sin and blindness of his people. He appealed to the nation to open its eyes in faith and behold its destiny, to let its sins be forgiven and washed away. When there was little response, he refused to give up his hope. Since his confidence was based, not on the nation's religious character, but upon the promises of God, he asserted that God would establish his great new era for the world in spite of Israel's stubborn sinfulness. However, as he and the faithful who stood with him were brutally persecuted for their faith and rejected officially by the community, he reluctantly abandoned his hopes for the whole nation and focused them upon the believing remnant. How could men who fought so bitterly against God have any participation in the coming day of salvation? But his faith and thought did not rest finally in this answer. In ch. 53 he saw in the suffering of the faithful Servant the means whereby God would yet break through the stubborn blindness of sinful men, win them to himself, and clothe them with a new righteousness. Therefore, the separation of the faithful from the sinners in Israel in chs. 65 and 66 was not to issue in a self-righteous minority holding itself aloof from the sinners, consigning them to destruction, and awaiting all manner of blessing for itself, but rather, in a community of believers who continued to intercede for the larger community that rejected them and who lived in hope that, through their humiliation in faithfulness to God, eventually the blindness would be struck from the eyes of the sinners (Israelites and non-Israelites), and God's righteousness would achieve its triumph.

V. 1. The RSV "I was ready to be sought" does not sufficiently express God's active outreach to Israel. "I would be sought—I would be found" is closer to the Hebrew and brings out better perhaps God's eagerness in love to be sought and found. The suffix "for me" has fallen away from the verb "ask" and must be replaced. The pointing of the verb "call" makes it passive, but in some versions the pointing is that of the active verb, "a nation that did not call upon my name." This was said of Israel in ch. 64:7 and elsewhere. The passive may have originated in a misunderstanding concerning the identity of the people condemned in ch. 65:1-16. *V. 2.* Read "a rebellious and disobedient people" with the LXX. That the Israelites follow "their own thoughts" means that they have no room in their minds for God's thoughts, which are so different from theirs (ch. 55:9). *V. 3.* The pagan practices described in vs. 3-5, 7, 11 cannot all be exactly identified, but they were undoubtedly an accumulation of popular superstitions, some indigenous to Palestine and some imported through the centuries from abroad. "Sacrificing in gardens" would be the licentious fertility cult that had such deep rootage in the land and that was condemned in ch. 57. "Sitting in tombs" (*v. 4*) suggests a consulting of the spirits of the dead and "spending the night in secret places" some form of incubation in which messages from the other world were sought by sleeping in a holy place. The people in their blindness seek help from beyond in superstitious ways when all the time God is reaching out to them to give them all that they need. They try to get messages from the spirits instead of opening their ears to the word that God is continually speaking to them. The eating of swine's flesh and other unclean things would seem in its context to be part of a pagan cult practice and not just a disregard of Israelite religious law. *V. 5.* Having performed his pagan practices, the devotee imagines himself to be so impregnated with supernatural power that it is dangerous for anyone to come near to him or to touch him. He is "taboo." He has attained a nearness to the deity that is denied to his fellows! The appeal of the pagan practices was that they enabled men to attain "a consciousness of God" liturgically without having to undergo any painful process of repentance and change within themselves. The forbidding character of Israel's God even to Israelites was that no ritual could command his presence. There was no device by which men could be sure of him. No promise or assurance was given except to a faith that laid itself open to him and clung to him through good and ill. *V. 6.* The judgment of God on such iniquity already stands written. There is an echo here of ch. 64:12. The prophet in his intercession asked, "Why art thou silent?" God now answers, "I will be silent no longer. I will speak and act, but in judgment and not for their redemption." One of the two verbs, "I will repay," is perhaps displaced from the last clause of v. 7, which would then read, "I will take the measure of their former sins and repay them into their bosom." *V. 7.* The suffixes to "sins" and "fathers" should be third instead of second person. Here it becomes plain that the practices condemned by Second Isaiah are a continuation of those with which the earlier prophets had battled, and that for him there is an unbroken continuity between the people who confront him and the preexilic Judean community. It is no newly introduced paganism of which the people are guilty, but rather, the same syncretistic practices that Jeremiah and Ezekiel condemned. It helps us to visualize Second Isaiah's situation when we remember that only a half century earlier, in the time of Jeremiah and Ezekiel, many priests and prophets who counted themselves official religious authorities in Judah, as well as many other prominent people, saw nothing wrong in these practices. Before Josiah's reform the fertility cult was established even in the precincts of the Jerusalem Temple, and its adherents would undoubtedly find ways and means of continuing it.

V. 8. The likening of Israel to a grapevine was firmly established in prophetic thought (Isa., ch. 5; Jer. 2:21; 6:9; Hos. 10:1). The fate of a vineyard that failed to produce good wine would be the rooting up of its vines (Isa., ch. 5). This has to be understood as the background of v. 8. The prophet has pronounced God's judgment upon Israel, but he has not stated it in these terms. His mind, however, leaps forward. The Israel he knows is not like a vineyard that is wholly corrupt and gives no promise of wine. God has faithful servants in the midst of the unfaithful nation. They are like good grapes among the wild and hopeless ones. From them will come a rich fruitfulness for God. Therefore, while the destroying judgment comes upon the nation as a whole, these must be spared. The use of the plural term "servants" throughout ch. 65 is significant, all the prophet's hopes for Israel the Servant being concentrated now upon the little persecuted group of servants. *V. 9.* That they "are brought forth from Jacob and Judah" and form the true succession indicates that they have been members of the Judean community until now. There is no suggestion that the faithful remnant consists in any way of exiles who have returned from abroad. They are promised an amazing augmentation of their numbers as more of God's true people are gathered from among the nations, but they themselves seem to have their origin in the Palestinian community. The promise that they are to "possess" the mountain of God has more than ordinary force when we read it in the light of ch. 66:5, where we learn that at the time the words of ch. 65 were addressed to the remnant, they had been denied a place in the Jerusalem community. The dispossessed are to be vindicated as the true inheritors. *V. 10.* Because they have sought God in truth, in contrast to their brothers (v. 1), not only the mountains of Jerusalem but the whole land, symbolized by the coastal plain of Sharon on the west and the inland valley of Achor on the east, will be covered with their flocks and herds.

Vs. 11-12. The prophet turns directly to his rebellious brethren and pronounces God's judgment on them. "Forget my holy hill" as a parallel to "forsake the Lord" is puzzling, since the "brethren" in ch. 66:5-6 are in possession of the Temple. It can only be that the prophet is thinking here of devotees of pagan shrines established in the countryside beyond Jerusalem. The preparation of food and wine in v. 11b is for a feast or feasts in honor of the god of fortune,

Gad, and the god of destiny, Meni. There is a play on words in v. 12 that gives a sharp edge to the judgment, the verb "destine" being used in the declaration of judgment and the consonants of the verb "spread" (a table) being reversed in the verb "bow down." The reference again to "I called and you did not answer" confirms the identification of the people addressed with the unresponsive community in which Second Isaiah was ministering in all the earlier chapters.

Vs. 13-16. The judgment concludes with a comparison of the future in store for the two divisions of the nation. The rebellious can look forward only to hunger, thirst, anguish, and death—and after death that their name should be used only as a curse. But the faithful inherit the agelong promises of God to his covenant people and have in prospect a fruitful land in which they shall rejoice unceasingly. *V. 15* is proof that until now the rebellious and the faithful have formed one community and have borne one name. Duhm can make no sense of the verse, since for him the rebels are Samaritans and he remarks that the prophet cannot mean that the name "Israel" is to be abandoned. Yet that is specifically what the text says. The faithful remnant is to be given a new name, and their God is to be known as the "God of truth" rather than the "God of Israel." Nothing could make clearer both the sharpness of the breach between the persecuted believers and the community as a whole and the fact that the persecuting community was the official Judean community that claimed for itself the name of "Israel." The phrase "The Lord Yahweh shall slay you" is suspect as an intrusion for several reasons: it breaks the connection between the turning of the name "Israel" into a curse and the giving of a new name to the "servants," but also it speaks of God in the third person in a passage in which God himself is speaking. Its intrusion has caused the suffix to "servants" to be changed from an original first person to third and the verb "call" to be changed in pointing from passive to active. The sentence should read, "You shall leave your name to my chosen for a curse, and my servants shall be called by a different name." The new name is "Amen," meaning true or faithful, a name to be borne only by a people that would maintain in sincerity and truth the covenant relation with God.

V. 17. The eschatological framework of Second Isaiah's thought here comes fully into view once more. He anticipates not just a change in the fortunes of the two divergent sections of the community but the speedy arrival of the day of the Lord when God's sovereignty will be openly revealed to all men. Already in ch. 51:6 he had seen the old heavens and the old earth vanishing like smoke to make way for the new and eternal order of God's redemption. Now he envisages a new creation, a universal new beginning. The term "former things," as in earlier passages, denotes the entire course of the world's history from the beginning until the approaching end. The glory of the new era will be such that the old sin-darkened era will be forgotten. In ch. 60:19-21 the sun and moon as sources of light were replaced by the luminous presence of God himself. Expecting the new day to dawn at any moment (cf. ch. 50:9), the prophet could face rejection and persecution unmoved and with absolute confidence. *V. 18.* Naturally for him the focal point of the new creation is a new Jerusalem (cf. ch. 60). The keynote of its life is joy, the joy of its people and the joy of God in it. No less than six words are used in vs. 18-19 to express joy. We are reminded by this of the exuberance of jubilation that breaks through at so many points in Second Isaiah's writings. It could be said of him as of Jesus Christ (Heb. 12:2) that for the joy that was set before him he was prepared to endure any measure of suffering. Torrey emends "for ever" to "ye eternal cities," which makes unnecessary the insertion of the preposition "in" (RSV) before the next clause. The sentence as it stands requires either the one emendation or the other. *V. 20.* A puzzling sentence, prosaic in form in contrast to the poetic character of the passage and difficult to understand, it is most likely a gloss. Perhaps the same person who inserted "The Lord Yahweh will slay you" in v. 15 to sharpen the judgment attempted here to elaborate rather clumsily the return of the earth to the conditions of paradise. The earliest age at which anyone will die, he says, will be one hundred years, perhaps intended to signify a lengthening of the life-span to that of the earlier patriarchs. That the sinner a hundred years old shall be accursed has no clear meaning. It contradicts the prophet's assertion in ch. 60:21 that the people of the New Jerusalem will all be righteous, which is certainly the implication also of ch. 65:9-16. It is peculiar that the age of one hundred should be set for the cursing of the sinner. *V. 21.* Security in home and in possession of the produce of the land was like a promise of paradise to Palestinians who had been so frequently driven from their homes and made to suffer under heavy exactions by foreign rulers. *V. 22.* "Like the days of a tree" does not mean that the people are to live as long as a tree lives. The tree with its roots deep in the soil and bearing its foliage and fruit year by year in spite of all vicissitudes was for the Palestinian a symbol of permanence (cf. Ps. 1:3; Jer. 17:7-8). *V. 24.* Another echo of ch. 64, where the complaint was that God gave no answer to the cries of his people for help. In the new day God will answer even before his people call to him. This may have been the original conclusion of the chapter. *V. 25,* which, except for its middle clause concerning the serpent, is identical with parts of Isa. 11:6-9, may be a further elaboration by a later hand of the features of the new paradise. Torrey thinks v. 25 originated with Second Isaiah and was copied by the author of Isa., ch. 11, and sees in the reference to the serpent still eating dust a touch of humor—all others, men and beasts, are well fed, but the serpent still has only dust to eat. It seems more likely that Second Isaiah would conclude the picture of the servants' felicity with a promise of God's readiness to help rather than with a general description of wild beasts at peace with each other in all Palestine.

CHAPTER 66 / The singular importance of this 66th chapter of the book should be obvious. It opens with a repudiation by God of a proposal by certain people who do *not* tremble at his word, the proposal that they should build a temple for him. This is followed by a harsh condemnation of the offering of sacrifices, equating them with pagan rites. An oracle is then addressed to those who *do* tremble at God's word and who are hated, mocked, and cast out by their brethren, an oracle containing a prediction of God's coming in judgment to punish such disobedience and cruelty. It should be evident at once that we have before us a his-

torical record of unique significance, acquainting us with events that are otherwise unknown, and throwing a beam of light not only upon the circumstances of Second Isaiah's ministry but into a shadowy period in the history of his people. And yet for one reason or another this passage has been passed over by all interpreters without any adequate realization of its momentous importance. Duhm's assumption that the proposed temple was the rival one of the Samaritans has been mentioned. Others have suggested that exiles in Egypt or Babylonia were planning to build themselves a temple and that the prophet, in loyalty to the Deuteronomic principle that centralized the sacrificial worship in Jerusalem, was protesting against it. All have taken it for granted that it was impossible for him to have been opposed to the rebuilding of the Jerusalem Temple. Torrey surprisingly passes over the events very lightly, making no attempt to assess their significance or to take account of them in his interpretation of the remainder of the book. He seems to interpret the passages as poetic expressions of the prophet's general philosophy, composed, like all the other chapters, in remoteness from any actual historical situation.

Since the persecuting brethren elsewhere in the book are the official Judean community, the reference in vs. 1-2 must be to a project to rebuild the Jerusalem Temple.[1] We know of two such projects from the Book of Ezra and the books of Haggai and Zechariah. In Ezra, chs. 1 to 4, the return of exiles from Babylon in 538 B.C. is said to be for the specific purpose of rebuilding the Temple. The priest Jeshua and the prince Zerubbabel are described as first building an altar on which to offer sacrifices (ch. 3:1-2) and then a

[1] It is curious how consistently the commentaries assume that the obvious meaning cannot be the right one. Skinner, *op. cit.,* is candid enough to admit that "the view which does fullest justice to the language of the verses" is that they are directed against the building of a temple in Jerusalem, but eventually he feels compelled to reject this. H. Gressmann, *Über die im Jes. 56–66 vorausgesetzten zeitgeschichtlichen Verhältnisse* (Göttingen: Dieterich, 1898), recognized the occasion that drew forth the condemnation of the prophet, but made nothing more of it. Smith, *op. cit.,* asserted dogmatically that the verses "do not condemn the building of the (Jerusalem) Temple. *This was not possible* (my italics) for a prophecy that contains ch. 60." The orthodox editor did his work well, by his few added touches to the book, to convince so many commentators that the prophet could have only warm regard for the Jerusalem Temple and its devotees and to persuade them to ignore all the evidence to the contrary.

year later laying the foundation of the Temple. But soon the work on the Temple was halted by the opposition of "the people of the land" (ch. 4:4) who are represented by the Chronicler as the descendants of the foreigners settled in Palestine by the Assyrians two hundred years before. This whole account is strongly suspect because of the neatness with which it fits into the Chronicler's artificial schema of Israel's history, according to which no true Israelites remained in Palestine after 587 B.C. and the renewal of the Jerusalem community and its worship was wholly the work of those who returned from Babylon. The conclusion of Torrey, however, that no return took place in 538 B.C., the account being wholly the creation of the Chronicler, is too extreme. On the other hand, it must be granted that the Chronicler's misrepresentation of the situation in the sixth century in Palestine is so palpable and his exaltation of the priestly Temple cult so dominant in the shaping of his story that all his statements must be used with great caution. In spite of this tendentiousness of the Chronicler's account, however, genuine traditions may lie behind his narrative of the return, just as they most certainly do lie behind his story of the rebuilding of the walls by Nehemiah. The fact that Cyrus permitted exiles from other nations to return to their homes and encouraged them to reestablish the cultus of their ancestral religion lends credence to the Chronicler's tradition of a return from Babylon in 538 B.C. and an abortive attempt to rebuild the Temple. But we must not follow him in his idealization of the returned exiles and his insistence at one point that they kept themselves pure in their religion and blood by refusing to mingle with the people of the land. He himself preserves a quite different tradition concerning them in Ezra 9:1-4, where Ezra is appalled that not only the people who returned in 538 B.C. but also their priests and Levites had intermarried with the people of the land and copied their pagan practices.

There is no reason to assume that Judeans who spent the years from 597 or 587 B.C. until 539 B.C. in Babylonia would be radically different in character from those who lived through those years in Palestine. They were of identical origin, and the preponderance of upper-class people in Babylon would not necessarily make one expect a greater purity in religion. Nor is there any reason to think

that the influence of the Deuteronomic historians and of those who
gathered and preserved the books of the prophets was exerted entirely upon the Babylonian exiles and not at all upon those who
remained in Palestine or went to live in Egypt. A close comparison
between the book of Deuteronomy and the writings of Second Isaiah
might suggest an intimate relation between the two and place them
both within the same milieu.[2] But what is of concern to us here is
that a return of exiles in 538 B.C. may have taken place without
changing in any appreciable degree the character of the community
confronting Second Isaiah. In fact, if it took place in his time, it
may have strengthened the priestly forces to which he was opposed
and inspired the project to rebuild the Temple, which he condemned.

We must ask what light the books of Haggai and Zechariah throw
upon our problem. At no point in the book of Haggai is there any
reference to a return from exile, and the community as a whole is
referred to as "the remnant of the people," i.e., those who have
been left when the remainder of the nation has been removed.[3] In
Hag. 2:4 they are addressed as "all you people of the land." They
seem to have been long settled in their homes. They are experienc-
ing difficult times, which Haggai attributes to their failure to rebuild the Temple. What strikes us most forcefully is that as a
prophet he represents a viewpoint that is precisely the one condemned by Second Isaiah. In the name of God, Haggai promises
the members of the community a better time if only they will rebuild the Temple! Zechariah, in the second year of Darius, 520
B.C., speaks of the anger of God against Jerusalem and the cities of
Judah that has persisted for seventy years and then proclaims the
beginning of a new era of mercy when God will return to his city
and both city and Temple will be rebuilt. One feature of this new
day is to be the return of exiles from "the land of the north" and
from Babylon (Zech. 2:6-7). A reference to three exiles who have
recently come from Babylon bringing with them silver and gold
that is used to make a crown (Zech. 6:10-11) indicates a close rela-

[2] Noth, *op. cit.*, considers the Deuteronomic history to have been composed in
Palestine.
[3] Kosters, *op. cit.*

tionship between the Jerusalem and Babylonian communities, the former receiving a measure of support from the latter. It suggests the probability that at least a small and influential group had already come from Babylon and taken its place in the community. But there is no word of any substantial return of exiles in the past such as the Chronicler describes nor of any earlier laying of foundations for the Temple. The project sponsored by the two prophets and by Jeshua and Zerubbabel is the first, so far as Zechariah is concerned. It is noteworthy that the high priest, Jeshua, has to be cleansed of a pollution before he can take his part in the new era. The Chronicler retains a tradition that the sons of Jeshua had married foreign women (Ezra 10:18). The likelihood is that in the period before 521 b.c., Jeshua had engaged in some of the syncretistic practices that are condemned by Second Isaiah. Zechariah, like Haggai, expects prosperity to be restored through the rebuilding of the Temple, but unlike Haggai, he also places a strong emphasis upon the need for repentance and faithfulness to God's commands.

The witness of Haggai and Zechariah increases our cautiousness in accepting the Chronicler's account of the period of restoration in Judah. The most we can affirm is that most likely some exiles returned in 538 b.c., mingling with the existing community, accentuating the priestly and sacrificial character of its worship, and instigating an attempt to rebuild the Temple, which for some reason came to nothing. Haggai is particularly valuable as the spokesman of a religious point of view that corresponds closely with that which Second Isaiah criticizes in chs. 58:1-5 and 66:1-4. This does not mean that we can identify the Temple rebuilding opposed by Second Isaiah as that of 521 b.c. or that we can make him and Haggai personal opponents, but only that Haggai's prophecies serve as evidence of the presence in Jerusalem in 521 b.c. of an influential and authoritative religious party that preserved the viewpoint that Second Isaiah condemned in his opponents. Perhaps it was the earlier attempt to rebuild the Temple in 538 b.c. that roused Second Isaiah's scorn, and a vague recollection of the opposition of his group of believers to the project may be preserved in the Chronicler's tradition that the "people of the land," i.e., people who were in the land when the exiles returned, brought the project to a halt.

Second Isaiah's opposition to the rebuilding of the Temple must not be generalized into a rejection of all worship in temples built with men's hands and an insistence that God asks for nothing more than humility and obedience. The prophet was not the enemy of all religious institutions and did not intend the abandonment of all places of worship any more than did the author of John's Gospel (John 4:21-24). Like some of his predecessors he repudiated animal sacrifices as essentially pagan (ch. 66:3-4) and as having never had any authority from the God of Israel (ch. 43:23-24), but more than once he speaks of the Temple in sympathetic terms. But for him it was a matter of life or death for the nation that it should realize the impossibility of God's satisfaction with anything less than a repentance and obedience that would permeate the entire common life of the people. Only a nation in covenant with God and willing to be cleansed of its sins by his forgiveness had any hope of a future. God asked of his people, not that they perform impressive ceremonies, or observe days of fasting, or build a Temple, but that they feed the hungry, clothe the naked, set the prisoner free, and establish truth and justice in all their relations. The nation was offering God something less than that surrender of itself in love by which alone it could be restored to its true existence as the covenant people of God. It was not the Temple in itself that was abhorrent to God, but the Temple conceived as a structure that would guarantee his presence in the midst of his people and serve as a substitute for the humble and contrite heart.

It is hard to understand how anyone could question the genuineness of ch. 66 as a writing of Second Isaiah. The loftiness of the conception of God as Lord of heaven and earth to whom all things belong, the promise of his presence with the humble and contrite (cf. ch. 57:15), the definition of the righteous as those "who tremble at his word" (cf. chs. 40:8; 50:10; 51:1, 7), and the vivid dramatic form are a combination of features that should be sufficient for identification. But what constitutes practically a signature is the phrase with which the faithful are mocked by their brethren in v. 5: "Let the Lord be glorified that we may see your joy." The mockers seize upon two salient characteristics of Second Isaiah's preaching: that God is about to come in glory and that his coming will usher in a day of great joy for all true believers. They felt that they could safely disregard a prophet who made such wild and incredible predictions on behalf of his little group of followers. One final link with Second Isaiah's writings in chs. 40 to 55 is the evident suffering of those who to the prophet were the faithful servants of the word of God. Chapter 66 belongs closely together with chs. 50 and 53 and is essential to a right understanding of both chapters. All three have their focus in a suffering servant or suffering servants of the word.

V. 1. Throughout Second Isaiah the constant emphasis upon God's transcendent power as Creator of the heavens and the earth is background and basis for the prophet's confidence in a new creative act of God that is to establish a wholly new order. The god of his opponents is too small and, like the pagan idols, can do nothing in history. Their proposal to build a house for Yahweh is part and parcel of their pagan way of thinking. The god cannot be present in the land if he has nowhere to live! That Israelites should speak thus of Yahweh, the Creator of all things and the Lord of history, was outrageous and blasphemous. The force of God's violent repudiation of the project is better preserved if we translate: "What is this? A house that you will build for me? What is this? A place for me to take my rest?" God has no intention of "resting" in Zion!

V. 2. "All these things" refers to the whole creation, the heavens and the earth. One can imagine a sweep of the prophet's hand as he speaks the words. The possessive preposition and suffix signifying "mine" has dropped out of the Hebrew text and must be supplied from the LXX.

V. 3. Amos and Jeremiah rejected the Temple sacrifices, but neither of them condemned them in such violent terms as are used by Second Isaiah. The ritual killing of an ox he equates with the murder of a man and the sacrifice of a lamb with the brutal breaking of a dog's neck. Cereal offerings and incense are no better than pagan practices. These elements in the customary worship of the Jerusalem community were so similar to parallel elements in the worship of false gods that they facilitated the syncretistic process, confusing the minds of the people and concealing from them the radical distinction between the God of Israel and the idols of the pagans. Looked at superficially, there seemed to be little difference between the worship of Yahweh and the worship of the idols. The prophetic condemnation of sacrifice was an attempt to clear away this source of confusion and to let the uniqueness of the God of Israel be evident in the character of the worship offered him. The Temple party "choose their own ways" in preference to God's ways (cf. chs. 53:6; 55:9), just as in ch. 65:2 they "follow their own thoughts" in preference to God's thoughts. *V. 4*. But *their* choice is followed by *God's* choice. They are free to choose their own road, but it is God who determines the outcome of their choice. The reference to "their fears" indicates that by their sacrifices they are trying to ward off misfortunes and secure prosperity. But their sacrifices are meaningless when in their way of life they themselves are totally unresponsive to the voice of God. God has been speaking his word to Israel through his prophet, calling his people to return to him and, as his covenant people, to fulfill a glorious destiny, but the community as a whole has turned a deaf ear to this call. The refusal to hear has been a constantly recurring complaint of Second Isaiah against his fellow countrymen.

V. 5. "Hear the word of the Lord" does not introduce a new oracle, but merely a shift of focus from the rebels to the faithful servants. V. 5 is linked closely with v. 4; mention of those who refuse to respond to God's word is followed directly by a message of encouragement to those who have responded to it and are suffering for their response. It is the word of God that has divided the community, and not the initiative of the prophet. Like Jesus or Paul or Luther, his intention is only to recall God's people to the fulfillment of the destiny that God established for them from the beginning and revealed in his word. The counting of heads or the noting of who retains possession of Jerusalem does not determine the true line of continuity in the Israel of God. The true church is present where there is a people that lives in utter dependence upon the word of God. Torrey weakens the force of the prophet's statement about the relation between the divided brethren by translating the second verb as "spurn you" rather than "cast you out." One would expect something more forceful after "hate." The Hebrew verb that is used came later to mean "excommunicate." "For my name's sake" makes clear that it is the servants' uncompromising loyalty to God that has made their continued presence in the community intolerable. The fact that their "brethren" could cast them out indicates that these brethren are not to be identified as certain lower elements in the community, but rather, as the official religious and civil authorities. The evils against which the prophet and his followers protested were entrenched in the highest quarters.

V. 6. To read this verse aright, it must be grasped that the prophet is now outside Jerusalem. His enemies occupy the city and the Temple site. But in imagination he hears a great uproar in the city like the noise of battle. The sound comes from the city and from the Temple, i.e., from the site where the altar of sacrifice stands and where the work has begun upon the building of the Temple. It is the sound of God executing judgment upon his enemies. It is a mistake to picture God as going forth from Jerusalem to punish his enemies somewhere else, as in Amos 1:2 (Duhm). The enemies this time are in Jerusalem itself.

V. 7. God's coming in judgment upon his enemies in Jerusalem is at the same time his coming to redeem the city and to transform its future. The emphasis is upon the speed and immediacy of the event, which indicates the intensity of expectation in the prophetic group. The dawn of the new day is likened here, as in ch. 42:14, to a woman giving birth to a child. Suddenly, without even the warning of the pains of childbirth, the new creature arrives. The unbelievable is about to happen: a new nation is to be born in a day (*v. 8*). Here, as in the New Testament, the eschatological hope seems pathetically doomed to disappointment. The prophet is inciting his followers to expect an event at any moment that simply will not happen. His opponents who ridicule his expectation seem to be the sensible realists who have their eyes open to the distinction between the possible and the impossible. Yet this expectation of the seemingly impossible is the faith that moves mountains, and the contrasting attitude issues in a religion that expects nothing of God and so receives nothing from God. The apparently irrational hopes expressed in this eschatological language have to be understood, not as a fixing of a timetable for God's action, but as the utterances of a faith that is so certain of God's sovereignty in human affairs that it lives moment by moment in expectation of God's vindication and fulfillment of his purpose. Modern imitations of prophetic eschatology that operate chiefly with a timetable for God's actions in the future are not to be confused with Biblical eschatology. The essential element in the Biblical hope is the openness of the believer constantly to the action of God and his certainty of God's triumph that enables him to live confidently and joyfully, even in times of darkness when the powers of evil have the upper hand. His faith does not depend upon the new nation being born tomorrow, but rather, is so rooted and grounded in the promise of God that it remains unshaken no matter how long the day of redemption is delayed.

V. 10. Those who love Jerusalem and are in mourning for her but are here promised a time of rejoicing are the excluded brethren. The entire chapter has to be read as addressed directly to them. In *vs. 11-13* they are likened to newborn babies of Mother Jerusalem in the new era: nursed at her breast, dandled on her knees, and comforted by her. The force of "You will be comforted in Jerusalem" is apparent only when we remember that those addressed have been driven out and are homeless.

Throughout ch. 66:1-14 the hand of Second Isaiah has been evident in many ways: the demand for faith and obedience and the repudiation of any lesser way of securing God's favor, the words of encouragement to faithful believers who are persecuted by their fellows, the highly dramatic style and the quotation of the mocking words of the persecutors, the use of the likeness of childbirth for the dawning of the new day, the suddenness of the transformation, the heaping up of rhetorical questions, the element of repetition, the likening of Jerusalem to a mother, the note of comfort, and finally the balancing of salvation for God's servants against vengeance for his enemies in *v. 14.* Verse 14 completes the oracle begun in v. 1.

Vs. 15-24 form a most unsatisfactory conclusion to the chapter and the book. There is no clear line of development within them and there are peculiar incoherencies. They are not addressed to the same situation as vs. 1-14. Muilenburg considers vs. 17-24 to have been added by a redactor. This may be true of vs. 15-16 as well. The fiery judgment in vs. 15-16 is upon all flesh in contrast to the judgment in vs. 4, 6, and 14 upon the unfaithful Israelites. But in v. 17 it is focused upon the idolators in Israel. Then in vs. 18 ff. a universal salvation is pictured, with echoes of Second Isaiah but also with elements of confusion, and some passages that sound much more like the orthodox editor with his enthusiasm for Temple, priesthood, and Sabbath. The whole section has about it the kind of clumsiness that was evident in chs. 44:28, 56:1-7, and 58:13-14. It looks very much as though in collecting the assorted oracles of Second Isaiah in chs. 56-66, the editor had added a preface and an appendix in order to express his own concern for the Temple as a place of worship for all nations and for the Sabbath as the primary observance of a true Israelite. His one point of agreement with Second Isaiah was his anticipation of a day of universal judgment and salvation.

Vs. 15-16. The fiery judgment is here universal. Therefore, *v. 17,* which echoes the denunciations of syncretistic idolaters in ch. 65, follows strangely. Volz considers it displaced.

V. 18. "Their works and their thoughts" interrupts the sequence between "I" and "am coming." The RSV introduces the verb "know" from the Septuagint in order to make sense. However reconstructed, it belongs to the thought of v. 17 rather than v. 18.

The ingathering of nations echoes Second Isaiah's eschatology, but in *v. 19* the picture becomes hopelessly confused. The nations that are gathered are termed "survivors," echoing ch. 45:20, but they are then dispatched as messengers to a series of nations that are said to have not yet "heard my fame or seen my glory." In Second Isaiah's eschatology all nations see the glory of God in his great day of judgment and salvation. But here the messengers have to take news of it to distant lands. They also bring exiles home from these lands as "an offering to the Lord . . . as the Israelites bring their cereal offering in a clean vessel to the house of the Lord." This latter phrase implies a Temple in existence, directly similar to ch. 56:7. The clumsiness of the editor is evident in the fact that he would use this language in an appendix to a chapter that began with a denunciation of the Temple and its sacrifices. His Temple-centered outlook had such authority for him that he was unaware that he was introducing contradictory elements into the chapter. In ch. 56:1-7 the Temple was to be a place of worship for all people; in ch. 66:21 the foreign nations are even to provide priests and Levites for the service of the Temple.

Vs. 22-23. The reference to the new heavens and earth echoes Second Isaiah, but in v. 23 the climax of the new creation is Sabbath worship, as in ch. 56:1-7, and we see how the editor bends the prophet's greatest thoughts to fit his orthodox schema. The consummation is not an era of justice and mercy in all the common relations of life, as it was for the prophet, but is the coming of all nations on new moons and Sabbaths to participate in the Temple worship.

V. 24. Again the clumsiness is evident. The chapter closes, not with a representation of God's judgment, but with the righteous worshipers going forth somewhere in the neighborhood of Jerusalem to look gloatingly on the dead bodies of the damned.

CHAPTER 35 /

How ch. 35 became separated from chs. 40 to 66 we cannot tell, but it bears all the marks of a genuine writing of Second Isaiah. If it stood at the end of the book, after ch. 66, interpreters would speak of it as the perfect lyrical conclusion of the prophet's work. Its contents are parallel at every point with Second Isaiah's message: the desert that is transformed into a fruitful land by the advent of God in glory; the good news of God's coming as the source of strength and confidence to a despairing people; the Day of the Lord as a day when the blind see, the deaf hear, and the lame walk; the likening of God's coming to the breaking forth of streams in the desert; the highway on which the ransomed of the Lord return to Jerusalem from the four corners of the earth; the absence of "ravenous beasts," symbolic of the peacefulness of the new day; and the everlasting joy of the redeemed that forms the crown and climax of the picture. Each of these features is typical of Second Isaiah, and among them there is no discordant note that would suggest another author. They are so perfectly blended in a lyrical poem of exquisite beauty, similar in many ways to ch. 55, that if the chapter were attributed to a later disciple of Second Isaiah, it would be necessary to assume that the disciple was his equal in both prophetic and poetic powers. It is much simpler to recognize it as an original oracle of Second Isaiah that in the process of the editing of The Book of Isaiah became separated from chs. 40 to 66 by the insertion of the historical material in chs. 36 to 39. Where it originally stood among the writings of Second Isaiah we can have no idea, but it does no violence to it to place it at the end and to let it form the conclusion of the book. It is unnecessary to make extended comments on the verses, since their thought content has already received full attention. The chapter is like a recapitulation in which nothing new is introduced.

V. 1. For Second Isaiah the desert is always symbolic of the world without God. The withdrawal of God is the withdrawal of the source of life. The RSV rightly makes "like the crocus" the opening of v. 2. At God's coming the whole world breaks into singing because his presence with man spells the end of death and the beginning of life. *V. 2.* The trees of Lebanon and the lush growth on Carmel and the plain of Sharon are likenesses of the fruitfulness of the new day. *V. 3.* The sudden change from joyful proclamation of God's coming to the commanding of unnamed persons to take the good news to a fainting and fearful people is familiar in Second Isaiah, and exactly parallel to ch. 40:1-11. The task is one of encouragement. The prophet in ch. 50:4 describes his own and the Servant's mission in similar terms as the speaking of a word from God that will sustain him who is weary. In ch. 40:27-31 and elsewhere, we hear him speaking this word passionately and convincingly. But always he calls for others to join with him in this work of spiritual restoration, and as we have seen, his call did not go unanswered. *V. 4.* The fear that he sought to combat was the despair into which his people were sinking in their hopelessness. They had ceased to hope for anything from God, and therefore the world and all the forces of the world that surrounded them became terrifying threats to their existence. Fear led to superstitious practices. In their fear they turned for help to any quarter where it was promised. Since Yahweh had apparently abandoned them, perhaps the queen of heaven would come to their rescue (cf. Jer. 44:15 ff.). In a real sense the whole message of Second Isaiah is summed up in the proclamation "Behold your God!", which should stand by itself here as in ch. 40:9, the sentence continuing "he will come with vengeance." The entire misery of man had its source in what can be described either as his blindness to God or God's absence from him. Therefore, nothing can be of help to him until he opens his mind and heart to the living power and glory of God. The prophet does not merely promise God's coming at a future date. To await his coming in faith was to know the joy of his coming already. To hope in him was to lay hold upon him and to be sustained by him now.

V. 5. The blind, the deaf, the dumb, and the lame are not just a few unfortunates among men, but are meant to describe the whole of humanity. Here as elsewhere Second Isaiah's outlook is universal (cf. the blind and deaf in chs. 42 to 44). Also he has in mind, not the physical infirmities, but the spiritual, the blindness and deafness to God that destroys man's understanding of all things in life, the dumbness that unfits him for the speaking of the word of truth, and the lameness that cripples him for walking in God's ways. *V. 7.* The first half of the second line neither gives adequate meaning nor corresponds to its parallel phrase. Torrey's suggestion "the haunt of jackals will become a marsh" involves only slight emendation.

V. 8. The prophet leaps from one image to another. Having described the coming day under the likenesses of a healing of human infirmities and a transformation of desert places into fruitful land, he finally envisages a great highway on which the redeemed from all the earth come to Zion. This is the miraculous highway of the day of redemption for which mountains are melted down and valleys are filled up. By it first of all God himself returns to his people (ch. 40:3-5). Then down it come the redeemed not only of Israel but of all the nations. To make it a highway from one specific place to Jerusalem is to lose sight of the fact that it brings God from heaven to earth and the people of God from the farthest corners of the earth, north, south, east, and west. The second line of v. 8 has a confusion of words at its center, yet its meaning is sufficiently clear; that the unclean and foolish (in the Hebrew sense of corrupted in mind) will not be found traveling this road. *Vs. 9-10.* The absence of wild beasts symbolizes the end of violence and the coming of peace. Only the redeemed will be found on the highway and in Zion. It will be a time of unbroken and unshadowed joy.

Appendix:

THE NEW TESTAMENT CONTEXT

IT WOULD be out of place in an exposition of the writings of Second
Isaiah to explore in detail the influence of those writings on the
New Testament. But it is important to draw attention to the close
similarities at many points between the mission and message of
Second Isaiah and the formulation of the Christian mission and
message in the New Testament. If it can be shown to be true that
Second Isaiah, on the one side, and Jesus with his followers, on the
other, had much in common and that an influence of Second Isaiah
can be traced with definiteness in the New Testament far beyond
that of any other of the prophets, then it may be that not only will
the parallels in Second Isaiah be of value in illuminating the New
Testament but also the parallels in the New Testament will help us
to understand better the intention of Second Isaiah. In short, if the
New Testament takes up and develops elements that were already
present in Second Isaiah so that the two are knit together in a very
intimate way in spite of the nearly six centuries that lie between,
then each forms an important part of the larger historical context
of the other. Sometimes the ritual of the Babylonian Marduk cult is
quoted to furnish analogies to the language of Second Isaiah, but
no one is likely to suggest that the analogies go deeper than the
imagery of the language. But surely the parallels not only in language and thought but in the very form of prophetic ministry between Second Isaiah and the New Testament are of much greater

importance. And yet they have rarely been drawn into consideration in the interpretation of the prophet. As John Marsh pointed out in an essay on "Christ in the Old Testament,"[1] we sometimes have to look to the later developments in a movement in order to understand the meaning of earlier phenomena.

There are wide differences of judgment among scholars concerning the part played by the writings of Second Isaiah in the thinking of Jesus and of the early church. Unfortunately the arguments have tended to center themselves upon the question of whether or not Jesus identified himself with the Suffering Servant of Isa., ch. 53 in such a way that this chapter influenced his understanding and interpretation of his own death. A number of scholars, such as T. W. Manson,[2] Vincent Taylor,[3] and J. W. Bowman,[4] have held that Jesus consciously combined the Old Testament concepts of Son of Man and Suffering Servant to express his own conception of the nature and task of the Messiah. Others, such as Jackson and Lake,[5] F. C. Burkitt,[6] Wilhelm Bousset,[7] and Rudolf Bultmann,[8] have denied that Isa., ch. 53 exerted any influence on Christian thinking until the period of Hellenistic Christianity. Recently R. H. Fuller[9] has argued that the passion sayings in Mark, placed together, form a clear description of the Suffering Servant of ch. 53, a direct consequence of Jesus' conceiving himself as Servant of God in his lifetime and Son of Man afterward, and Oscar Cullmann[10] has traced the faint lines of an early Servant Christology that was taught perhaps by Peter, but most likely was based on Jesus' own conception of himself. In criticism of these conclusions Miss M. D. Hooker[11]

[1] J. Marsh, "Christ in the Old Testament," *Essays in Christology for Karl Barth*, ed. by T. H. L. Parker (London: Lutterworth Press, 1956).

[2] T. W. Manson, *The Servant-Messiah* (Cambridge: Cambridge University Press, 1953).

[3] Vincent Taylor, *Jesus and His Sacrifice* (London: The Macmillan Company, 1937).

[4] John Wick Bowman, *The Intention of Jesus* (The Westminster Press, 1943).

[5] F. J. Foakes-Jackson and Kirsopp Lake, *The Beginnings of Christianity* (London: Macmillan and Co., Ltd., 1920).

[6] F. C. Burkitt, *Christian Beginnings* (London: University of London Press, 1924).

[7] Wm. Bousset, *Kyrios Christos*, 2d ed. (Göttingen: Vandenhoeck & Ruprecht, 1921).

[8] Rudolf Bultmann, *Jesus and the Word* (Charles Scribner's Sons, 1934).

[9] R. H. Fuller, *The Mission and Achievement of Jesus* (Alec R. Allenson, Inc., 1954).

[10] Oscar Cullmann, *The Christology of the New Testament*, Revised Edition (The Westminster Press, 1964).

[11] Hooker, *op. cit.*

has made a very thorough examination of the New Testament records to show how little basis there is for an identification of Jesus with the Suffering Servant of ch. 53 either by Jesus himself or by the early church.

Miss Hooker's argument is at its strongest when she is exposing the lack of evidence that Jesus specifically identified himself as the Suffering Servant of ch. 53 or was so identified by Peter, Paul, or any of the earliest Christians. She explains that although modern scholars think of the Servant as an individual, neither Second Isaiah himself nor any Jewish writers in the following centuries used "Servant" as the title of an individual. Rather, it expressed a vision of the nature of Israel's vocation. The collective concept predominated and would be the background against which both Jesus and the early Jewish Christians read the Servant passages. But both Miss Hooker and those with whom she contends focus their attention too exclusively upon the Suffering Servant of ch. 53. No right perspective for the consideration of the problem can be gained unless the whole relation between Second Isaiah and the early Christian movement is explored and the question faced whether the points of contact with the Old Testament prophet began in the early church or with Jesus himself.

It is not sufficient merely to examine passages where the New Testament quotes directly from Second Isaiah. Jesus differed from the rabbis and from a rabbinically trained Christian such as Paul in the manner in which the Old Testament came to expression in his teaching and preaching. Direct quotations are rare, and when they occur, as in the temptation story or in Luke's account of Jesus' teaching in the synagogue in Nazareth (Luke 4:18-19), they are not proof texts, but rather, Old Testament words that have been incorporated in the most vital fashion into the mind and teaching of Jesus. It is striking that although Jesus does not base himself upon the authority of the Old Testament as the rabbis did (so much so that he was exposed to the accusation of abolishing the Torah [Matt. 5:17]), he takes up into himself and his gospel the very substance of the Old Testament and becomes the climactic expression of the word from God that was ever its hidden center. Walther Eichrodt[12]

---

[12] Walther Eichrodt, *Theology of the Old Testament,* Vol. I, tr. by J. A. Baker (The Westminster Press, 1961), p. 8.

points out that the Old Testament rather than the intertestamental literature has first place in the minds of the New Testament writers, and Paul Minear[13] notes that the imagery in which the mind of the early Christian community expresses itself is in direct continuity with preexilic and exilic Old Testament images, but shows little influence from postexilic Judaism. The Old Testament came alive in a new way in the Christian movement. Closely connected with this remarkable phenomenon is the fact that in John the Baptist and Jesus the great line of the Old Testament prophets that had faded out after the exile was suddenly revived. John was consciously a prophet who took up once more the task of an Elijah and an Amos. The fragmentary records of his ministry are in danger of concealing the dimensions of his prophetic stature. Jesus' deliberate associating of himself with John is in itself a massive affirmation of the rebirth of the prophetic office in John, and a careful examination of Jesus' own ministry and teaching shows it to be interwoven at countless points with the prophetic tradition. Here then we have the most reasonable explanation of the fact that the New Testament writings are more closely linked with the Old Testament than with the literature of Judaism, and the explanation suggests that this establishment of continuity in a new and living way with the central prophetic concerns of the Old Testament was the work of Jesus himself and not a later development of the church.

The continuity of Jesus with the Old Testament is not to be interpreted as though he consciously drew certain elements from the Old Testament and others from elsewhere to combine them into his own unique message and ministry. He did not take the Suffering Servant idea from Second Isaiah and the Son of Man idea from Daniel and Enoch and blend them together to form a new concept of Messiah. Rather, what he was in himself was primary. He did not deliberately revive the prophetic tradition. A word from God sounded in his being as it had in the ears of John, a word to which he could not be unfaithful without surrendering his very life in God, and although it made him speak and act differently from John and differently at many points from any of the earlier prophets, that word nevertheless bound him to John and to them in a common life

[13] Paul S. Minear, *Images of the Church in the New Testament* (The Westminster Press, 1960), p. 106.

and a common task. The earlier prophets and John and their message came alive again in Jesus, not as something that was copied or adopted, but as elements of a life in God that had once possessed them and now possessed him in a uniquely new way. Thus we might say that the Old Testament entered into his being like metal into a furnace to be melted, to be combined with other elements, and to come forth in a wholly new form, even though it remained the same metal. Thus, to demonstrate the elements in Second Isaiah that appear also in the New Testament is not to suggest that Jesus "took over" certain ideas from Second Isaiah, but only that he recognized an unusually close continuity between himself and the prophet who speaks in that portion of the book of Isaiah, similar to the continuity between himself and John the Baptist.

That the chapters which we now assign to Second Isaiah should have had a strong appeal for Jesus and the early church is not remarkable when we consider certain of their basic features. It is not just the figure of the Suffering Servant that provides an interest. Before all else was the intense eschatological expectation of the prophet, awaiting at any moment the appearance of God in power and glory to establish his universal rule and to destroy all the forces of evil. The hour was at hand, and the prophet sustained his own soul and the souls of all who were open to him with the confidence that God would soon vindicate his agelong purpose, bringing forth justice to the nations. It is no accident that Isa. 40:3 is found in the mouth of John the Baptist and is so often quoted in the New Testament. It has been too lightly assumed that the roots of the New Testament eschatology are wholly in Jewish apocalyptic.[14] Apocalyptic has undoubtedly exerted its influence, whether on Jesus or on the Jewish Christian church is open to question, but it is possible that both John the Baptist and Jesus were closer to Second Isaiah in the primary shaping of the forms of their eschatological hope. The influence of Second Isaiah's imagery in the book of Revelation is also to be noted. Second is the fact that Second Isaiah is the prophet who beyond all others has a vision of God's purpose that takes in the

[14] G. Ebeling, *Theologie und Verkündigung* (Tübingen: J. C. B. Mohr, 1963), p. 66, thinks Jesus may have burst through the forms of contemporary Jewish apocalyptic just as Paul and John did, but he takes no account of the possibility of prophetic continuity in this.

whole world. Israel is to be gathered from among the nations and is
to experience a glorious restoration but only that she may become
a nation of priests and ministers of God through whom he will be
made known to all men. Israel is to be a light to the nations. Believers from far beyond Israel are to be built into the people of God.
Most striking at this point is the fact that although Jesus addressed
his disciples as "the light of the world" (Matt. 5:14) and his gospel
has upon it from the beginning the stamp of universality (not by
any means a Jewish gospel that had later to be universalized by Paul
and the Gentile church!), in his lifetime he deliberately confined his
mission and that of his disciples to the ingathering of "the lost sheep
of the house of Israel." It is unlikely to be proposed that Jesus intended this to be a permanent limitation upon the mission instituted
by him. Paul was certain that he himself rather than the Judaizers
was the valid interpreter of Jesus' intention when he took the gospel
freely to the Gentiles. The question may at least be asked whether
these two stages in the Christian mission, first the ingathering of the
lost sheep of the house of Israel and then the building in of the Gentiles as a graft upon the olive tree of Israel (Rom. 11:17) correspond
directly to the two stages in the mission of the Servant Israel in Isa.,
ch. 49, first the restoration of the tribes of Jacob and then the shining
forth of light to the nations.

Perhaps we should have placed first the use of the term "gospel"
for the Christian message, a use that few would deny originated with
Jesus himself and a term that comes directly from such passages as
Isa. 40:9; 52:7. "Gospel," however, cannot be detached from its
eschatological context. It is, both in Second Isaiah and in the New
Testament, the unbelievably good news that God has forgiven his
sinful people, thereby restoring them to a fellowship with himself
that opens to them a wholly new possibility of life. This restoration
of the covenant relation can also be described as a "coming" of God
to his people so that the good news is "Behold your God!", i.e., God
no longer distant but present. Also this coming of God, in Second
Isaiah as in the New Testament, although it is still future, transforms the present situation of those who wait for it in faith. They
walk, run, and mount up on wings like eagles *now* because their
vision of God's coming enables them to live in a dark and fearful

present as though the glorious day of vindication had already come. Thus, no matter how discouraging the outlook, Second Isaiah exhibits an irrepressible joyousness in his faith that has its parallel in the joyousness of New Testament faith.

Whether Luke 4:16-30 be taken as the description of an actual incident or as a story by which the church represented to itself the origins of its ministry, it bears witness to the church's conviction that Jesus himself saw a continuity between the mission of the Servant in Second Isaiah (Isa. 61:1-2) and his own mission. The play upon the same passage in Jesus' answer to the disciples of John the Baptist in Matt. 11:4-5 lends force to the conviction that it was Jesus himself rather than the church who recognized the continuity, and it is noteworthy that in this dialogue two other features of the Servant's mission, familiar elsewhere in Second Isaiah, the giving of sight to the blind and hearing to the deaf, are combined with the preaching of the gospel to the poor from Isa., ch. 61.[15] Yet another theme from Second Isaiah that enters here is that of promise and fulfillment. Jesus understood his own mission, according to Luke 4:21, as the "fulfillment" of what was promised in Isa. 61:1-2. The words "the time is fulfilled" (Mark 1:15) can hardly be denied to Jesus himself as summarizing a part of his original preaching. In short, the conviction of the early Christians that they were living in the time of fulfillment, the last days, was a faithful reflection of Jesus' preaching from the beginning. But it was in the last days that according to Second Isaiah the poor, broken, sinful Servant Israel was to become the glorious and triumphant Servant through whom God would bring all men to the light and make his will prevail to the ends of the earth. This was promised "from of old," i.e., in the earlier revelations of God's purpose in Israel, and the goal of history was the fulfillment of these promises.

The predominance of the term "Servant" (or servants) in Second

[15] Hooker, op. cit., underestimates the importance of these two passages as demonstrating the presence of the figure of the Servant in Jesus' mind because she continues to distinguish four special "Servant Songs," an unfortunate legacy from Duhm, and denies the connection of Isa. 61:1-2 with the figure of the Servant. We dare not proceed as though even Jesus accepted Duhm's assumptions in advance! The unity of chs. 40 to 66, once established, makes it impossible to disassociate ch. 61:1-2 from chs. 42 and 49.

Isaiah in order to express the true nature and destiny of Israel in its covenant relation with God is a correlative of the emphasis upon God's absolute sovereignty. It has a double aspect: on the one hand, *'ebed* signifies a slave with no rights even over his own family because of the completeness with which he belongs to his master, but on the other hand, it is the title of the most trusted confidant of the sovereign and the ready instrument of his purpose. Israel as God's Servant or Slave owes him complete and unconditional obedience, but in this intimate relation with God is the agent of a worldwide redemption, sharing the glory of his ultimate triumph and rule. Parallel to this we note the emphasis upon God's sovereignty in Jesus' gospel of the Kingdom and his insistent claim upon men that they should surrender themselves unconditionally to God's rule. The death of self meant the end of all self-sovereignty and the yielding of all rights to a life of one's own outside the scope of God's rule. Therefore, it is not surprising that also for Jesus the correlative of God's sovereignty is man's servanthood and that he uses the figure of the servant to express not only his own relation with God and that of his disciples but also that of all true believers through the ages. "Servant" is thus never for him a title that he reserves for himself, but rather it describes what he and all men with him must be when their eyes are open to the reality of God's sovereignty. To suggest that Jesus was unaware of the similarity between his own use of these terms and that of the relevant chapters in Isaiah is to say that he was singularly obtuse in his reading of the Old Testament.

The application of the image of the Servant by Jesus to *both* himself and the disciples suggests why the church never used it clearly and specifically as a Messianic title. He himself had given it a broader reference. In Luke 22:27, "I am among you as one who serves" establishes not merely a unique office of Jesus in the perfectness of his obedience but a ministry into which he intends that every disciple should enter, however haltingly. In John, ch. 13, Jesus does the work of a slave in relation to his disciples, but specifically that they may have impressed upon their minds the nature of the ministry into which they have entered in fellowship with him. Also, in Phil., ch. 2, Jesus' "taking the form of a servant" is the incentive for all Christians to recognize that no true life is open to them in faith except that of servants. This broader reference is in complete harmony with the use of the term "Servant" (and servants) by Second Isaiah. The Servant may be an individual, such as Abraham or any one of the prophets, or he may be the people of God in all ages, or he may be a specific group of believers in the present moment. The meaning shifts as the reality is seen from various aspects. But the reality itself is the human person or persons, chosen by God to be the instrument of his purpose in the world, entrusted with his word in all its fearful wonder and power, and willing, if need be, to be trodden on and utterly humiliated by the world in order to fulfill the appointed destiny. Lucien Cerfaux[16] has suggested that Paul considered himself to be the Servant who would take the light to the Gentiles, continuing the work of the Servant begun by Jesus, and has pointed in support of this theory to a number of echoes of Second Isaiah both in Paul's letters and in references to Paul in Acts. The only objection one might make to this would be if Cerfaux were representing Paul as thinking of Jesus and himself as exclusively the Servants of God. This would be an individualizing of the Servant that has no support either in Second Isaiah or in the New Testament.

The multiple points of contact adduced thus far between Second Isaiah and the New Testament and the strong indications that Jesus himself was aware of these points of contact would make it strange and almost inexplicable if the suffering of the Servant in Second Isaiah (by no means in Isa., ch. 53 alone) had exerted no influence upon the mind of Jesus. The suffering of the Servant in Second Isaiah is intrinsic to his destiny and inescapable for him as the bearer of God's word. Because he hears this word from God and speaks what he hears, men seek to humiliate him (ch. 50:4 ff.). God wills his suffering (ch. 53:10) because God wills a redemption of all mankind that cannot be accomplished unless there is a Servant who will speak the word that judges and redeems, no matter what it may cost him in suffering. Jesus had sufficient evidence before him in the experience of John the Baptist and in the reactions of the religious authorities to his own teaching and actions to be able to count the

---

[16] Lucien Cerfaux, *Recueil Lucien Cerfaux*, Vol. II (Gembloux: J. Duculot, 1954), pp. 439–454.

cost of complete faithfulness to the Word that had been entrusted to him. He expected suffering not only for himself but also for his disciples. This suffering he saw in continuity with the sufferings of the prophets in the distant past (Matt. 5:12), i.e., in continuity with the sufferings of the Servant in whose figure the whole prophetic destiny of Israel was comprehended. But here again we find the Suffering Servant of Jesus to be no more an individual than he is in Second Isaiah, but rather to be Jesus and his disciples in the service of God that they had in common. We may therefore posit an influence of the Suffering Servant passages upon Jesus without expecting as a consequence that he should have identified himself as an individual with an exclusive figure, *the* Suffering Servant.[17]

Large problems are here touched upon that require a much more careful and detailed examination, but perhaps enough has been said for the present purpose to establish the intimacy of the relation that existed between the writings of the last great Old Testament prophet and the movement beginning with John the Baptist and flaming forth in Jesus and his church, which was in essence a picking up of the long-neglected lines of the prophetic tradition to carry it to its climax and decisive fruition. There must be no reading back of the Christian gospel into Second Isaiah. He must remain an Old Testament prophet for whom the end of the ages had not yet come and who lived by hope. But neither should there be any concealment of his closeness in mind and spirit, in ministry and destiny, to Jesus Christ, so close that he seems to occupy a position *before* Christ similar to that which the apostle Paul was to occupy *after* him. We dare not ever forget that Jesus was able to take the words of Second Isaiah and speak them as his own.

[17] Hooker, *op. cit.* In denying that Jesus identified himself in any way with the Suffering Servant, Miss Hooker seems anxious to negate any suggestion that the substitutionary interpretation of the suffering in Isa., ch. 53, had a place in Jesus' understanding of his suffering. To admit an identification that was not exclusive, as I do, would open the door that she is determined to close.